MIN[...] WAGE

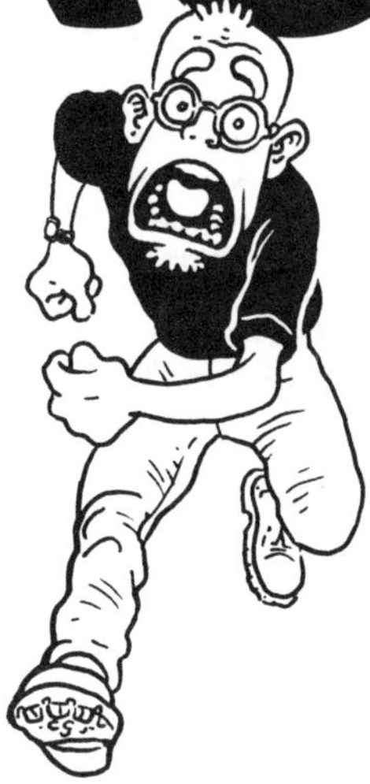

MINIMUM WAGE

BOOK ONE

EDITED by GARY GROTH
DESIGNED, WRITTEN and CREATED by
BOB FINGERMAN   PUBLISHED by GARY GROTH
and KIM THOMPSON   MINIMUM WAGE, July, 1995.
MINIMUM WAGE is published by Fantagraphics Books, Inc.,
and is copyright ©1995 Fantagraphics Books. All characters,
stories, and art ©1995 Bob Fingerman. No part of this publica-
tion may be reproduced without written permission from Fantagraphics books or Bob Fingerman. No similarity between any of the
names, characters, persons, and institutions in MINIMUM WAGE
and those of any living or dead person is intended, and any such
similarity that may exist is purely coincidental. First printing:
July,1995. ISBN: 1-56097-187-8. Available from the publisher for $9.95 + $1.00 postage & handling. Fantagraphics Books, 7563 Lake City Way N.E.,
Seattle, WA 98115. Printed
in Canada.

MINIMUM WAGE
BOOK ONE

By
BOB
FINGERMAN

FANTAGRAPHICS BOOKS

MINIMUM WAGE
BOOK ONE

BY BOB FINGERMAN

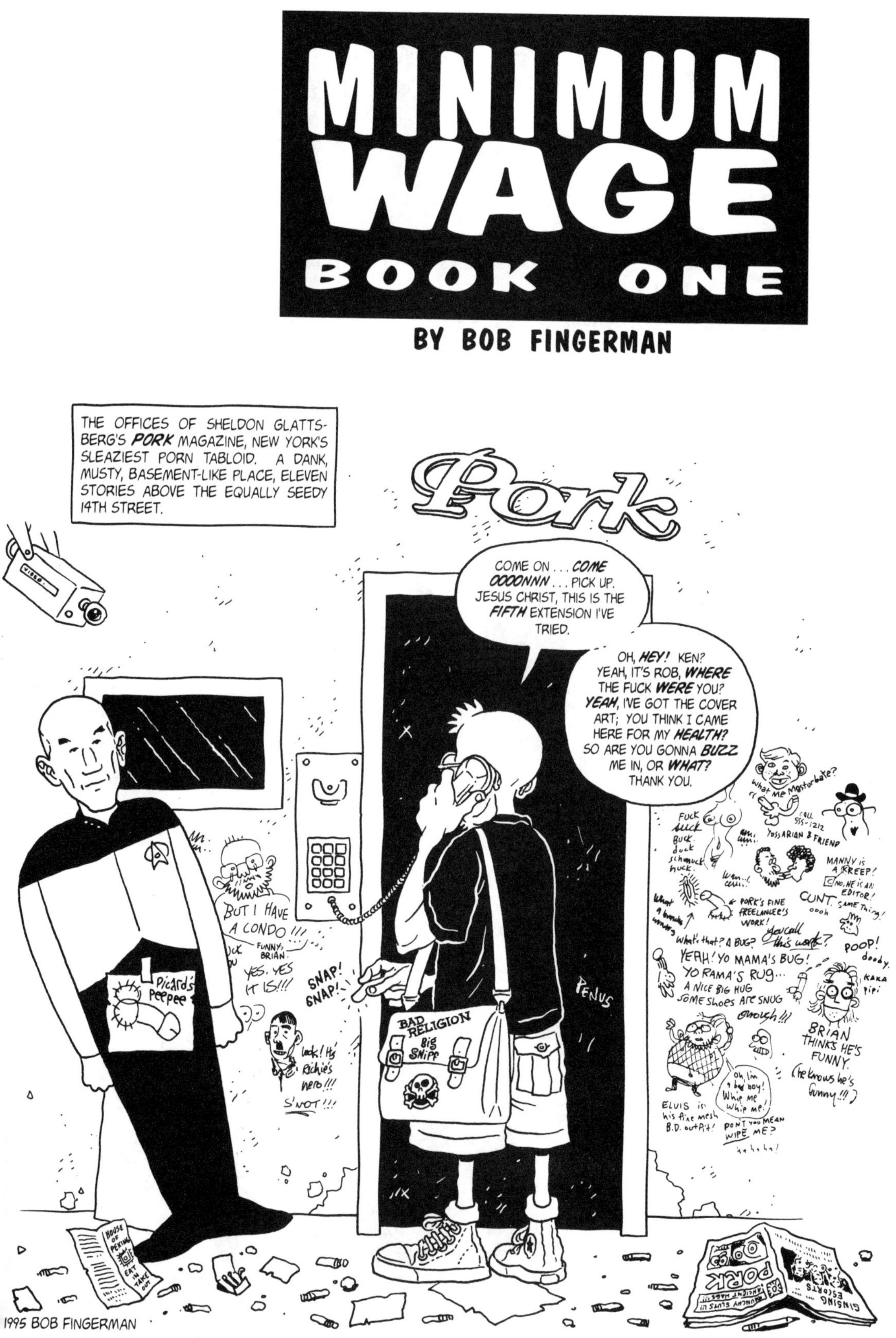
THE OFFICES OF SHELDON GLATTSBERG'S *PORK* MAGAZINE, NEW YORK'S SLEAZIEST PORN TABLOID. A DANK, MUSTY, BASEMENT-LIKE PLACE, ELEVEN STORIES ABOVE THE EQUALLY SEEDY 14TH STREET.
Pork
VIDEO
COME ON . . . ***COME OOOONNN*** . . . PICK UP. JESUS CHRIST, THIS IS THE ***FIFTH*** EXTENSION I'VE TRIED.
OH, ***HEY!*** KEN? YEAH, IT'S ROB, ***WHERE*** THE FUCK ***WERE*** YOU? ***YEAH***, I'VE GOT THE COVER ART; YOU THINK I CAME HERE FOR MY ***HEALTH?*** SO ARE YOU GONNA ***BUZZ*** ME IN, OR ***WHAT?*** THANK YOU.
SNAP! SNAP!
BUT I HAVE A CONDO!!!
FUNNY, BRIAN.
YES. YES IT IS!!!
Picard's peepee
look! H's Richie's hero!!!
S'NOT!!!
PENUS
BAD RELIGION
Big Snipp
What me Mastorbate?
CALL 555-1212
YOSSARIAN & FRIEND
Fuck suck Buck. duck schmuck huck.
MANNY IS A KREEP!
NO, HE IS AN EDITOR!
SAME Thing!
CUNT.
oooh
PORK'S FINE FREELANCER'S WORK!
What's that? A BUG?
you call this work?
YEAH! YO MAMA'S BUG! YO RAMA'S RUG... A NICE BIG HUG SOME SHOES ARE SNUG
enough!!!
POOP! doody.
KAKA pipi
BRIAN THINKS HE'S FUNNY.
(he knows he's funny!!!)
Oh, I'm a bad boy! Whip me Whip me!
ELVIS is his fine mesh B.D. outfit!
DON'T YOU MEAN WIPE ME?
ha ha ha!
HOUSE OF PEKING EAT IN TAKE OUT
PORK
GINSING ESCORTS
RAUNCHY SLUTS!!!

1995 BOB FINGERMAN

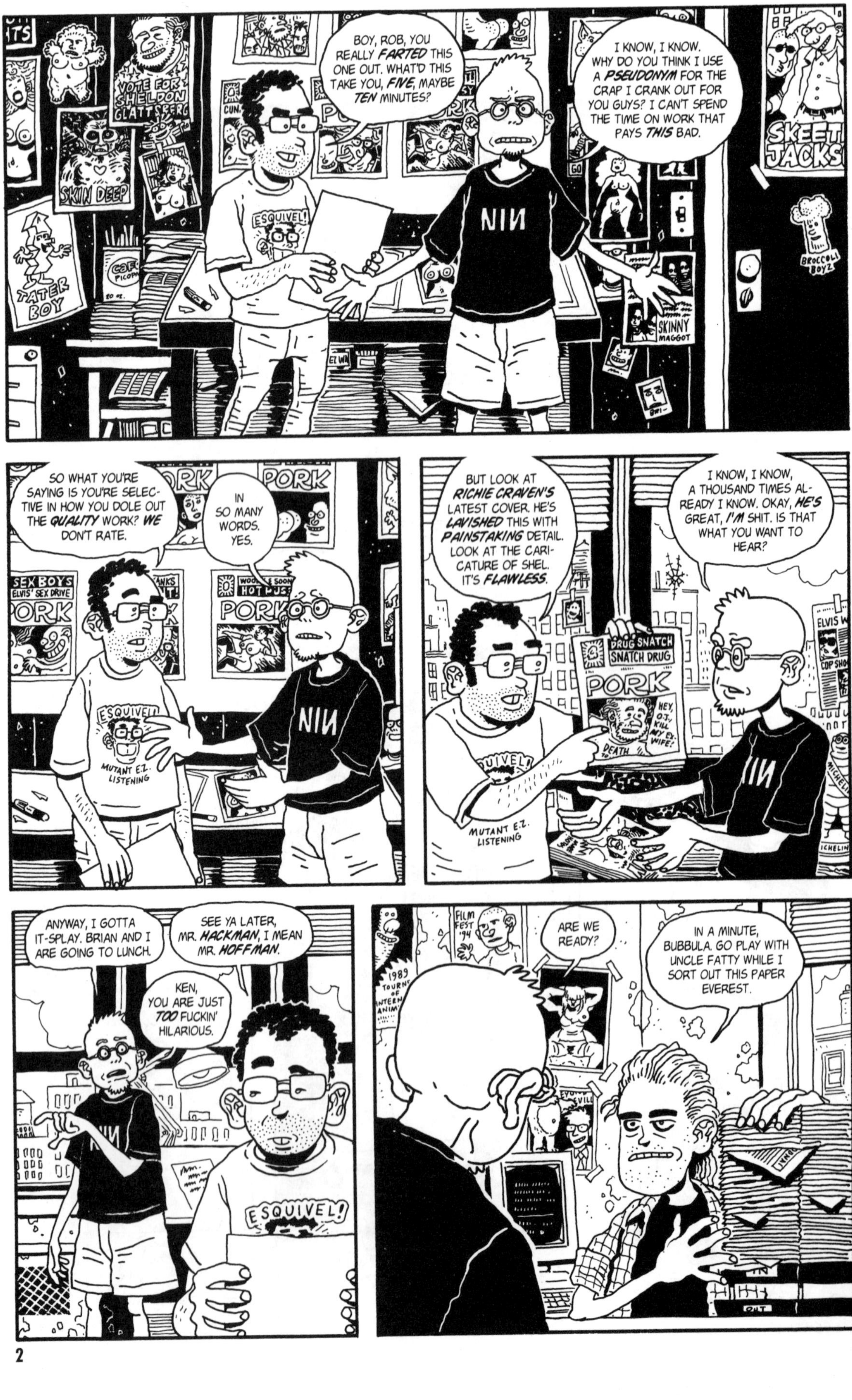
BOY, ROB, YOU REALLY FARTED THIS ONE OUT. WHAT'D THIS TAKE YOU, FIVE, MAYBE TEN MINUTES?
I KNOW, I KNOW. WHY DO YOU THINK I USE A PSEUDONYM FOR THE CRAP I CRANK OUT FOR YOU GUYS? I CAN'T SPEND THE TIME ON WORK THAT PAYS THIS BAD.
SO WHAT YOU'RE SAYING IS YOU'RE SELECTIVE IN HOW YOU DOLE OUT THE QUALITY WORK? WE DON'T RATE.
IN SO MANY WORDS. YES.
BUT LOOK AT RICHIE CRAVEN'S LATEST COVER. HE'S LAVISHED THIS WITH PAINSTAKING DETAIL. LOOK AT THE CARICATURE OF SHEL. IT'S FLAWLESS.
I KNOW, I KNOW, A THOUSAND TIMES ALREADY I KNOW. OKAY, HE'S GREAT, I'M SHIT. IS THAT WHAT YOU WANT TO HEAR?
ANYWAY, I GOTTA IT-SPLAY. BRIAN AND I ARE GOING TO LUNCH.
SEE YA LATER, MR. HACKMAN, I MEAN MR. HOFFMAN.
KEN, YOU ARE JUST TOO FUCKIN' HILARIOUS.
ARE WE READY?
IN A MINUTE, BUBBULA. GO PLAY WITH UNCLE FATTY WHILE I SORT OUT THIS PAPER EVEREST.

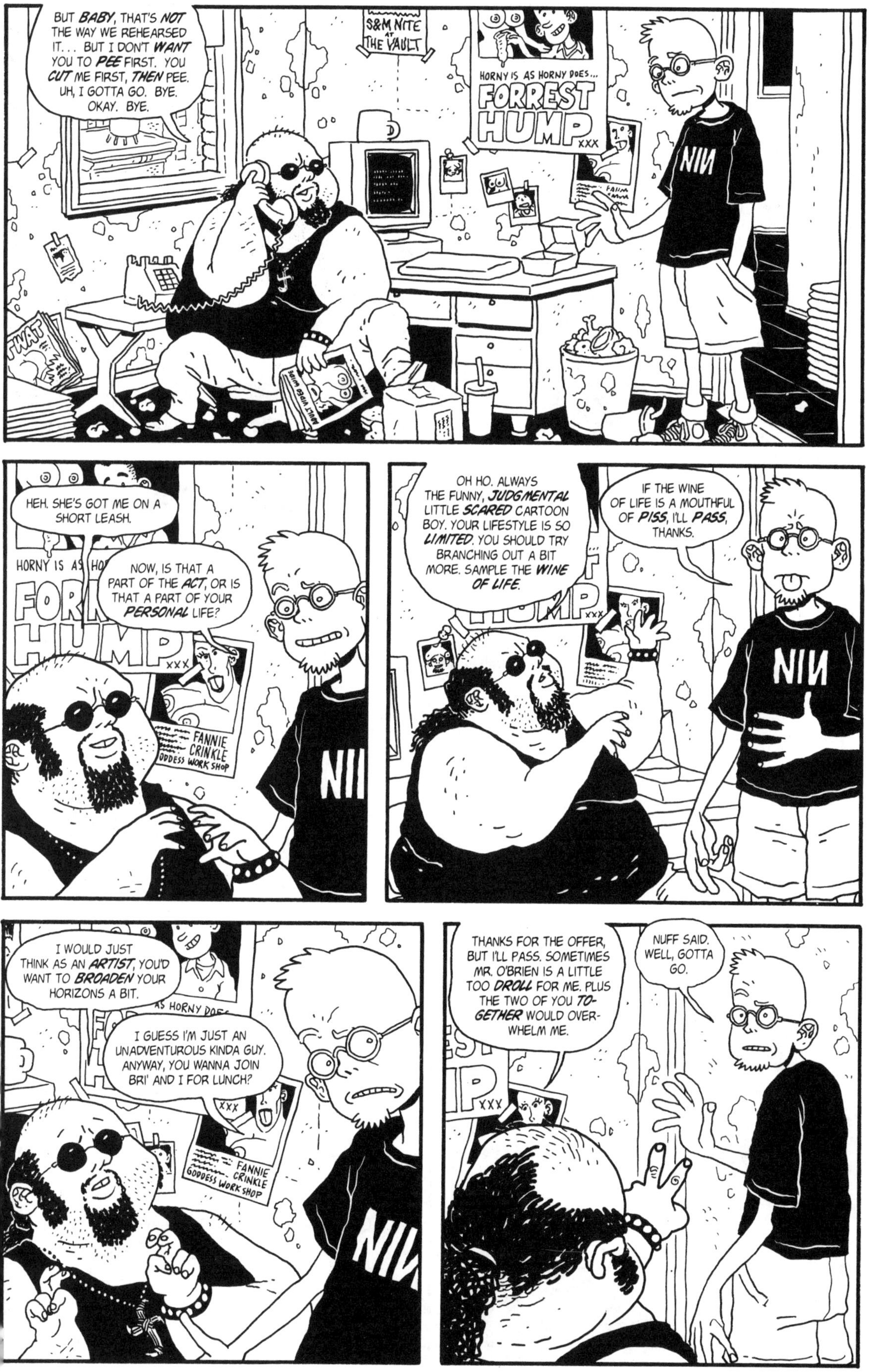
BUT BABY, THAT'S NOT THE WAY WE REHEARSED IT... BUT I DON'T WANT YOU TO PEE FIRST. YOU CUT ME FIRST, THEN PEE. UH, I GOTTA GO. BYE. OKAY. BYE.
S&M NITE AT THE VAULT
HORNY IS AS HORNY DOES...
FORREST HUMP XXX
NIN
TWAT
HEH. SHE'S GOT ME ON A SHORT LEASH.
NOW, IS THAT A PART OF THE ACT, OR IS THAT A PART OF YOUR PERSONAL LIFE?
FANNIE CRINKLE GODDESS WORK SHOP
OH HO. ALWAYS THE FUNNY, JUDGMENTAL LITTLE SCARED CARTOON BOY. YOUR LIFESTYLE IS SO LIMITED. YOU SHOULD TRY BRANCHING OUT A BIT MORE. SAMPLE THE WINE OF LIFE.
IF THE WINE OF LIFE IS A MOUTHFUL OF PISS, I'LL PASS, THANKS.
I WOULD JUST THINK AS AN ARTIST, YOU'D WANT TO BROADEN YOUR HORIZONS A BIT.
I GUESS I'M JUST AN UNADVENTUROUS KINDA GUY. ANYWAY, YOU WANNA JOIN BRI' AND I FOR LUNCH?
THANKS FOR THE OFFER, BUT I'LL PASS. SOMETIMES MR. O'BRIEN IS A LITTLE TOO DROLL FOR ME. PLUS THE TWO OF YOU TOGETHER WOULD OVERWHELM ME.
NUFF SAID. WELL, GOTTA GO.

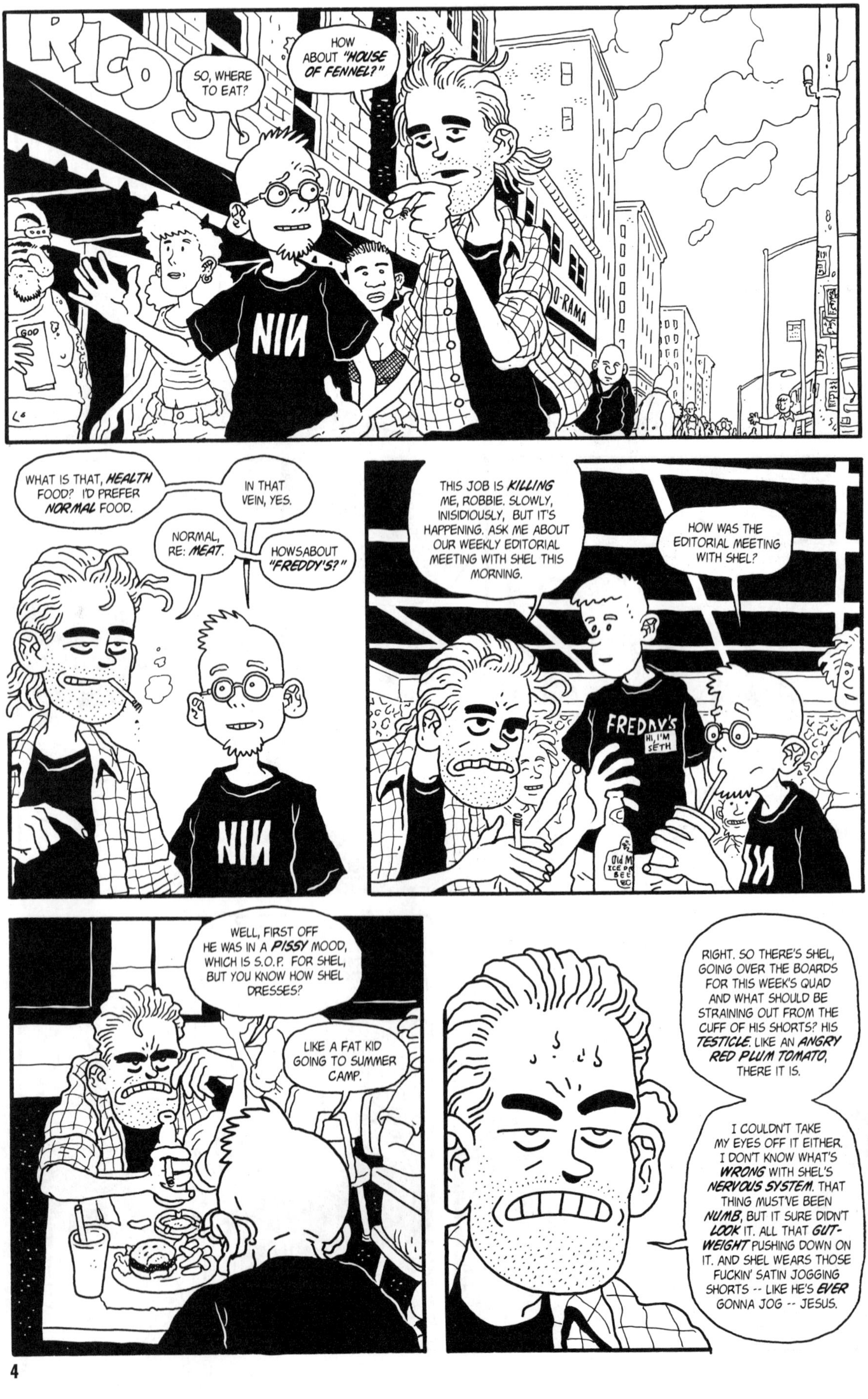
SO, WHERE TO EAT?
HOW ABOUT "HOUSE OF FENNEL?"
NIN
WHAT IS THAT, HEALTH FOOD? I'D PREFER NORMAL FOOD.
IN THAT VEIN, YES.
NORMAL, RE: MEAT.
HOWSABOUT "FREDDY'S?"
NIN
THIS JOB IS KILLING ME, ROBBIE. SLOWLY, INISIDIOUSLY, BUT IT'S HAPPENING. ASK ME ABOUT OUR WEEKLY EDITORIAL MEETING WITH SHEL THIS MORNING.
HOW WAS THE EDITORIAL MEETING WITH SHEL?
FREDDY'S
HI, I'M SETH
WELL, FIRST OFF HE WAS IN A PISSY MOOD, WHICH IS S.O.P. FOR SHEL, BUT YOU KNOW HOW SHEL DRESSES?
LIKE A FAT KID GOING TO SUMMER CAMP.
RIGHT. SO THERE'S SHEL, GOING OVER THE BOARDS FOR THIS WEEK'S QUAD AND WHAT SHOULD BE STRAINING OUT FROM THE CUFF OF HIS SHORTS? HIS TESTICLE. LIKE AN ANGRY RED PLUM TOMATO, THERE IT IS.
I COULDN'T TAKE MY EYES OFF IT EITHER. I DON'T KNOW WHAT'S WRONG WITH SHEL'S NERVOUS SYSTEM. THAT THING MUST'VE BEEN NUMB, BUT IT SURE DIDN'T LOOK IT. ALL THAT GUT-WEIGHT PUSHING DOWN ON IT. AND SHEL WEARS THOSE FUCKIN' SATIN JOGGING SHORTS -- LIKE HE'S EVER GONNA JOG -- JESUS.

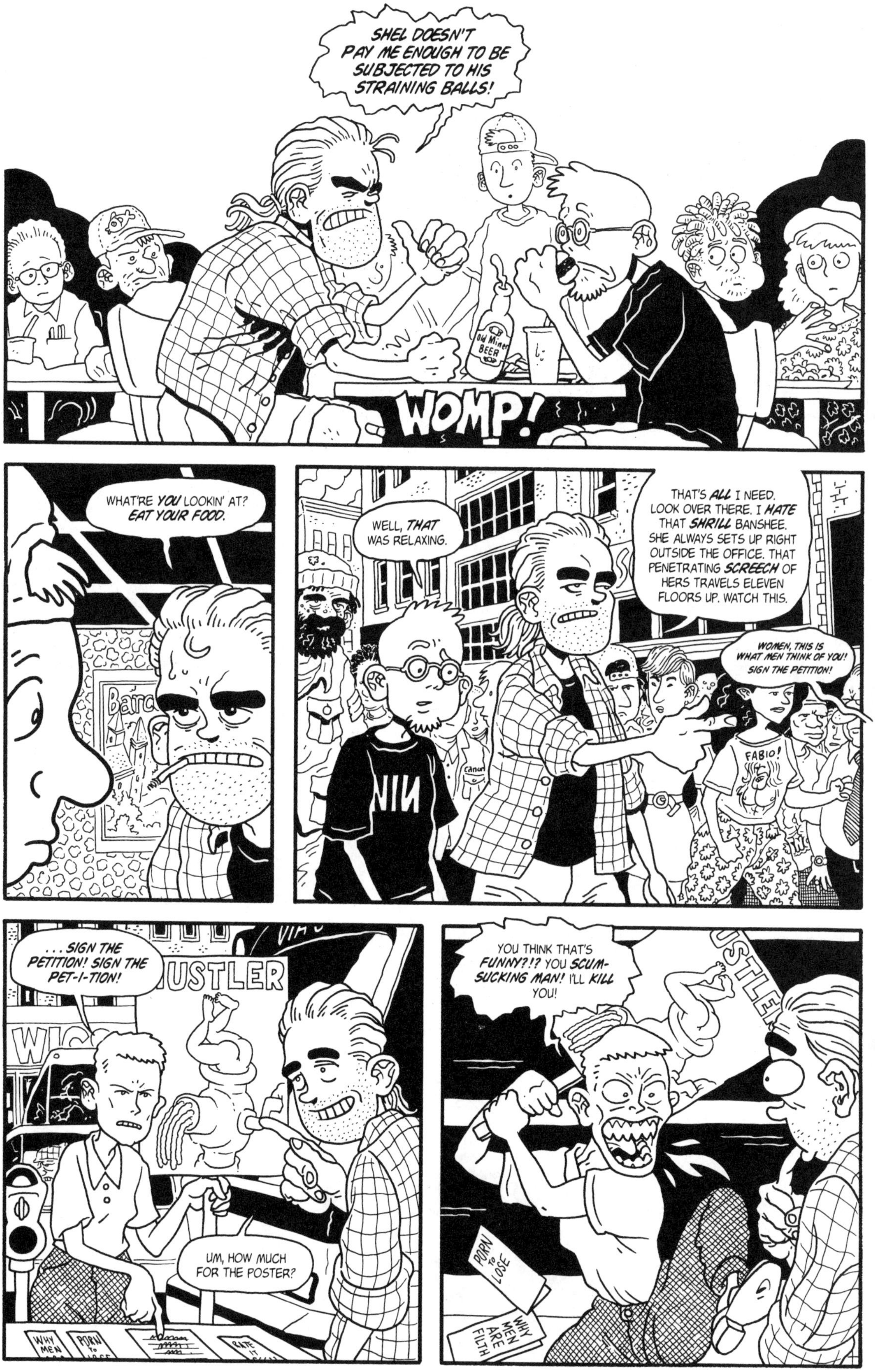

SHEL DOESN'T PAY ME ENOUGH TO BE SUBJECTED TO HIS STRAINING BALLS!
Old Miner BEER
WOMP!
WHAT'RE YOU LOOKIN' AT? EAT YOUR FOOD.
WELL, THAT WAS RELAXING.
THAT'S ALL I NEED. LOOK OVER THERE. I HATE THAT SHRILL BANSHEE. SHE ALWAYS SETS UP RIGHT OUTSIDE THE OFFICE. THAT PENETRATING SCREECH OF HERS TRAVELS ELEVEN FLOORS UP. WATCH THIS.
WOMEN, THIS IS WHAT MEN THINK OF YOU! SIGN THE PETITION!
FABIO!
NIN
. . . SIGN THE PETITION! SIGN THE PET-I-TION!
USTLER
UM, HOW MUCH FOR THE POSTER?
PORN TO LOSE
YOU THINK THAT'S FUNNY?!? YOU SCUM-SUCKING MAN! I'LL KILL YOU!
WHY MEN ARE FILTH

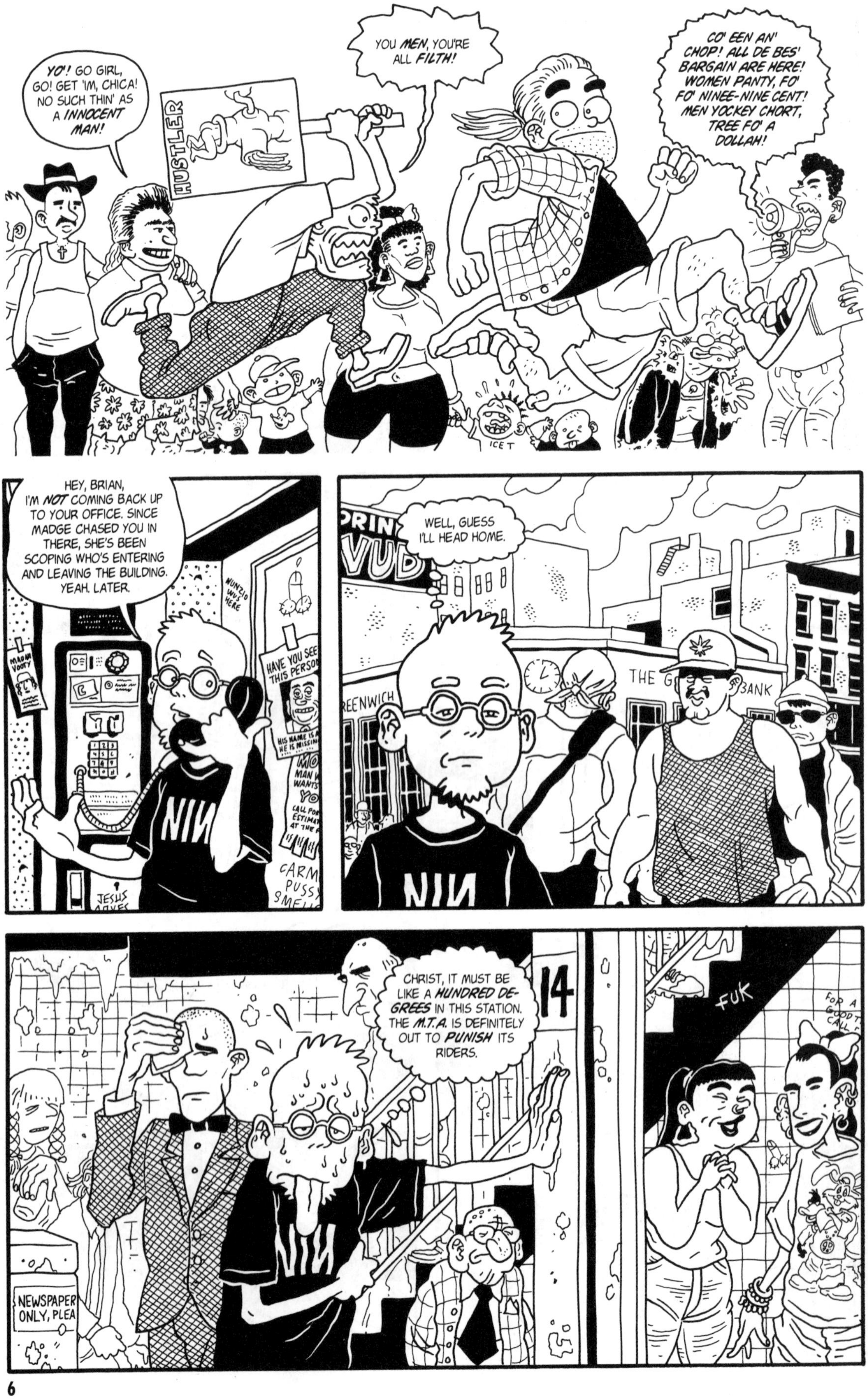
YO'! GO GIRL, GO! GET 'IM, CHICA! NO SUCH THIN' AS A INNOCENT MAN!
HUSTLER
YOU MEN, YOU'RE ALL FILTH!
CO' EEN AN' CHOP! ALL DE BES' BARGAIN ARE HERE! WOMEN PANTY, FO' FO' NINEE-NINE CENT! MEN YOCKEY CHORT, TREE FO' A DOLLAH!
ICE T
HEY, BRIAN, I'M NOT COMING BACK UP TO YOUR OFFICE. SINCE MADGE CHASED YOU IN THERE, SHE'S BEEN SCOPING WHO'S ENTERING AND LEAVING THE BUILDING. YEAH. LATER.
NIN
WELL, GUESS I'LL HEAD HOME.
NIN
CHRIST, IT MUST BE LIKE A HUNDRED DEGREES IN THIS STATION. THE M.T.A. IS DEFINITELY OUT TO PUNISH ITS RIDERS.
14
FUK
NIN
NEWSPAPER ONLY, PLEA

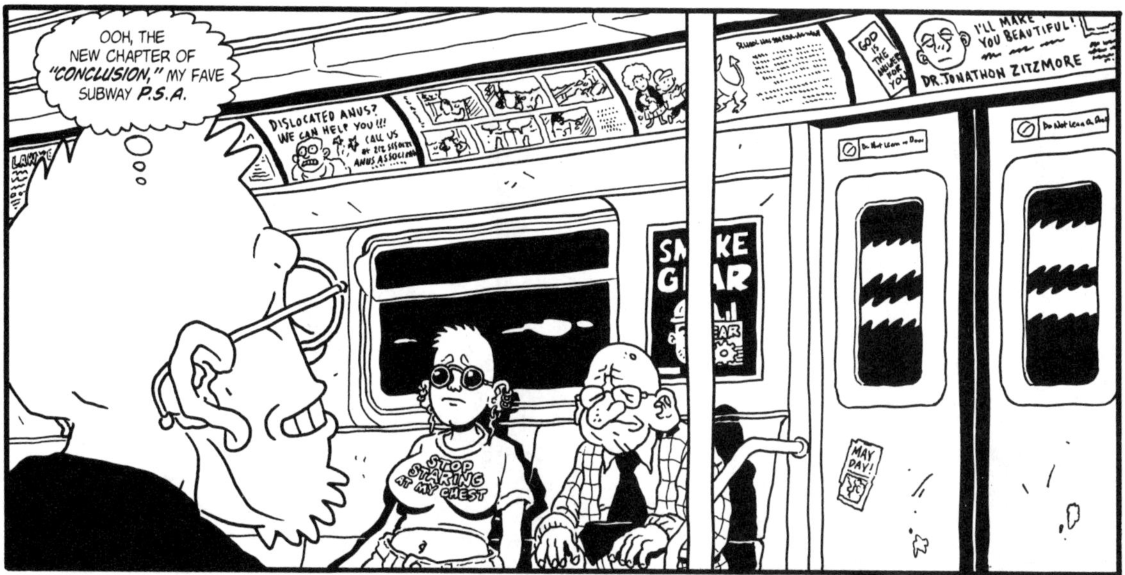

OOH, THE NEW CHAPTER OF "CONCLUSION," MY FAVE SUBWAY P.S.A.
DISLOCATED ANUS? WE CAN HELP YOU!!! CALL US
GOD IS THE ANSWER FOR YOU
I'LL MAKE YOU BEAUTIFUL!
DR. JONATHON ZITZMORE
SMOKE GEAR
STOP STARING AT MY CHEST
MAY DAY!

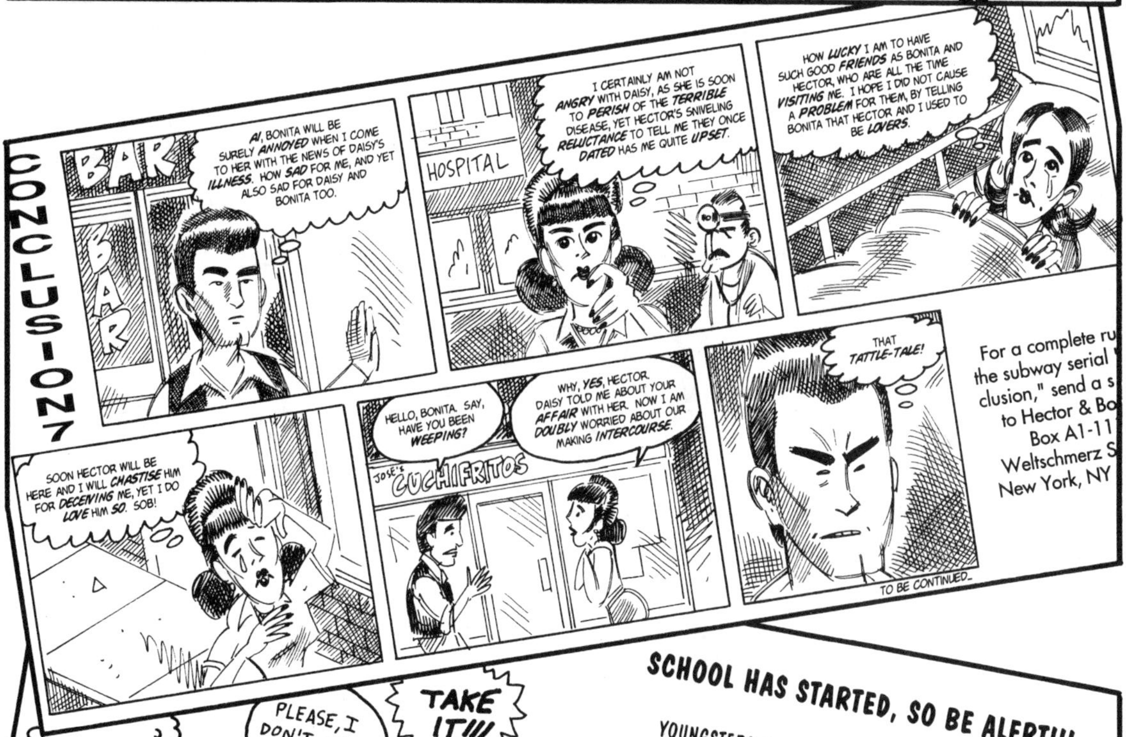

CONCLUSION 7
BAR
AI, BONITA WILL BE SURELY ANNOYED WHEN I COME TO HER WITH THE NEWS OF DAISY'S ILLNESS. HOW SAD FOR ME, AND YET ALSO SAD FOR DAISY AND BONITA TOO.
HOSPITAL
I CERTAINLY AM NOT ANGRY WITH DAISY, AS SHE IS SOON TO PERISH OF THE TERRIBLE DISEASE, YET HECTOR'S SNIVELING RELUCTANCE TO TELL ME THEY ONCE DATED HAS ME QUITE UPSET.
HOW LUCKY I AM TO HAVE SUCH GOOD FRIENDS AS BONITA AND HECTOR, WHO ARE ALL THE TIME VISITING ME. I HOPE I DID NOT CAUSE A PROBLEM FOR THEM, BY TELLING BONITA THAT HECTOR AND I USED TO BE LOVERS.
SOON HECTOR WILL BE HERE AND I WILL CHASTISE HIM FOR DECEIVING ME, YET I DO LOVE HIM SO. SOB!
HELLO, BONITA. SAY, HAVE YOU BEEN WEEPING?
WHY, YES, HECTOR. DAISY TOLD ME ABOUT YOUR AFFAIR WITH HER. NOW I AM DOUBLY WORRIED ABOUT OUR MAKING INTERCOURSE.
JOSE'S CUCHIFRITOS
THAT TATTLE-TALE!
TO BE CONTINUED...
For a complete ru
the subway serial
clusion," send a s
to Hector & Bo
Box A1-11
Weltschmerz S
New York, NY

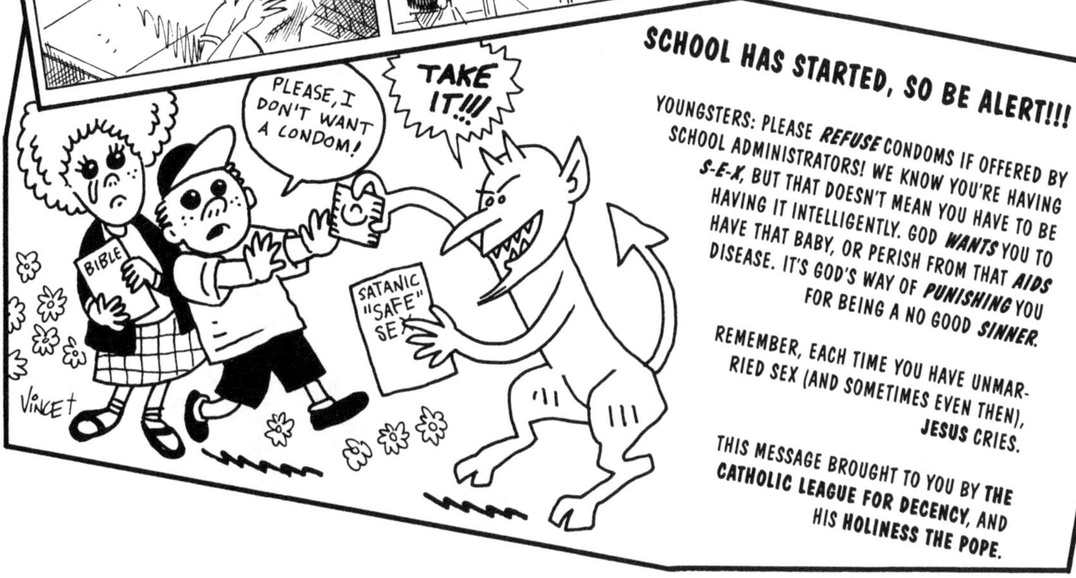

PLEASE, I DON'T WANT A CONDOM!
TAKE IT!!!
BIBLE
SATANIC "SAFE" SEX
VINCE+
SCHOOL HAS STARTED, SO BE ALERT!!!
YOUNGSTERS: PLEASE REFUSE CONDOMS IF OFFERED BY SCHOOL ADMINISTRATORS! WE KNOW YOU'RE HAVING S-E-X, BUT THAT DOESN'T MEAN YOU HAVE TO BE HAVING IT INTELLIGENTLY. GOD WANTS YOU TO HAVE THAT BABY, OR PERISH FROM THAT AIDS DISEASE. IT'S GOD'S WAY OF PUNISHING YOU FOR BEING A NO GOOD SINNER.
REMEMBER, EACH TIME YOU HAVE UNMARRIED SEX (AND SOMETIMES EVEN THEN), JESUS CRIES.
THIS MESSAGE BROUGHT TO YOU BY THE CATHOLIC LEAGUE FOR DECENCY, AND HIS HOLINESS THE POPE.

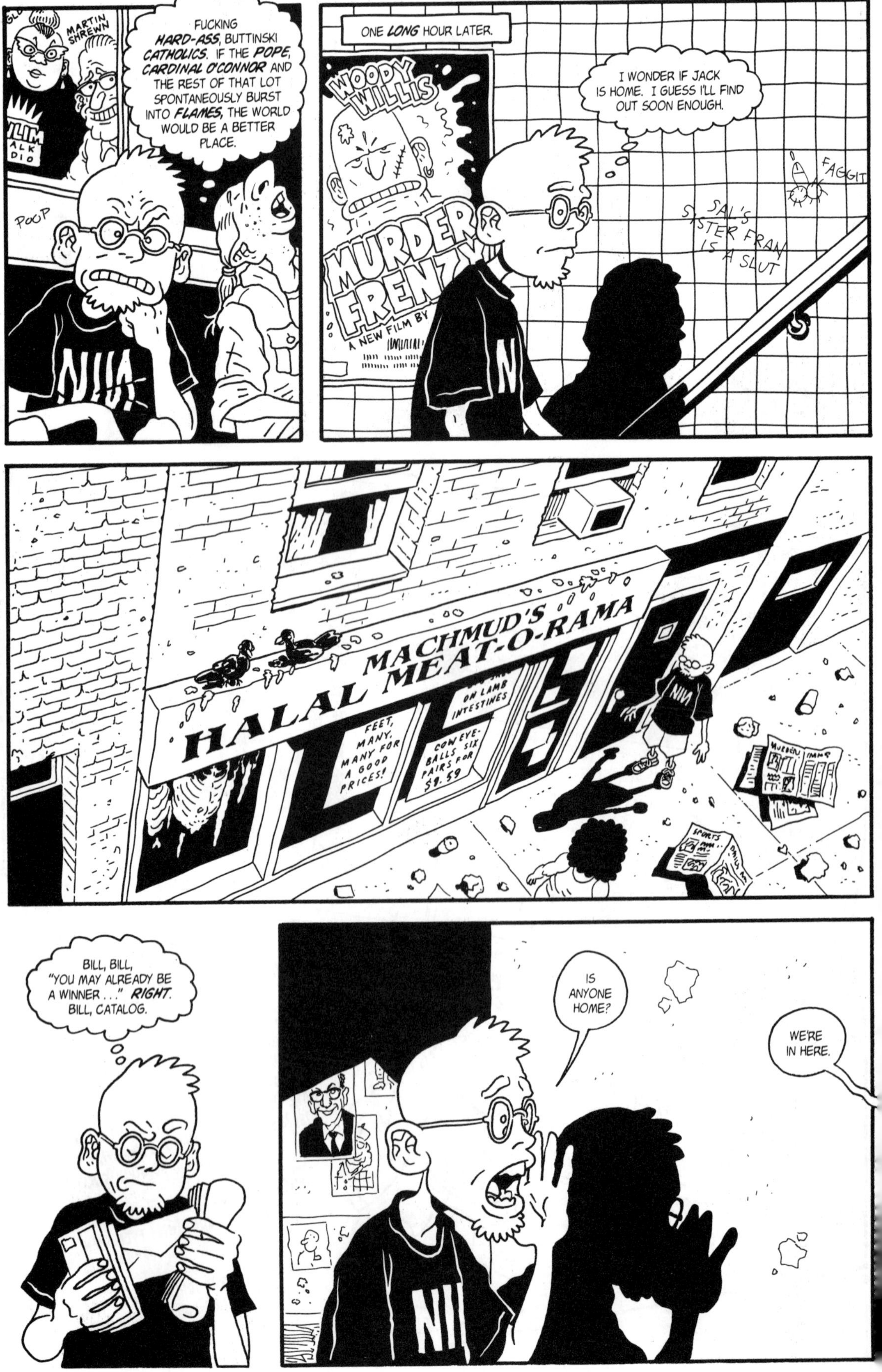
MARTIN SHREWN
FUCKING HARD-ASS, BUTTINSKI CATHOLICS. IF THE POPE, CARDINAL O'CONNOR AND THE REST OF THAT LOT SPONTANEOUSLY BURST INTO FLAMES, THE WORLD WOULD BE A BETTER PLACE.
POOP
ONE LONG HOUR LATER.
WOODY WILLIS
MURDER FRENZY
A NEW FILM BY
I WONDER IF JACK IS HOME. I GUESS I'LL FIND OUT SOON ENOUGH.
FAGGIT
SAL'S SISTER FRAN IS A SLUT
MACHMUD'S
HALAL MEAT-O-RAMA
FEET, MANY, MANY FOR A GOOD PRICES!
ON LAMB INTESTINES
COW EYE-BALLS SIX PAIRS FOR $9.59
SPORTS
BILL, BILL, "YOU MAY ALREADY BE A WINNER . . ." RIGHT. BILL, CATALOG.
IS ANYONE HOME?
WE'RE IN HERE.

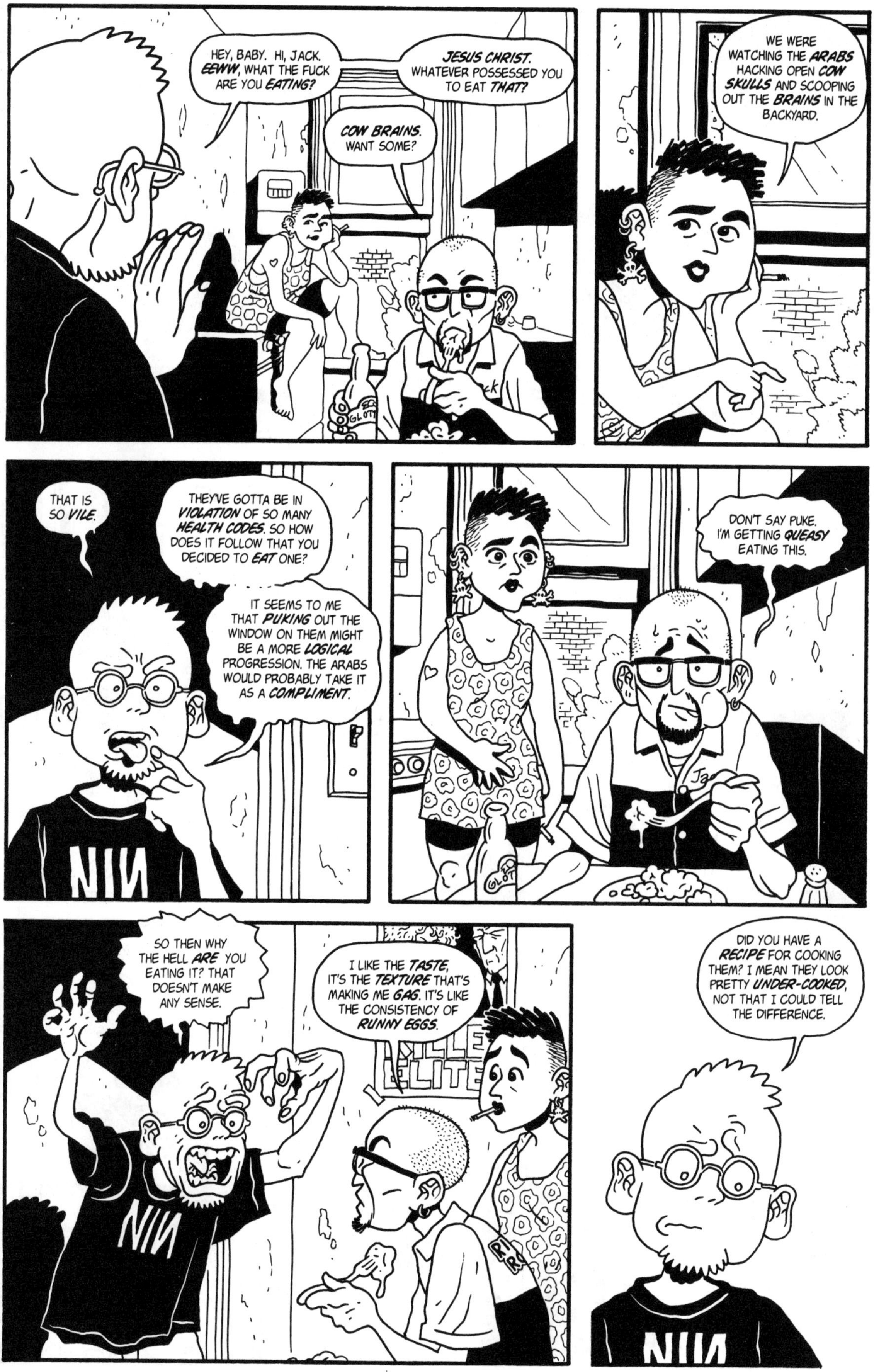
HEY, BABY. HI, JACK. EEWW, WHAT THE FUCK ARE YOU EATING?
JESUS CHRIST. WHATEVER POSSESSED YOU TO EAT THAT?
COW BRAINS. WANT SOME?
WE WERE WATCHING THE ARABS HACKING OPEN COW SKULLS AND SCOOPING OUT THE BRAINS IN THE BACKYARD.
THAT IS SO VILE.
THEY'VE GOTTA BE IN VIOLATION OF SO MANY HEALTH CODES. SO HOW DOES IT FOLLOW THAT YOU DECIDED TO EAT ONE?
IT SEEMS TO ME THAT PUKING OUT THE WINDOW ON THEM MIGHT BE A MORE LOGICAL PROGRESSION. THE ARABS WOULD PROBABLY TAKE IT AS A COMPLIMENT.
NIN
DON'T SAY PUKE. I'M GETTING QUEASY EATING THIS.
SO THEN WHY THE HELL ARE YOU EATING IT? THAT DOESN'T MAKE ANY SENSE.
I LIKE THE TASTE, IT'S THE TEXTURE THAT'S MAKING ME GAG. IT'S LIKE THE CONSISTENCY OF RUNNY EGGS.
NIN
DID YOU HAVE A RECIPE FOR COOKING THEM? I MEAN THEY LOOK PRETTY UNDER-COOKED, NOT THAT I COULD TELL THE DIFFERENCE.
NIN

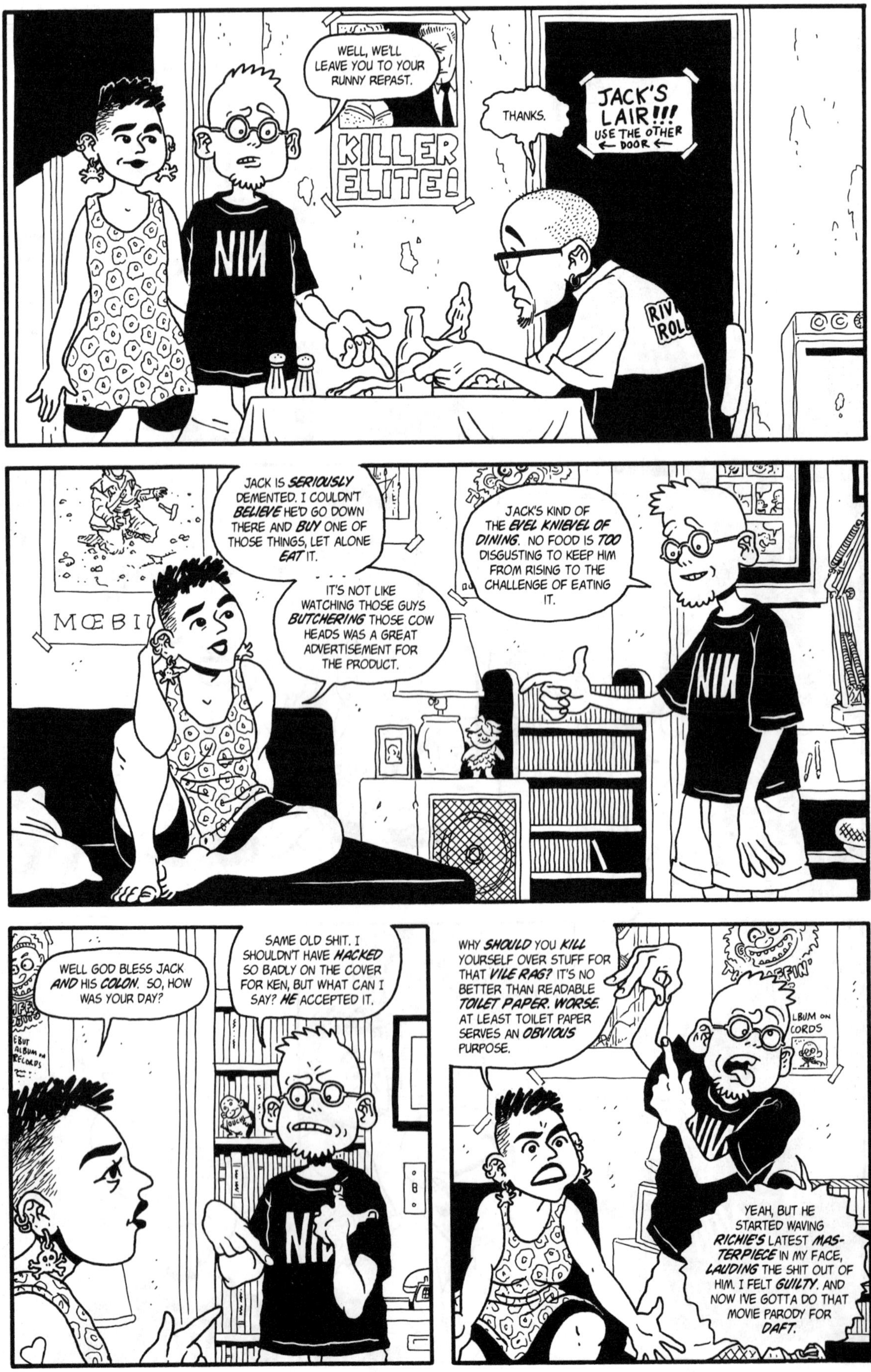

WELL, WE'LL LEAVE YOU TO YOUR RUNNY REPAST.
KILLER ELITE!
THANKS.
JACK'S LAIR!!! USE THE OTHER ← DOOR ←
JACK IS SERIOUSLY DEMENTED. I COULDN'T BELIEVE HE'D GO DOWN THERE AND BUY ONE OF THOSE THINGS, LET ALONE EAT IT.
IT'S NOT LIKE WATCHING THOSE GUYS BUTCHERING THOSE COW HEADS WAS A GREAT ADVERTISEMENT FOR THE PRODUCT.
JACK'S KIND OF THE EVEL KNIEVEL OF DINING. NO FOOD IS TOO DISGUSTING TO KEEP HIM FROM RISING TO THE CHALLENGE OF EATING IT.
MŒBIU
WELL GOD BLESS JACK AND HIS COLON. SO, HOW WAS YOUR DAY?
SAME OLD SHIT. I SHOULDN'T HAVE HACKED SO BADLY ON THE COVER FOR KEN, BUT WHAT CAN I SAY? HE ACCEPTED IT.
WHY SHOULD YOU KILL YOURSELF OVER STUFF FOR THAT VILE RAG? IT'S NO BETTER THAN READABLE TOILET PAPER. WORSE. AT LEAST TOILET PAPER SERVES AN OBVIOUS PURPOSE.
YEAH, BUT HE STARTED WAVING RICHIE'S LATEST MASTERPIECE IN MY FACE, LAUDING THE SHIT OUT OF HIM. I FELT GUILTY. AND NOW I'VE GOTTA DO THAT MOVIE PARODY FOR DAFT.

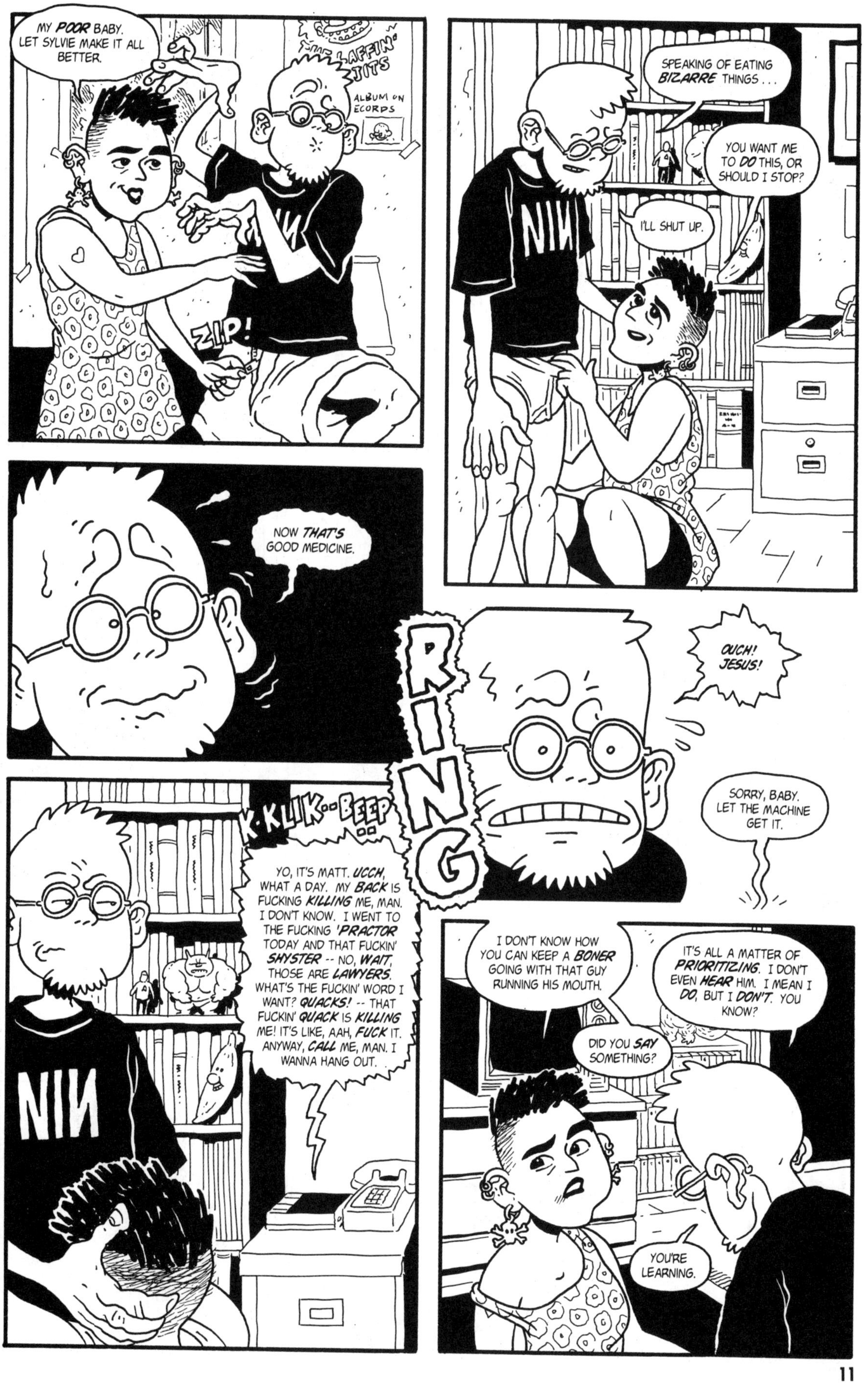
MY POOR BABY. LET SYLVIE MAKE IT ALL BETTER.
THE LAFFIN' JITS
ALBUM ON RECORDS
ZIP!
SPEAKING OF EATING BIZARRE THINGS . . .
YOU WANT ME TO DO THIS, OR SHOULD I STOP?
I'LL SHUT UP.
NOW THAT'S GOOD MEDICINE.
RING
OUCH! JESUS!
SORRY, BABY. LET THE MACHINE GET IT.
K-KLIK--BEEP
YO, IT'S MATT. UCCH, WHAT A DAY. MY BACK IS FUCKING KILLING ME, MAN. I DON'T KNOW. I WENT TO THE FUCKING 'PRACTOR TODAY AND THAT FUCKIN' SHYSTER -- NO, WAIT, THOSE ARE LAWYERS. WHAT'S THE FUCKIN' WORD I WANT? QUACKS! -- THAT FUCKIN' QUACK IS KILLING ME! IT'S LIKE, AAH, FUCK IT. ANYWAY, CALL ME, MAN. I WANNA HANG OUT.
I DON'T KNOW HOW YOU CAN KEEP A BONER GOING WITH THAT GUY RUNNING HIS MOUTH.
IT'S ALL A MATTER OF PRIORITIZING. I DON'T EVEN HEAR HIM. I MEAN I DO, BUT I DON'T. YOU KNOW?
DID YOU SAY SOMETHING?
YOU'RE LEARNING.

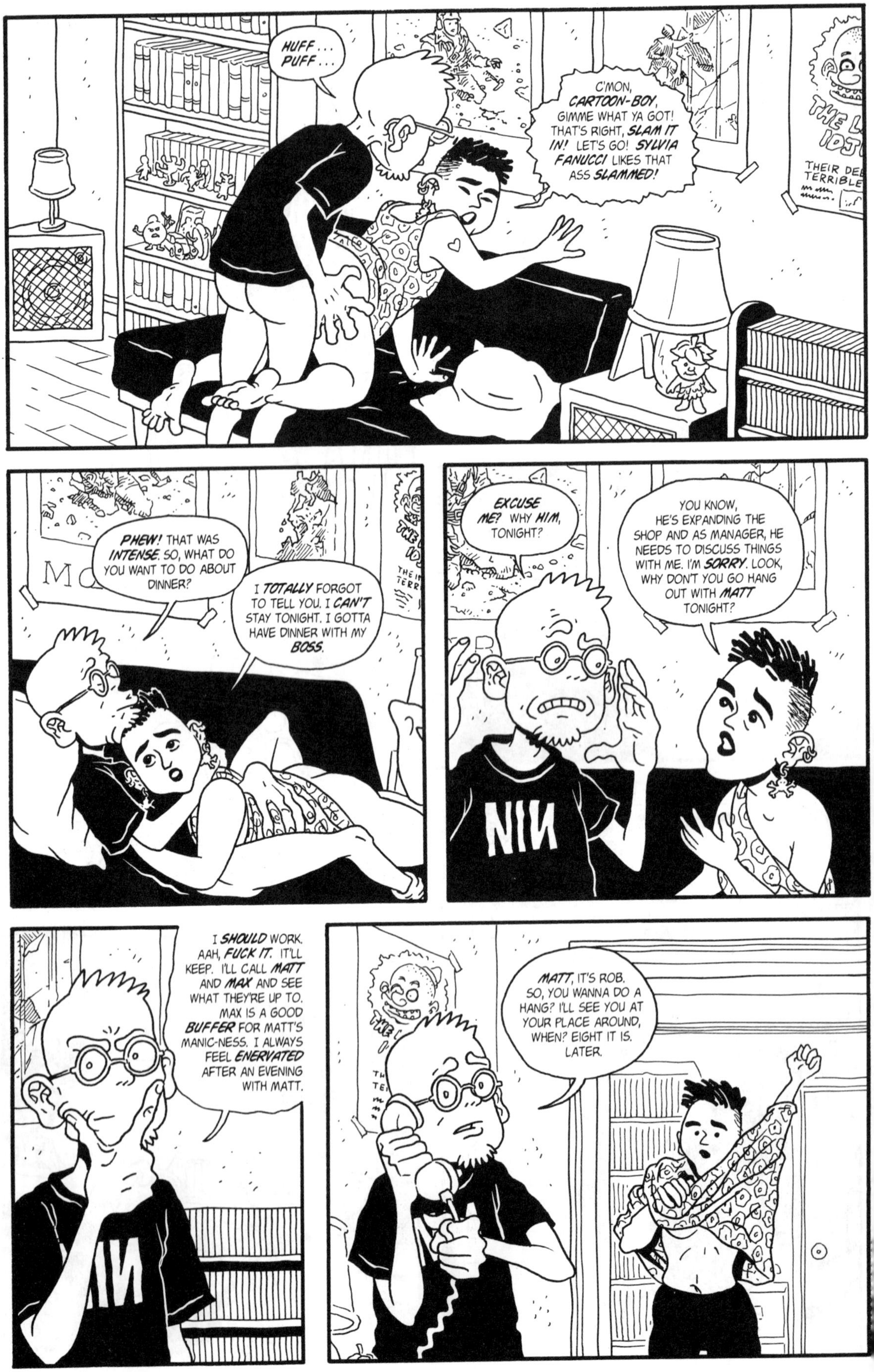
HUFF... PUFF...
C'MON, CARTOON-BOY, GIMME WHAT YA GOT! THAT'S RIGHT, SLAM IT IN! LET'S GO! SYLVIA FANUCCI LIKES THAT ASS SLAMMED!
PHEW! THAT WAS INTENSE. SO, WHAT DO YOU WANT TO DO ABOUT DINNER?
I TOTALLY FORGOT TO TELL YOU. I CAN'T STAY TONIGHT. I GOTTA HAVE DINNER WITH MY BOSS.
EXCUSE ME? WHY HIM, TONIGHT?
YOU KNOW, HE'S EXPANDING THE SHOP AND AS MANAGER, HE NEEDS TO DISCUSS THINGS WITH ME. I'M SORRY. LOOK, WHY DON'T YOU GO HANG OUT WITH MATT TONIGHT?
NIN
I SHOULD WORK. AAH, FUCK IT. IT'LL KEEP. I'LL CALL MATT AND MAX AND SEE WHAT THEY'RE UP TO. MAX IS A GOOD BUFFER FOR MATT'S MANIC-NESS. I ALWAYS FEEL ENERVATED AFTER AN EVENING WITH MATT.
MATT, IT'S ROB. SO, YOU WANNA DO A HANG? I'LL SEE YOU AT YOUR PLACE AROUND, WHEN? EIGHT IT IS. LATER.

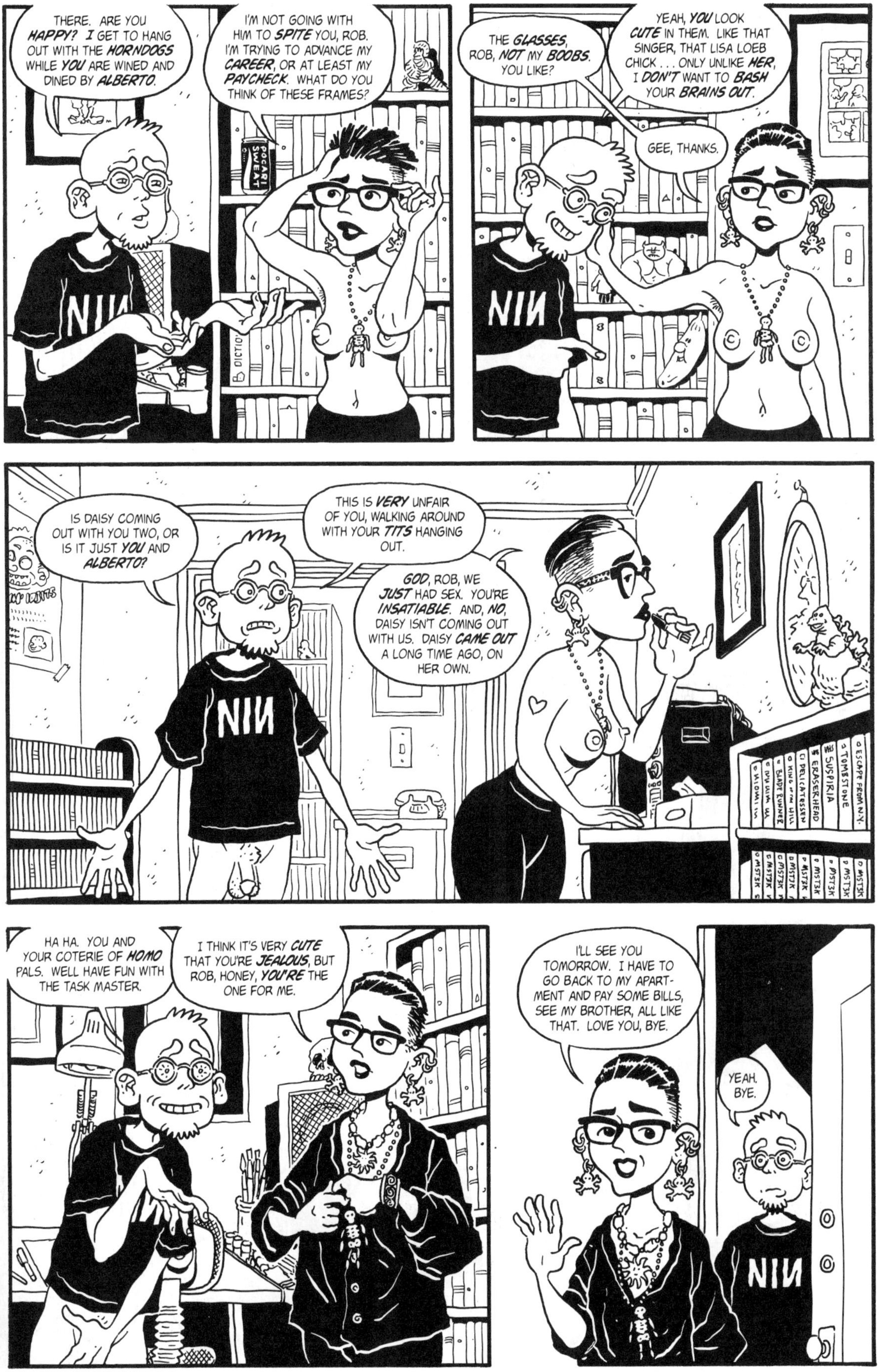
THERE. ARE YOU HAPPY? I GET TO HANG OUT WITH THE HORNDOGS WHILE YOU ARE WINED AND DINED BY ALBERTO.
I'M NOT GOING WITH HIM TO SPITE YOU, ROB. I'M TRYING TO ADVANCE MY CAREER, OR AT LEAST MY PAYCHECK. WHAT DO YOU THINK OF THESE FRAMES?
POCARI SWEAT
THE GLASSES, ROB, NOT MY BOOBS. YOU LIKE?
YEAH, YOU LOOK CUTE IN THEM. LIKE THAT SINGER, THAT LISA LOEB CHICK . . . ONLY UNLIKE HER, I DON'T WANT TO BASH YOUR BRAINS OUT.
GEE, THANKS.
IS DAISY COMING OUT WITH YOU TWO, OR IS IT JUST YOU AND ALBERTO?
THIS IS VERY UNFAIR OF YOU, WALKING AROUND WITH YOUR TITS HANGING OUT.
GOD, ROB, WE JUST HAD SEX. YOU'RE INSATIABLE. AND, NO, DAISY ISN'T COMING OUT WITH US. DAISY CAME OUT A LONG TIME AGO, ON HER OWN.
ESCAPE FROM N.Y.
TOMBSTONE
SUSPIRIA
ERASERHEAD
DELICATESSEN
BLADE RUNNER
MST3K
HA HA. YOU AND YOUR COTERIE OF HOMO PALS. WELL HAVE FUN WITH THE TASK MASTER.
I THINK IT'S VERY CUTE THAT YOU'RE JEALOUS, BUT ROB, HONEY, YOU'RE THE ONE FOR ME.
I'LL SEE YOU TOMORROW. I HAVE TO GO BACK TO MY APART-MENT AND PAY SOME BILLS, SEE MY BROTHER, ALL LIKE THAT. LOVE YOU, BYE.
YEAH. BYE.

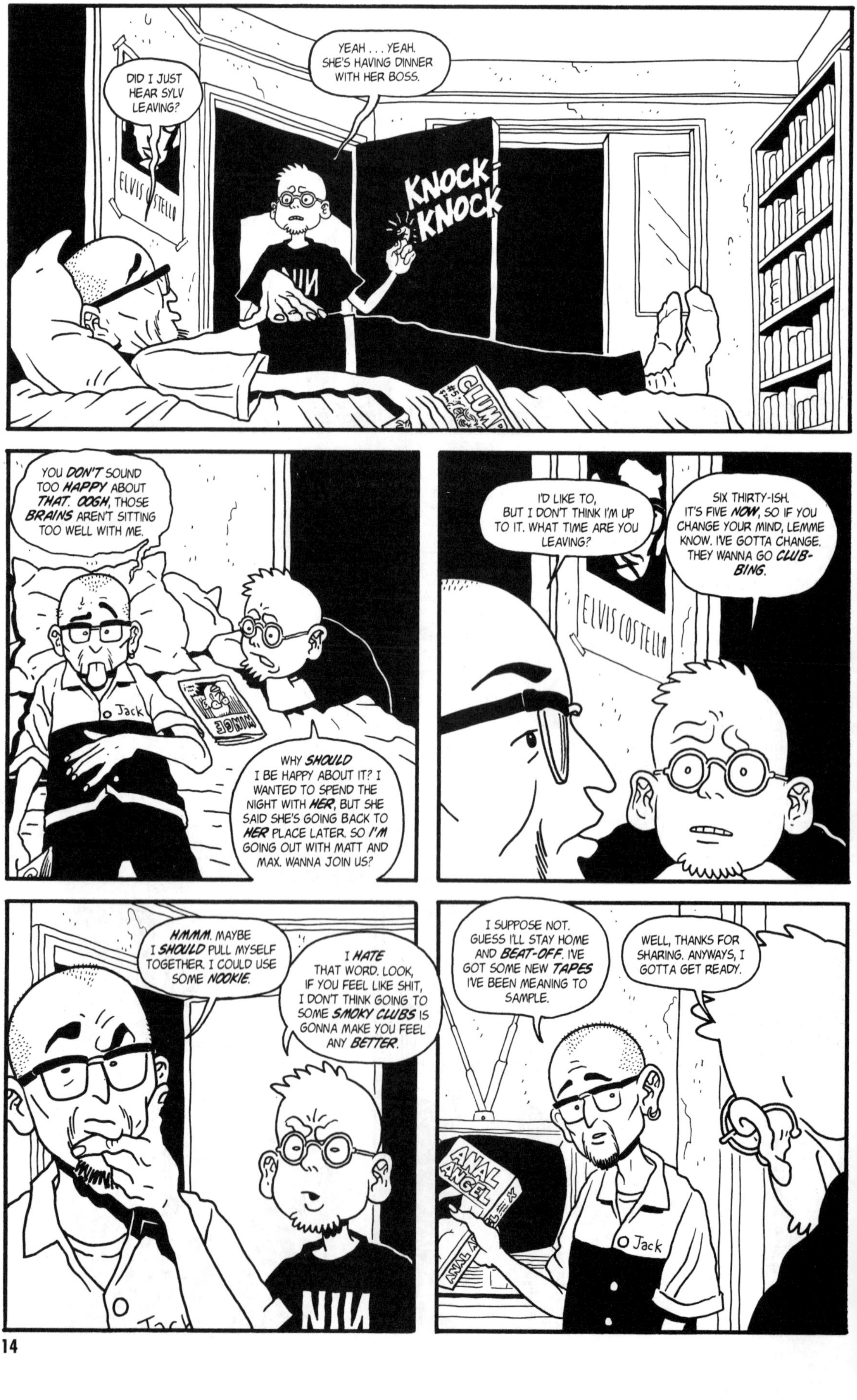
DID I JUST HEAR SYLV LEAVING?
YEAH . . . YEAH. SHE'S HAVING DINNER WITH HER BOSS.
KNOCK KNOCK
ELVIS COSTELLO
CLUMP #5
YOU DON'T SOUND TOO HAPPY ABOUT THAT. OOGH, THOSE BRAINS AREN'T SITTING TOO WELL WITH ME.
Jack
MINGE
WHY SHOULD I BE HAPPY ABOUT IT? I WANTED TO SPEND THE NIGHT WITH HER, BUT SHE SAID SHE'S GOING BACK TO HER PLACE LATER. SO I'M GOING OUT WITH MATT AND MAX. WANNA JOIN US?
I'D LIKE TO, BUT I DON'T THINK I'M UP TO IT. WHAT TIME ARE YOU LEAVING?
SIX THIRTY-ISH. IT'S FIVE NOW, SO IF YOU CHANGE YOUR MIND, LEMME KNOW. I'VE GOTTA CHANGE. THEY WANNA GO CLUB-BING.
ELVIS COSTELLO
HMMM. MAYBE I SHOULD PULL MYSELF TOGETHER. I COULD USE SOME NOOKIE.
I HATE THAT WORD. LOOK, IF YOU FEEL LIKE SHIT, I DON'T THINK GOING TO SOME SMOKY CLUBS IS GONNA MAKE YOU FEEL ANY BETTER.
NIN
I SUPPOSE NOT. GUESS I'LL STAY HOME AND BEAT-OFF. I'VE GOT SOME NEW TAPES I'VE BEEN MEANING TO SAMPLE.
WELL, THANKS FOR SHARING. ANYWAYS, I GOTTA GET READY.
ANAL ANGEL
Jack

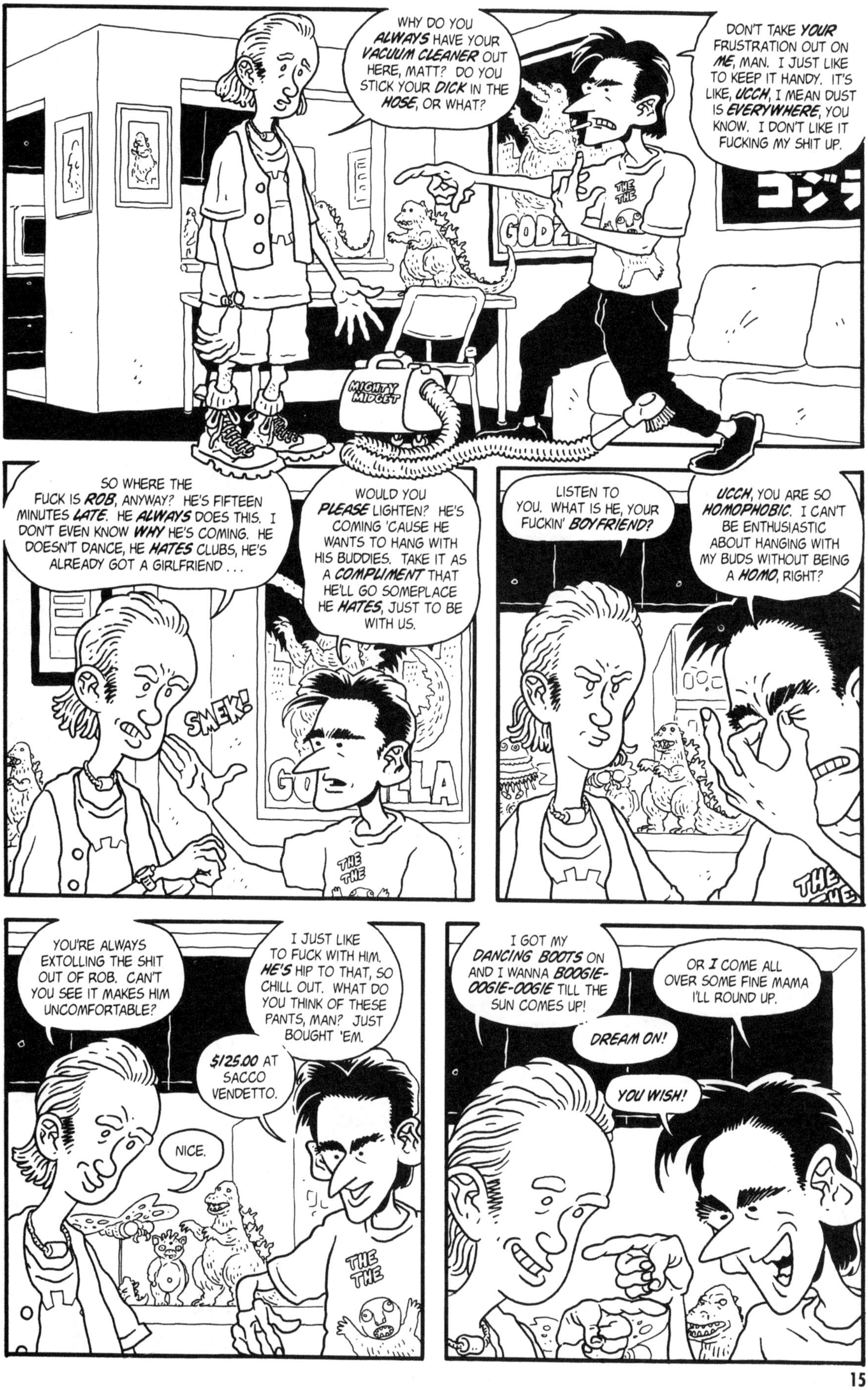
WHY DO YOU ALWAYS HAVE YOUR VACUUM CLEANER OUT HERE, MATT? DO YOU STICK YOUR DICK IN THE HOSE, OR WHAT?
DON'T TAKE YOUR FRUSTRATION OUT ON ME, MAN. I JUST LIKE TO KEEP IT HANDY. IT'S LIKE, UCCH, I MEAN DUST IS EVERYWHERE, YOU KNOW. I DON'T LIKE IT FUCKING MY SHIT UP.
THE THE
GODZ
MIGHTY MIDGET
SO WHERE THE FUCK IS ROB, ANYWAY? HE'S FIFTEEN MINUTES LATE. HE ALWAYS DOES THIS. I DON'T EVEN KNOW WHY HE'S COMING. HE DOESN'T DANCE, HE HATES CLUBS, HE'S ALREADY GOT A GIRLFRIEND . . .
WOULD YOU PLEASE LIGHTEN? HE'S COMING 'CAUSE HE WANTS TO HANG WITH HIS BUDDIES. TAKE IT AS A COMPLIMENT THAT HE'LL GO SOMEPLACE HE HATES, JUST TO BE WITH US.
SMEK!
GO ZILLA
THE THE
LISTEN TO YOU. WHAT IS HE, YOUR FUCKIN' BOYFRIEND?
UCCH, YOU ARE SO HOMOPHOBIC. I CAN'T BE ENTHUSIASTIC ABOUT HANGING WITH MY BUDS WITHOUT BEING A HOMO, RIGHT?
THE
YOU'RE ALWAYS EXTOLLING THE SHIT OUT OF ROB. CAN'T YOU SEE IT MAKES HIM UNCOMFORTABLE?
I JUST LIKE TO FUCK WITH HIM. HE'S HIP TO THAT, SO CHILL OUT. WHAT DO YOU THINK OF THESE PANTS, MAN? JUST BOUGHT 'EM.
$125.00 AT SACCO VENDETTO.
NICE.
THE THE
I GOT MY DANCING BOOTS ON AND I WANNA BOOGIE-OOGIE-OOGIE TILL THE SUN COMES UP!
OR I COME ALL OVER SOME FINE MAMA I'LL ROUND UP.
DREAM ON!
YOU WISH!

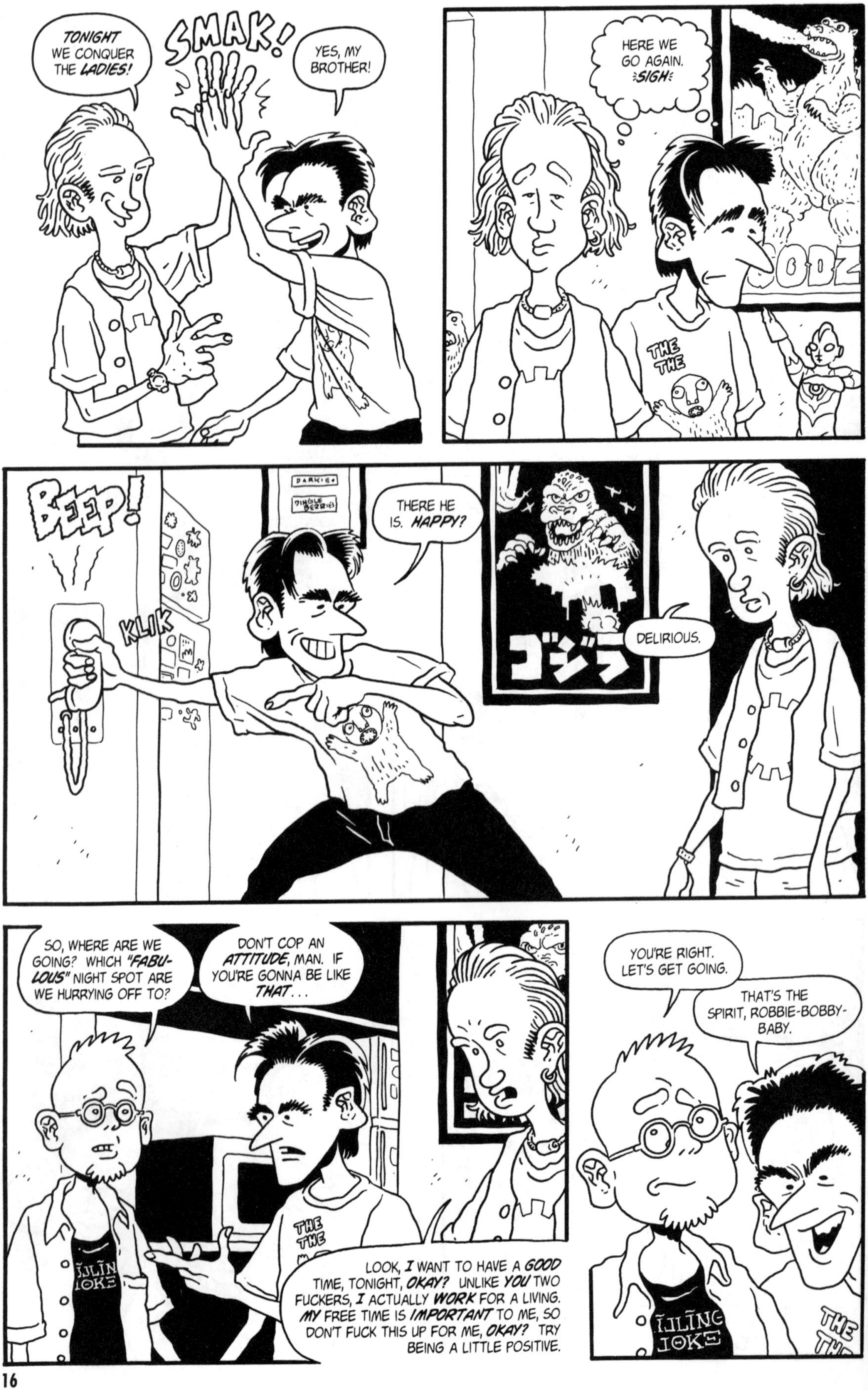
TONIGHT WE CONQUER THE LADIES!
SMAK!
YES, MY BROTHER!
HERE WE GO AGAIN. SIGH
BEEP!
KLIK
THERE HE IS. HAPPY?
DELIRIOUS.
SO, WHERE ARE WE GOING? WHICH "FABULOUS" NIGHT SPOT ARE WE HURRYING OFF TO?
DON'T COP AN ATTITUDE, MAN. IF YOU'RE GONNA BE LIKE THAT...
LOOK, I WANT TO HAVE A GOOD TIME, TONIGHT, OKAY? UNLIKE YOU TWO FUCKERS, I ACTUALLY WORK FOR A LIVING. MY FREE TIME IS IMPORTANT TO ME, SO DON'T FUCK THIS UP FOR ME, OKAY? TRY BEING A LITTLE POSITIVE.
YOU'RE RIGHT. LET'S GET GOING.
THAT'S THE SPIRIT, ROBBIE-BOBBY-BABY.

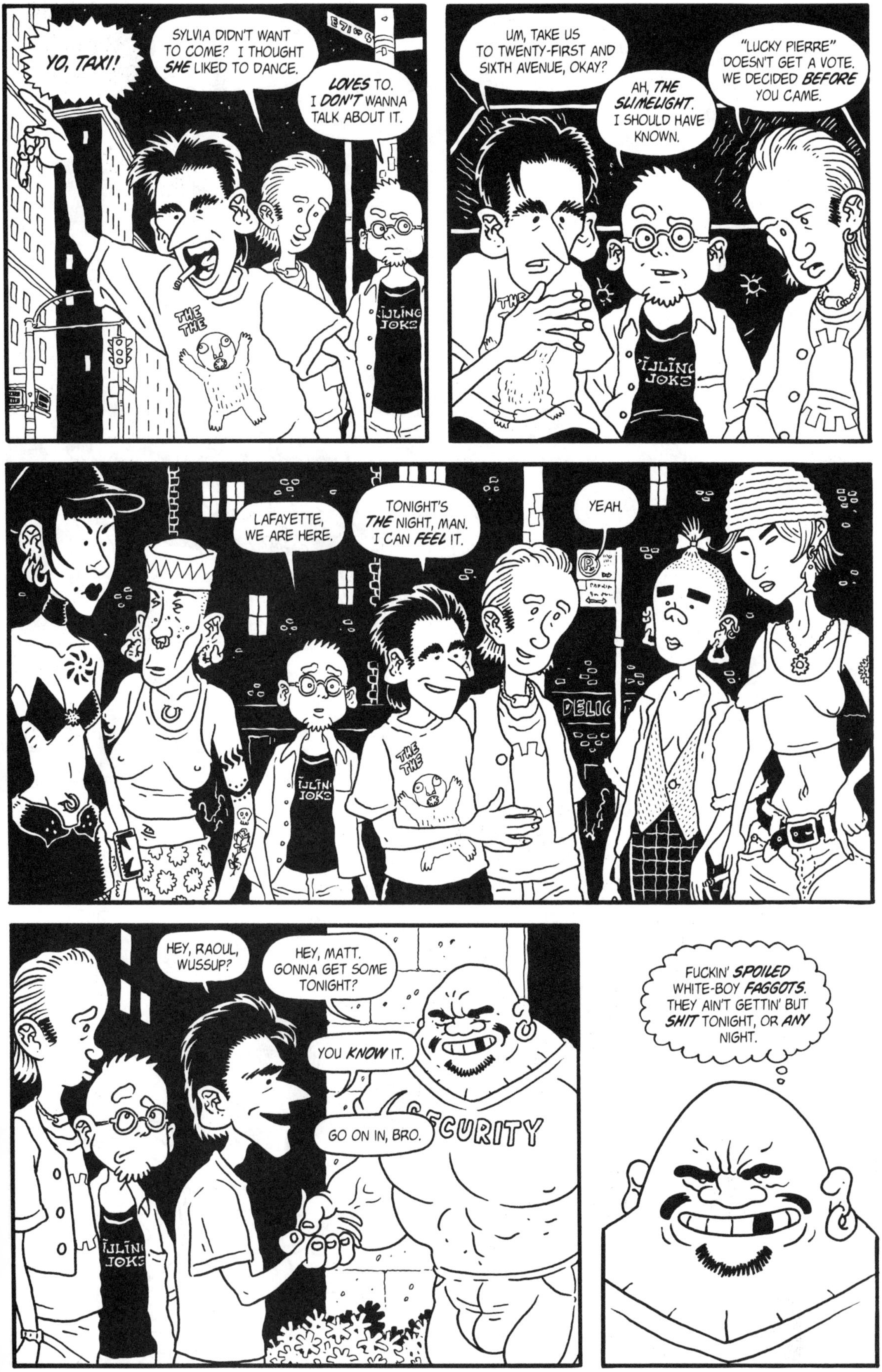
YO, TAXI!
SYLVIA DIDN'T WANT TO COME? I THOUGHT SHE LIKED TO DANCE.
LOVES TO. I DON'T WANNA TALK ABOUT IT.
UM, TAKE US TO TWENTY-FIRST AND SIXTH AVENUE, OKAY?
AH, THE SLIMELIGHT. I SHOULD HAVE KNOWN.
"LUCKY PIERRE" DOESN'T GET A VOTE. WE DECIDED BEFORE YOU CAME.
LAFAYETTE, WE ARE HERE.
TONIGHT'S THE NIGHT, MAN. I CAN FEEL IT.
YEAH.
HEY, RAOUL, WUSSUP?
HEY, MATT. GONNA GET SOME TONIGHT?
YOU KNOW IT.
GO ON IN, BRO.
SECURITY
FUCKIN' SPOILED WHITE-BOY FAGGOTS. THEY AIN'T GETTIN' BUT SHIT TONIGHT, OR ANY NIGHT.

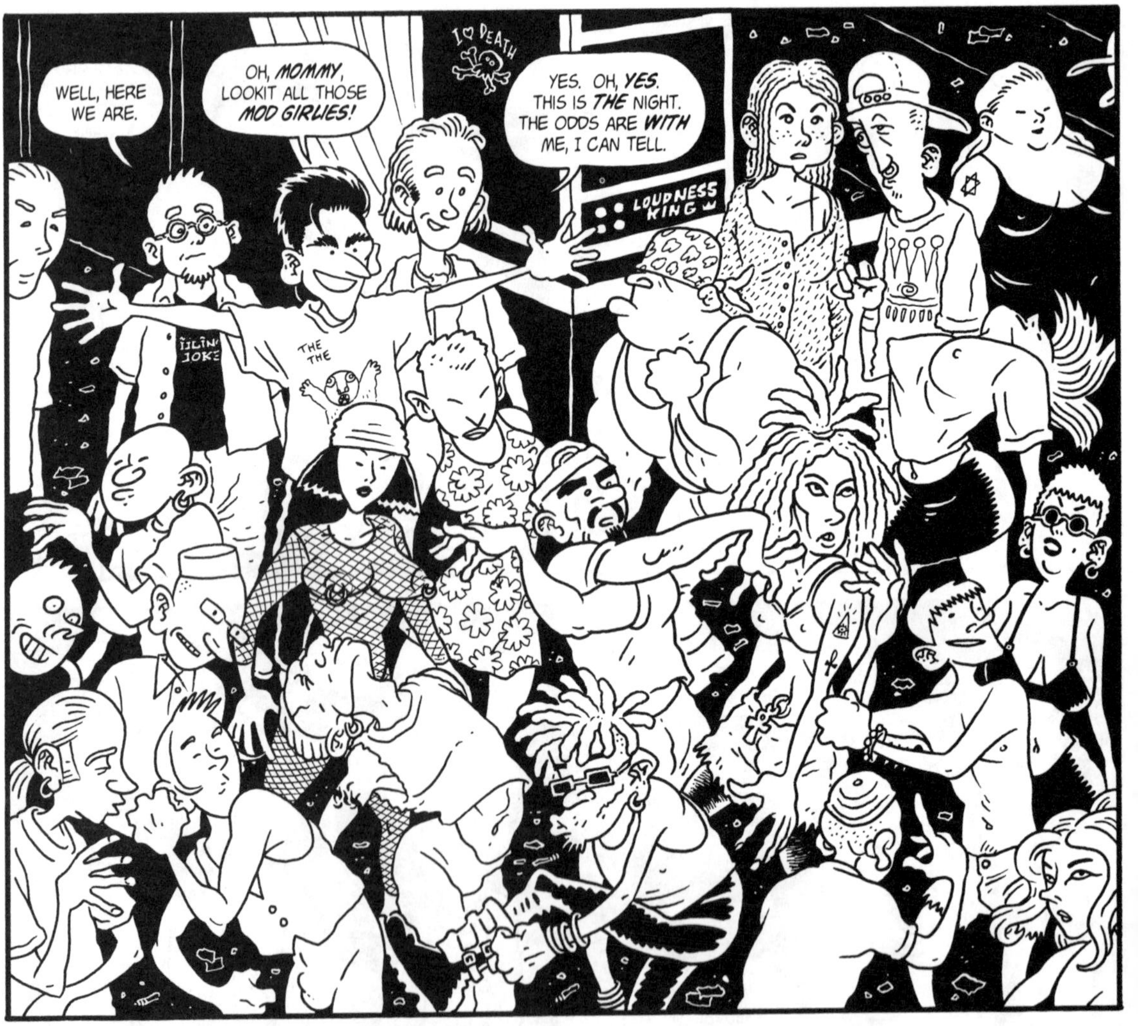
WELL, HERE WE ARE.
OH, MOMMY, LOOKIT ALL THOSE MOD GIRLIES!
YES. OH, YES. THIS IS THE NIGHT. THE ODDS ARE WITH ME, I CAN TELL.
I ♡ DEATH
LOUDNESS KING
THE THE

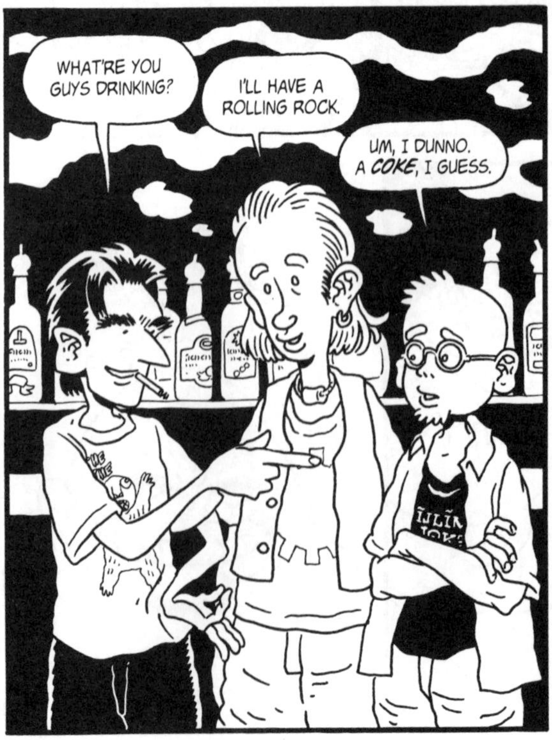
WHAT'RE YOU GUYS DRINKING?
I'LL HAVE A ROLLING ROCK.
UM, I DUNNO. A COKE, I GUESS.

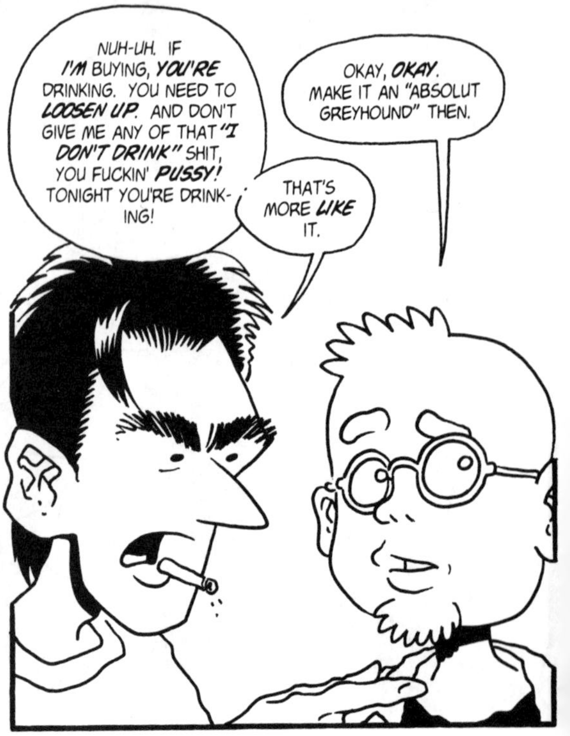
NUH-UH. IF I'M BUYING, YOU'RE DRINKING. YOU NEED TO LOOSEN UP. AND DON'T GIVE ME ANY OF THAT "I DON'T DRINK" SHIT, YOU FUCKIN' PUSSY! TONIGHT YOU'RE DRINK-ING!
OKAY, OKAY. MAKE IT AN "ABSOLUT GREYHOUND" THEN.
THAT'S MORE LIKE IT.

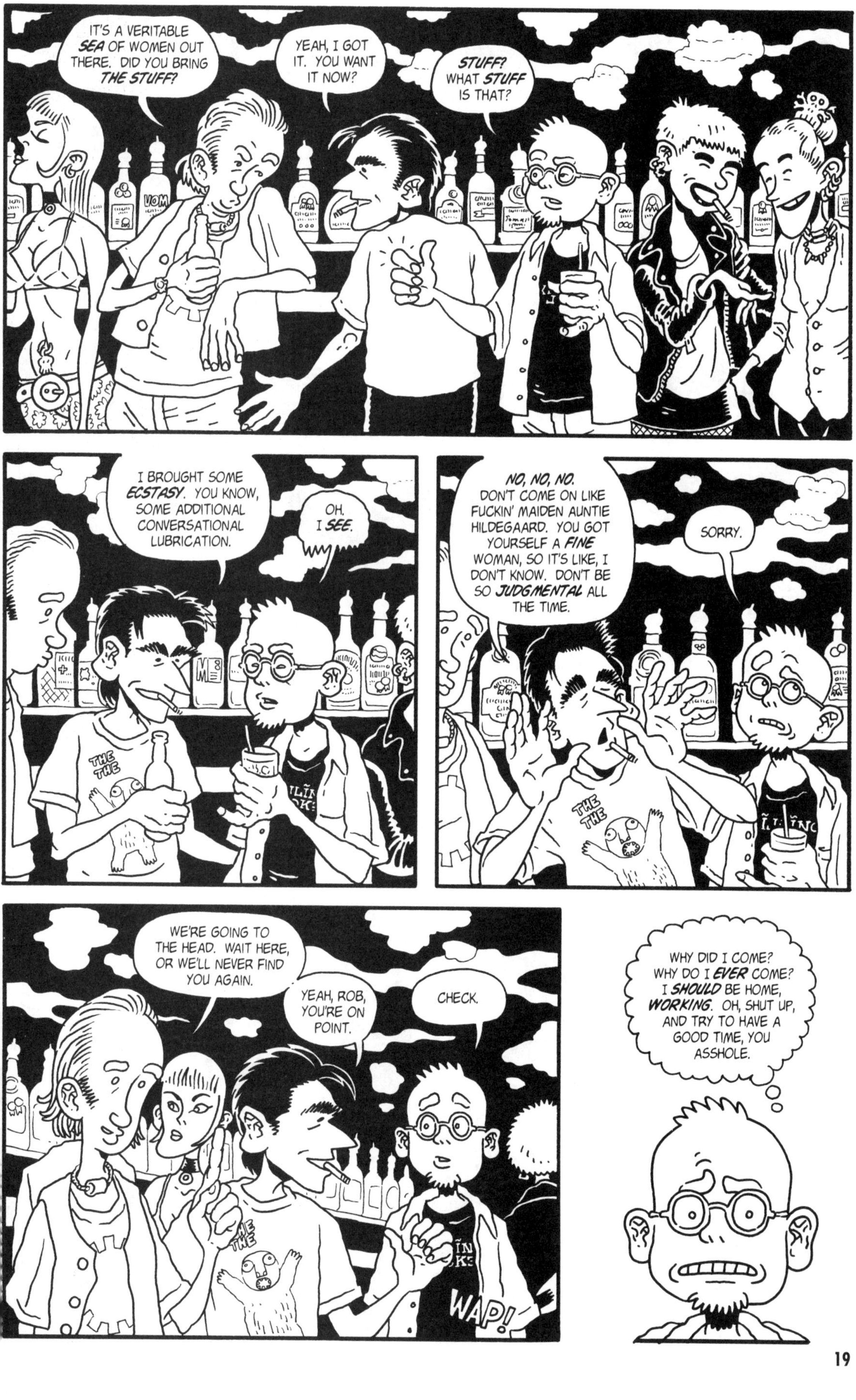
IT'S A VERITABLE SEA OF WOMEN OUT THERE. DID YOU BRING THE STUFF?
YEAH, I GOT IT. YOU WANT IT NOW?
STUFF? WHAT STUFF IS THAT?
VOM
I BROUGHT SOME ECSTASY. YOU KNOW, SOME ADDITIONAL CONVERSATIONAL LUBRICATION.
OH. I SEE.
THE THE
NO, NO, NO. DON'T COME ON LIKE FUCKIN' MAIDEN AUNTIE HILDEGAARD. YOU GOT YOURSELF A FINE WOMAN, SO IT'S LIKE, I DON'T KNOW. DON'T BE SO JUDGMENTAL ALL THE TIME.
SORRY.
THE THE
WE'RE GOING TO THE HEAD. WAIT HERE, OR WE'LL NEVER FIND YOU AGAIN.
YEAH, ROB, YOU'RE ON POINT.
CHECK.
WAP!
WHY DID I COME? WHY DO I EVER COME? I SHOULD BE HOME, WORKING. OH, SHUT UP, AND TRY TO HAVE A GOOD TIME, YOU ASSHOLE.

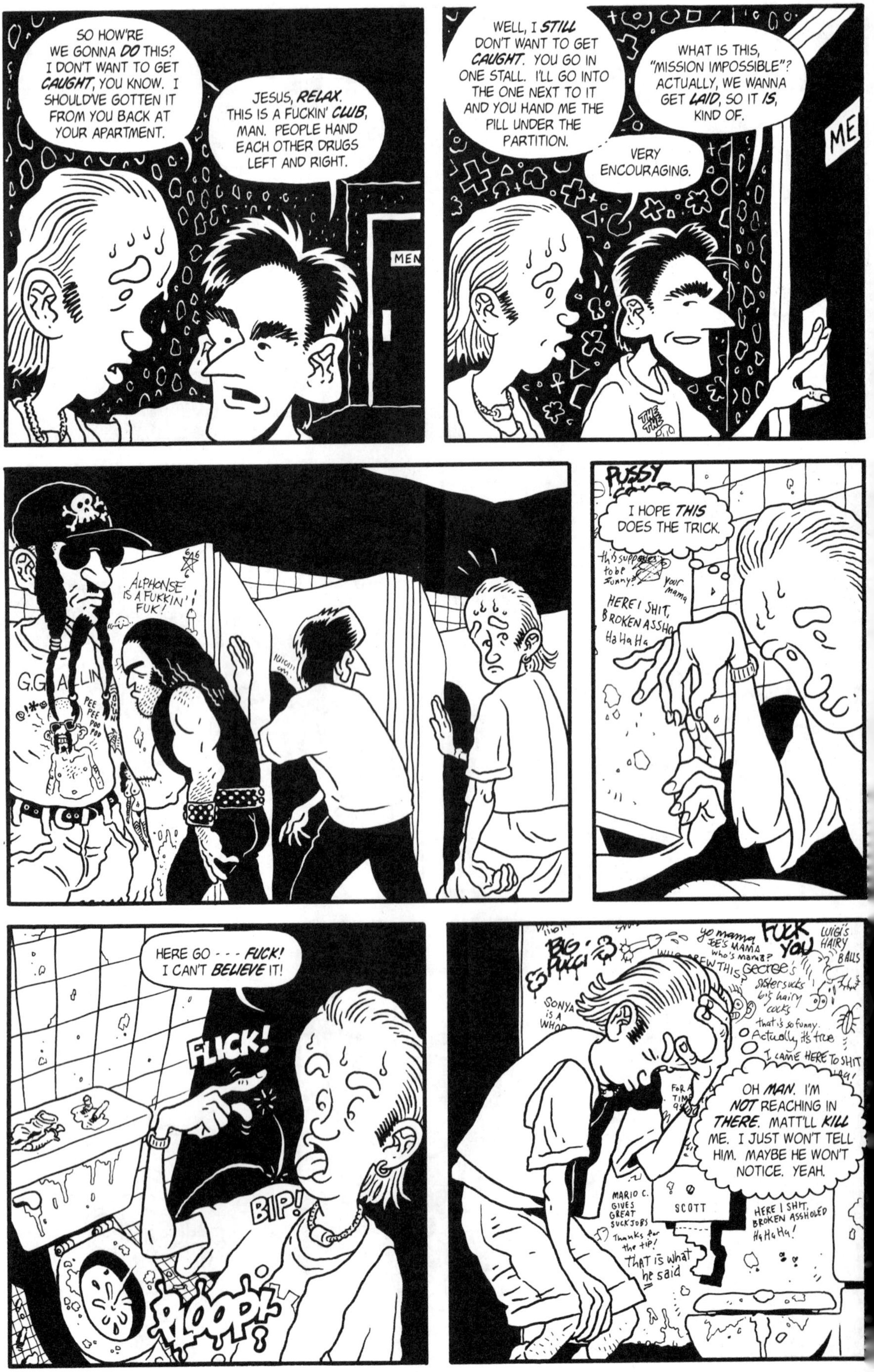
SO HOW'RE WE GONNA DO THIS? I DON'T WANT TO GET CAUGHT, YOU KNOW. I SHOULD'VE GOTTEN IT FROM YOU BACK AT YOUR APARTMENT.
JESUS, RELAX. THIS IS A FUCKIN' CLUB, MAN. PEOPLE HAND EACH OTHER DRUGS LEFT AND RIGHT.
MEN
WELL, I STILL DON'T WANT TO GET CAUGHT. YOU GO IN ONE STALL. I'LL GO INTO THE ONE NEXT TO IT AND YOU HAND ME THE PILL UNDER THE PARTITION.
WHAT IS THIS, "MISSION IMPOSSIBLE"? ACTUALLY, WE WANNA GET LAID, SO IT IS, KIND OF.
VERY ENCOURAGING.
ME
ALPHONSE IS A FUKKIN' FUK!
G.G. ALLIN
PEE PEE POO POO
PUSSY
I HOPE THIS DOES THE TRICK.
this supposed to be funny?
your mama
HERE I SHIT, BROKEN ASSHO
Ha Ha Ha
HERE GO - - - FUCK! I CAN'T BELIEVE IT!
FLICK!
BIP!
PLOOP!
BIG PUCCI
yo mama
JOE'S MAMA
Who's mama?
WHO DREW THIS?
FUCK YOU
LUIGI'S HAIRY BALLS
SONYA IS A WHO
George's sister sucks 6" hairy cocks
that's so funny.
Actually, it's true
I CAME HERE TO SHIT
OH MAN. I'M NOT REACHING IN THERE. MATT'LL KILL ME. I JUST WON'T TELL HIM. MAYBE HE WON'T NOTICE. YEAH.
MARIO C. GIVES GREAT SUCK JOBS
Thanks for the tip!
THAT is what he said
SCOTT
HERE I SHIT, BROKEN ASSHOLED Ha Ha Ha!

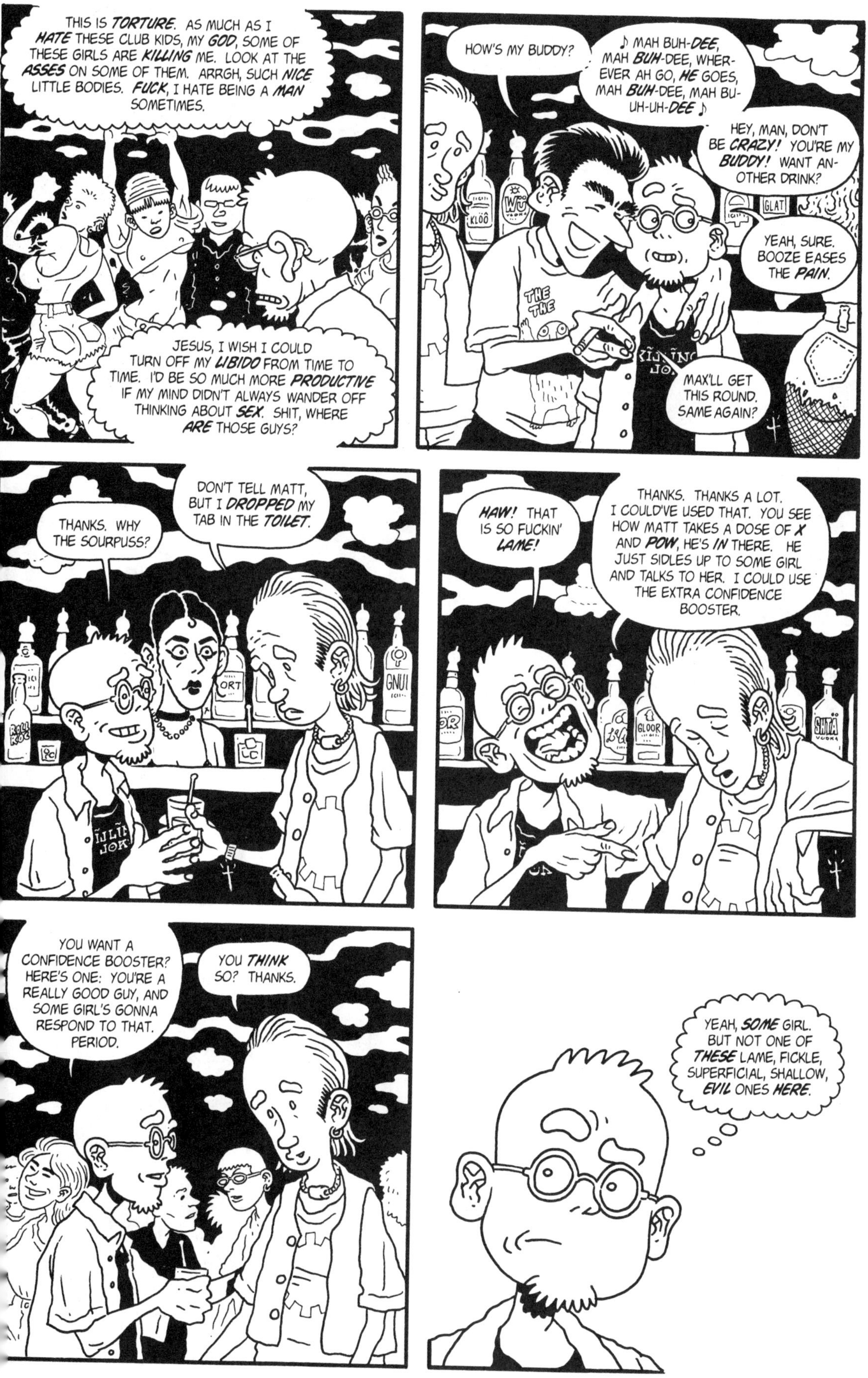
THIS IS TORTURE. AS MUCH AS I HATE THESE CLUB KIDS, MY GOD, SOME OF THESE GIRLS ARE KILLING ME. LOOK AT THE ASSES ON SOME OF THEM. ARRGH, SUCH NICE LITTLE BODIES. FUCK, I HATE BEING A MAN SOMETIMES.
JESUS, I WISH I COULD TURN OFF MY LIBIDO FROM TIME TO TIME. I'D BE SO MUCH MORE PRODUCTIVE IF MY MIND DIDN'T ALWAYS WANDER OFF THINKING ABOUT SEX. SHIT, WHERE ARE THOSE GUYS?
HOW'S MY BUDDY?
♪ MAH BUH-DEE, MAH BUH-DEE, WHER-EVER AH GO, HE GOES, MAH BUH-DEE, MAH BU-UH-UH-DEE ♪
HEY, MAN, DON'T BE CRAZY! YOU'RE MY BUDDY! WANT AN-OTHER DRINK?
YEAH, SURE. BOOZE EASES THE PAIN.
THE THE
MAX'LL GET THIS ROUND. SAME AGAIN?
THANKS. WHY THE SOURPUSS?
DON'T TELL MATT, BUT I DROPPED MY TAB IN THE TOILET.
HAW! THAT IS SO FUCKIN' LAME!
THANKS. THANKS A LOT. I COULD'VE USED THAT. YOU SEE HOW MATT TAKES A DOSE OF X AND POW, HE'S IN THERE. HE JUST SIDLES UP TO SOME GIRL AND TALKS TO HER. I COULD USE THE EXTRA CONFIDENCE BOOSTER.
YOU WANT A CONFIDENCE BOOSTER? HERE'S ONE: YOU'RE A REALLY GOOD GUY, AND SOME GIRL'S GONNA RESPOND TO THAT. PERIOD.
YOU THINK SO? THANKS.
YEAH, SOME GIRL. BUT NOT ONE OF THESE LAME, FICKLE, SUPERFICIAL, SHALLOW, EVIL ONES HERE.

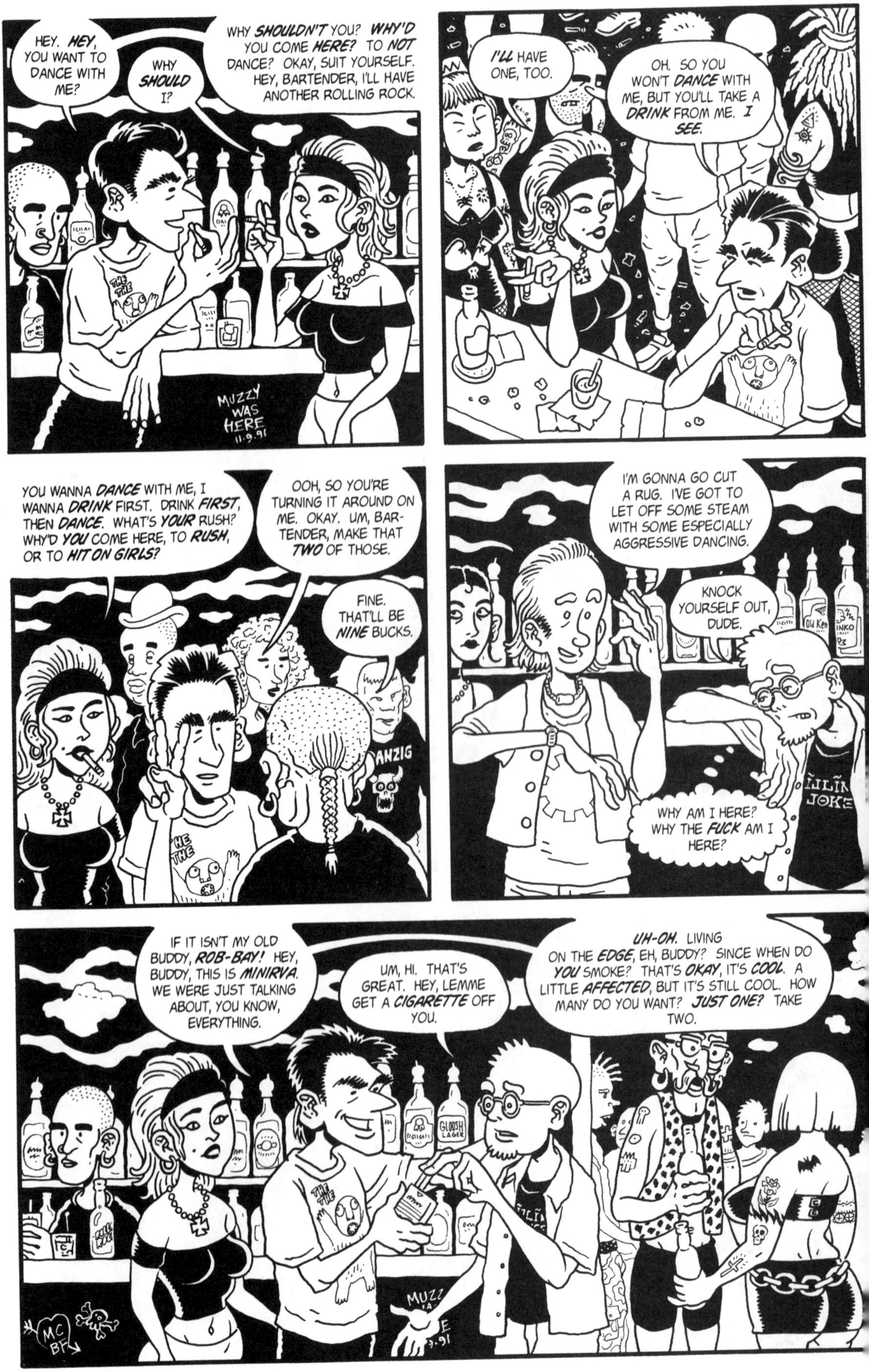
HEY. HEY, YOU WANT TO DANCE WITH ME?
WHY SHOULD I?
WHY SHOULDN'T YOU? WHY'D YOU COME HERE? TO NOT DANCE? OKAY, SUIT YOURSELF. HEY, BARTENDER, I'LL HAVE ANOTHER ROLLING ROCK.
MUZZY WAS HERE 11.9.91
I'LL HAVE ONE, TOO.
OH. SO YOU WON'T DANCE WITH ME, BUT YOU'LL TAKE A DRINK FROM ME. I SEE.
YOU WANNA DANCE WITH ME, I WANNA DRINK FIRST. DRINK FIRST, THEN DANCE. WHAT'S YOUR RUSH? WHY'D YOU COME HERE, TO RUSH, OR TO HIT ON GIRLS?
OOH, SO YOU'RE TURNING IT AROUND ON ME. OKAY. UM, BAR-TENDER, MAKE THAT TWO OF THOSE.
FINE. THAT'LL BE NINE BUCKS.
I'M GONNA GO CUT A RUG. I'VE GOT TO LET OFF SOME STEAM WITH SOME ESPECIALLY AGGRESSIVE DANCING.
KNOCK YOURSELF OUT, DUDE.
WHY AM I HERE? WHY THE FUCK AM I HERE?
IF IT ISN'T MY OLD BUDDY, ROB-BAY! HEY, BUDDY, THIS IS MINIRVA. WE WERE JUST TALKING ABOUT, YOU KNOW, EVERYTHING.
UM, HI. THAT'S GREAT. HEY, LEMME GET A CIGARETTE OFF YOU.
UH-OH. LIVING ON THE EDGE, EH, BUDDY? SINCE WHEN DO YOU SMOKE? THAT'S OKAY, IT'S COOL. A LITTLE AFFECTED, BUT IT'S STILL COOL. HOW MANY DO YOU WANT? JUST ONE? TAKE TWO.

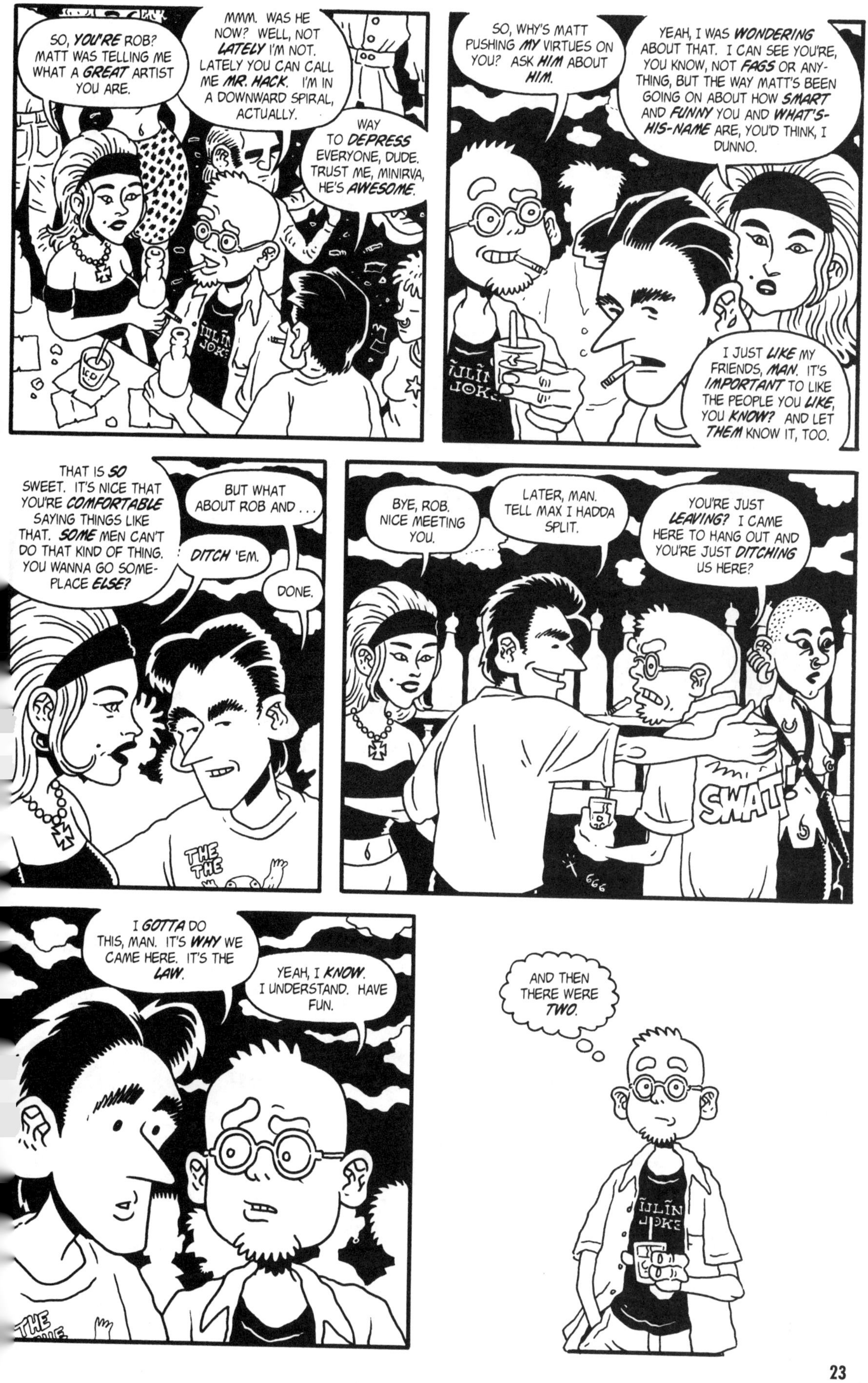
SO, YOU'RE ROB? MATT WAS TELLING ME WHAT A GREAT ARTIST YOU ARE.
MMM. WAS HE NOW? WELL, NOT LATELY I'M NOT. LATELY YOU CAN CALL ME MR. HACK. I'M IN A DOWNWARD SPIRAL, ACTUALLY.
WAY TO DEPRESS EVERYONE, DUDE. TRUST ME, MINIRVA, HE'S AWESOME.
SO, WHY'S MATT PUSHING MY VIRTUES ON YOU? ASK HIM ABOUT HIM.
YEAH, I WAS WONDERING ABOUT THAT. I CAN SEE YOU'RE, YOU KNOW, NOT FAGS OR ANYTHING, BUT THE WAY MATT'S BEEN GOING ON ABOUT HOW SMART AND FUNNY YOU AND WHAT'S-HIS-NAME ARE, YOU'D THINK, I DUNNO.
I JUST LIKE MY FRIENDS, MAN. IT'S IMPORTANT TO LIKE THE PEOPLE YOU LIKE, YOU KNOW? AND LET THEM KNOW IT, TOO.
THAT IS SO SWEET. IT'S NICE THAT YOU'RE COMFORTABLE SAYING THINGS LIKE THAT. SOME MEN CAN'T DO THAT KIND OF THING. YOU WANNA GO SOMEPLACE ELSE?
BUT WHAT ABOUT ROB AND . . .
DITCH 'EM.
DONE.
THE THE
BYE, ROB. NICE MEETING YOU.
LATER, MAN. TELL MAX I HADDA SPLIT.
YOU'RE JUST LEAVING? I CAME HERE TO HANG OUT AND YOU'RE JUST DITCHING US HERE?
SWAT!
666
I GOTTA DO THIS, MAN. IT'S WHY WE CAME HERE. IT'S THE LAW.
YEAH, I KNOW. I UNDERSTAND. HAVE FUN.
THE
AND THEN THERE WERE TWO.

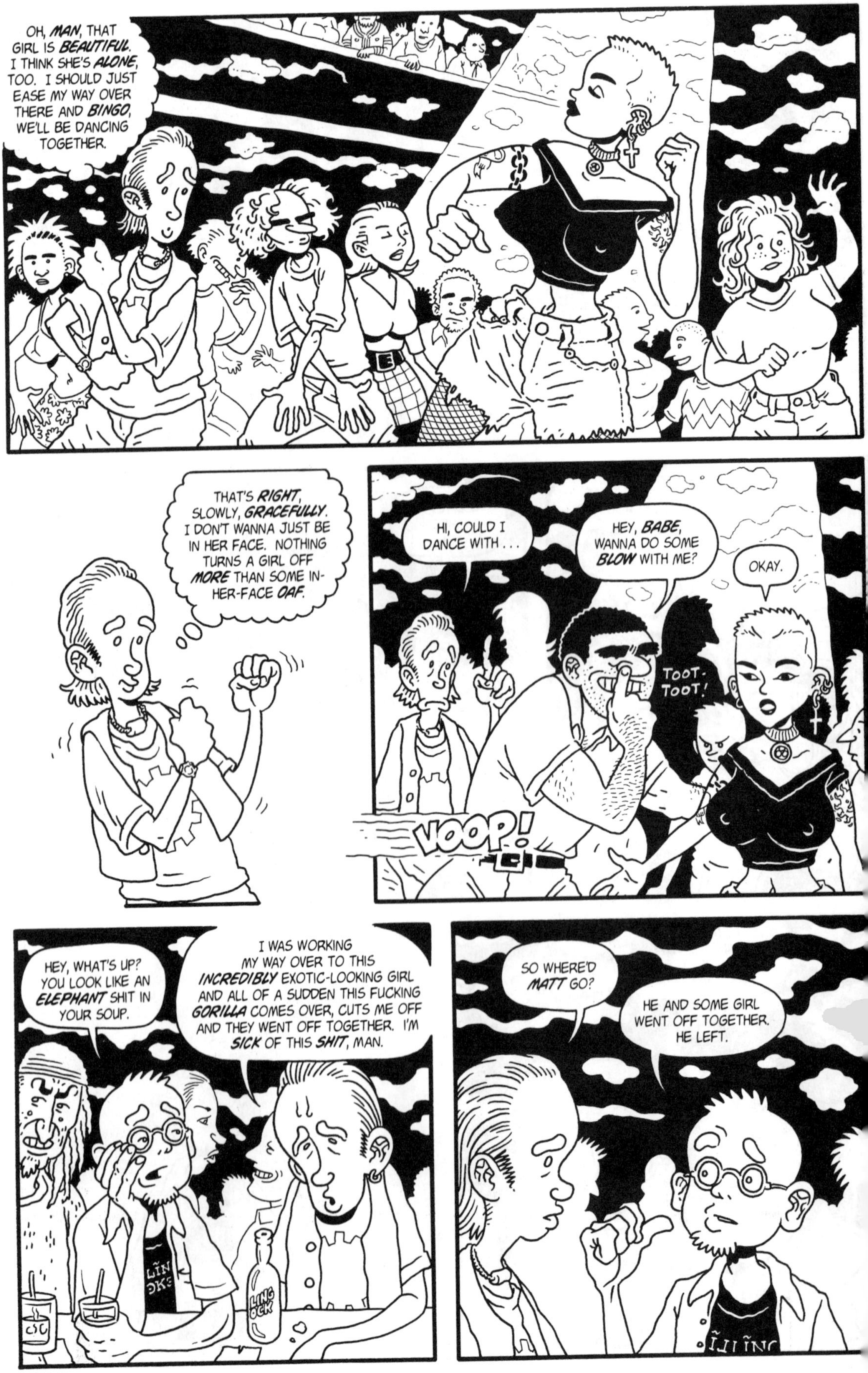

OH, MAN, THAT GIRL IS BEAUTIFUL. I THINK SHE'S ALONE, TOO. I SHOULD JUST EASE MY WAY OVER THERE AND BINGO, WE'LL BE DANCING TOGETHER.
THAT'S RIGHT, SLOWLY, GRACEFULLY. I DON'T WANNA JUST BE IN HER FACE. NOTHING TURNS A GIRL OFF MORE THAN SOME IN-HER-FACE OAF.
HI, COULD I DANCE WITH . . .
HEY, BABE, WANNA DO SOME BLOW WITH ME?
OKAY.
TOOT-TOOT!
VOOP!
HEY, WHAT'S UP? YOU LOOK LIKE AN ELEPHANT SHIT IN YOUR SOUP.
I WAS WORKING MY WAY OVER TO THIS INCREDIBLY EXOTIC-LOOKING GIRL AND ALL OF A SUDDEN THIS FUCKING GORILLA COMES OVER, CUTS ME OFF AND THEY WENT OFF TOGETHER. I'M SICK OF THIS SHIT, MAN.
SO WHERE'D MATT GO?
HE AND SOME GIRL WENT OFF TOGETHER. HE LEFT.

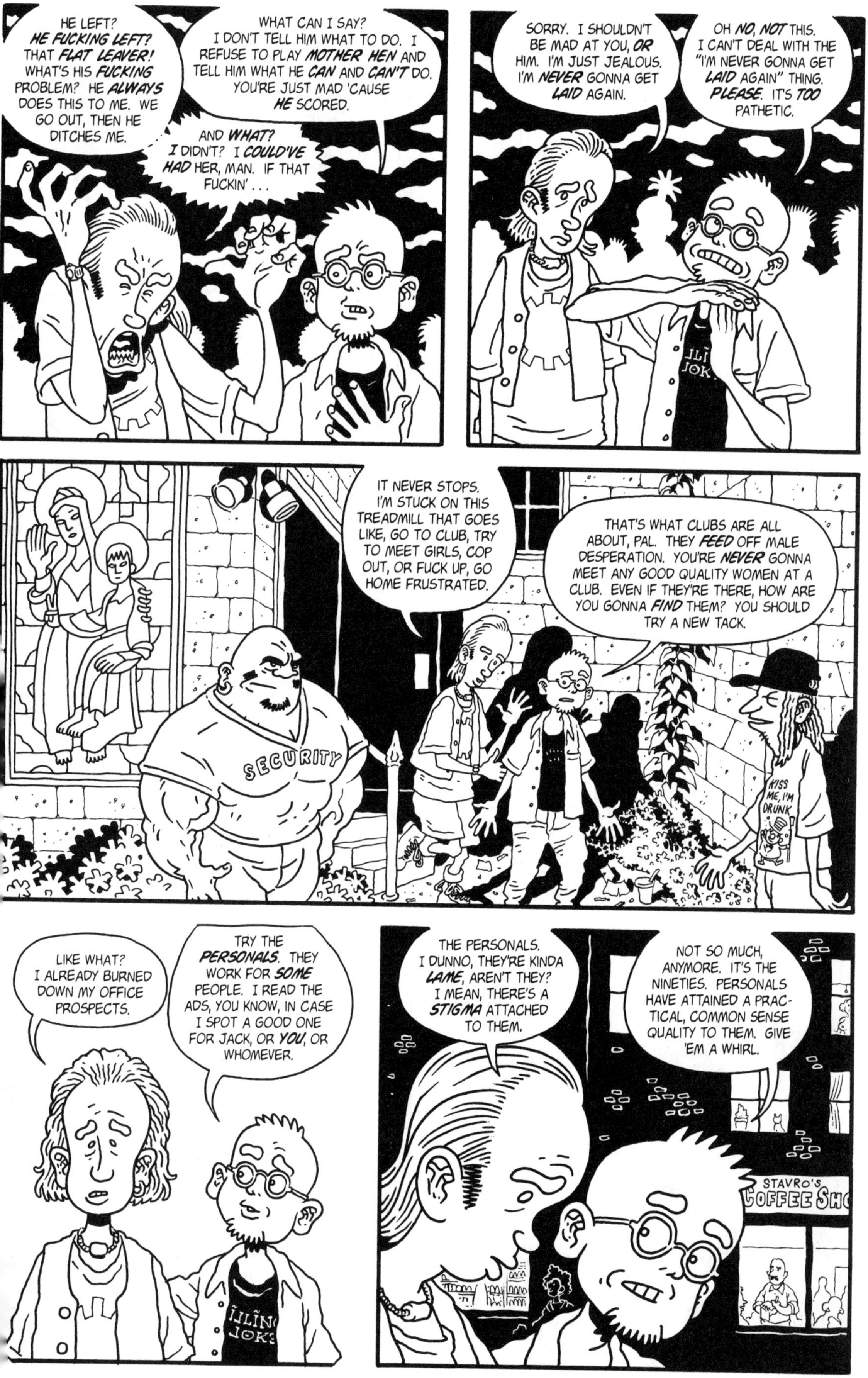
HE LEFT? HE FUCKING LEFT? THAT FLAT LEAVER! WHAT'S HIS FUCKING PROBLEM? HE ALWAYS DOES THIS TO ME. WE GO OUT, THEN HE DITCHES ME.
WHAT CAN I SAY? I DON'T TELL HIM WHAT TO DO. I REFUSE TO PLAY MOTHER HEN AND TELL HIM WHAT HE CAN AND CAN'T DO. YOU'RE JUST MAD 'CAUSE HE SCORED.
AND WHAT? I DIDN'T? I COULD'VE HAD HER, MAN. IF THAT FUCKIN' . . .
SORRY. I SHOULDN'T BE MAD AT YOU, OR HIM. I'M JUST JEALOUS. I'M NEVER GONNA GET LAID AGAIN.
OH NO, NOT THIS. I CAN'T DEAL WITH THE "I'M NEVER GONNA GET LAID AGAIN" THING. PLEASE. IT'S TOO PATHETIC.
IT NEVER STOPS. I'M STUCK ON THIS TREADMILL THAT GOES LIKE, GO TO CLUB, TRY TO MEET GIRLS, COP OUT, OR FUCK UP, GO HOME FRUSTRATED.
SECURITY
THAT'S WHAT CLUBS ARE ALL ABOUT, PAL. THEY FEED OFF MALE DESPERATION. YOU'RE NEVER GONNA MEET ANY GOOD QUALITY WOMEN AT A CLUB. EVEN IF THEY'RE THERE, HOW ARE YOU GONNA FIND THEM? YOU SHOULD TRY A NEW TACK.
KISS ME, I'M DRUNK
LIKE WHAT? I ALREADY BURNED DOWN MY OFFICE PROSPECTS.
TRY THE PERSONALS. THEY WORK FOR SOME PEOPLE. I READ THE ADS, YOU KNOW, IN CASE I SPOT A GOOD ONE FOR JACK, OR YOU, OR WHOMEVER.
THE PERSONALS. I DUNNO, THEY'RE KINDA LAME, AREN'T THEY? I MEAN, THERE'S A STIGMA ATTACHED TO THEM.
NOT SO MUCH, ANYMORE. IT'S THE NINETIES. PERSONALS HAVE ATTAINED A PRACTICAL, COMMON SENSE QUALITY TO THEM. GIVE 'EM A WHIRL.
STAVRO'S COFFEE SH

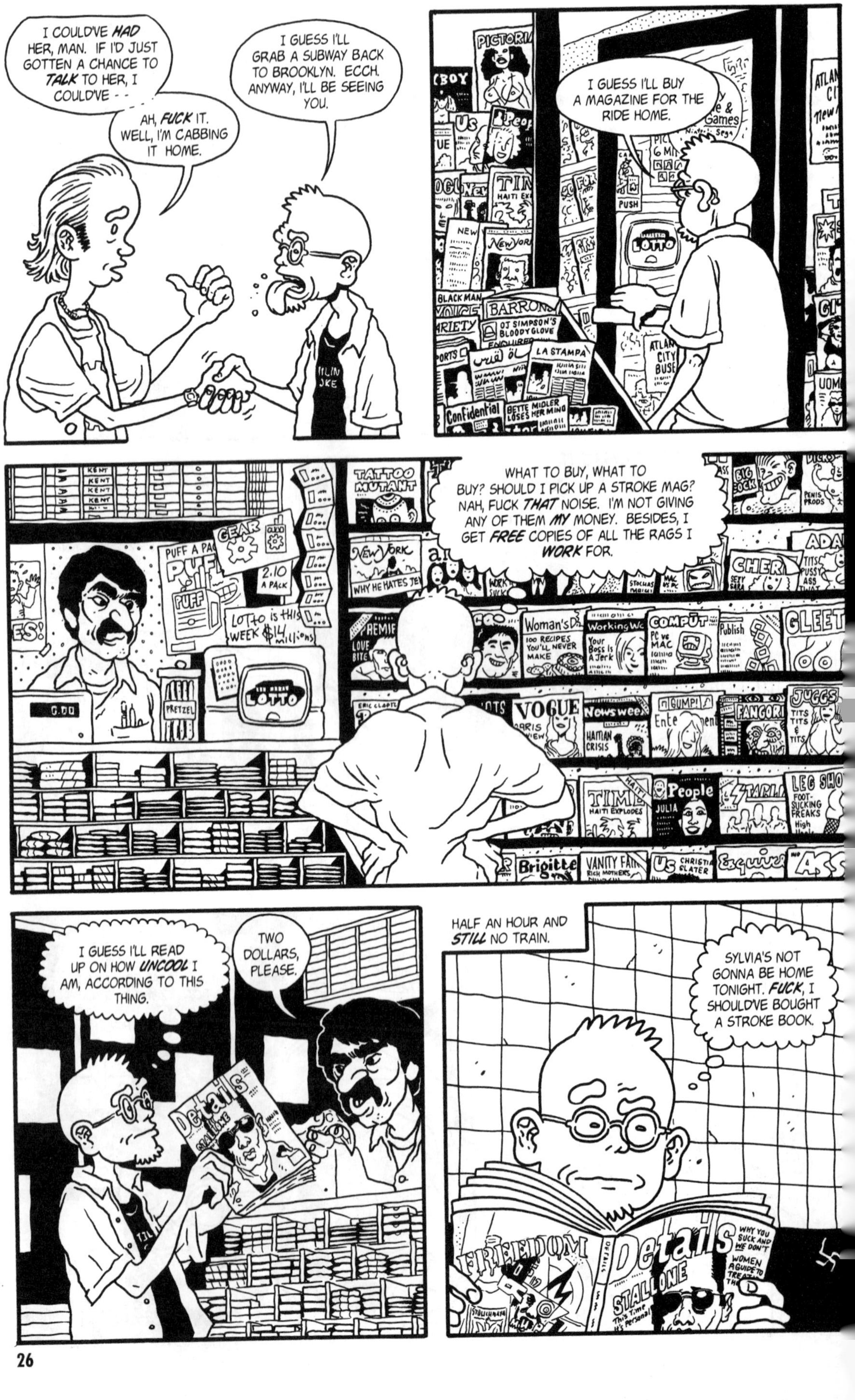
I COULD'VE HAD HER, MAN. IF I'D JUST GOTTEN A CHANCE TO TALK TO HER, I COULD'VE - -
AH, FUCK IT. WELL, I'M CABBING IT HOME.
I GUESS I'LL GRAB A SUBWAY BACK TO BROOKLYN. ECCH. ANYWAY, I'LL BE SEEING YOU.
I GUESS I'LL BUY A MAGAZINE FOR THE RIDE HOME.
WHAT TO BUY, WHAT TO BUY? SHOULD I PICK UP A STROKE MAG? NAH, FUCK THAT NOISE. I'M NOT GIVING ANY OF THEM MY MONEY. BESIDES, I GET FREE COPIES OF ALL THE RAGS I WORK FOR.
I GUESS I'LL READ UP ON HOW UNCOOL I AM, ACCORDING TO THIS THING.
TWO DOLLARS, PLEASE.
HALF AN HOUR AND STILL NO TRAIN.
SYLVIA'S NOT GONNA BE HOME TONIGHT. FUCK, I SHOULD'VE BOUGHT A STROKE BOOK.

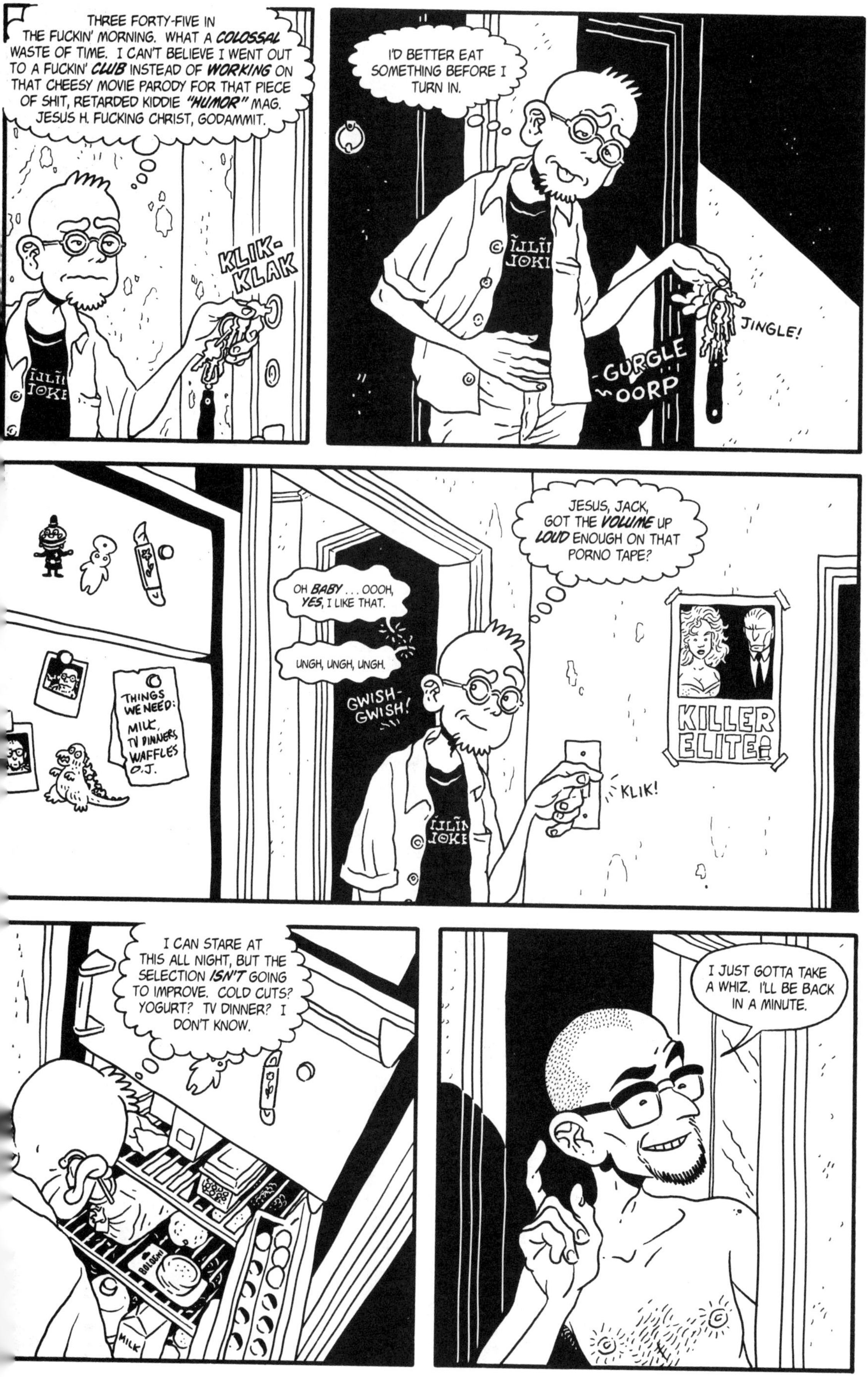
THREE FORTY-FIVE IN THE FUCKIN' MORNING. WHAT A *COLOSSAL* WASTE OF TIME. I CAN'T BELIEVE I WENT OUT TO A FUCKIN' *CLUB* INSTEAD OF *WORKING* ON THAT CHEESY MOVIE PARODY FOR THAT PIECE OF SHIT, RETARDED KIDDIE *"HUMOR"* MAG. JESUS H. FUCKING CHRIST, GODAMMIT.
KLIK-KLAK
I'D BETTER EAT SOMETHING BEFORE I TURN IN.
JINGLE!
GURGLE OORP
THINGS WE NEED: MILK, TV DINNERS, WAFFLES, O.J.
OH *BABY* . . . OOOH, *YES*, I LIKE THAT.
UNGH, UNGH, UNGH.
GWISH-GWISH!
JESUS, JACK, GOT THE *VOLUME* UP *LOUD* ENOUGH ON THAT PORNO TAPE?
KILLER ELITE
KLIK!
I CAN STARE AT THIS ALL NIGHT, BUT THE SELECTION *ISN'T* GOING TO IMPROVE. COLD CUTS? YOGURT? TV DINNER? I DON'T KNOW.
MILK
I JUST GOTTA TAKE A WHIZ. I'LL BE BACK IN A MINUTE.

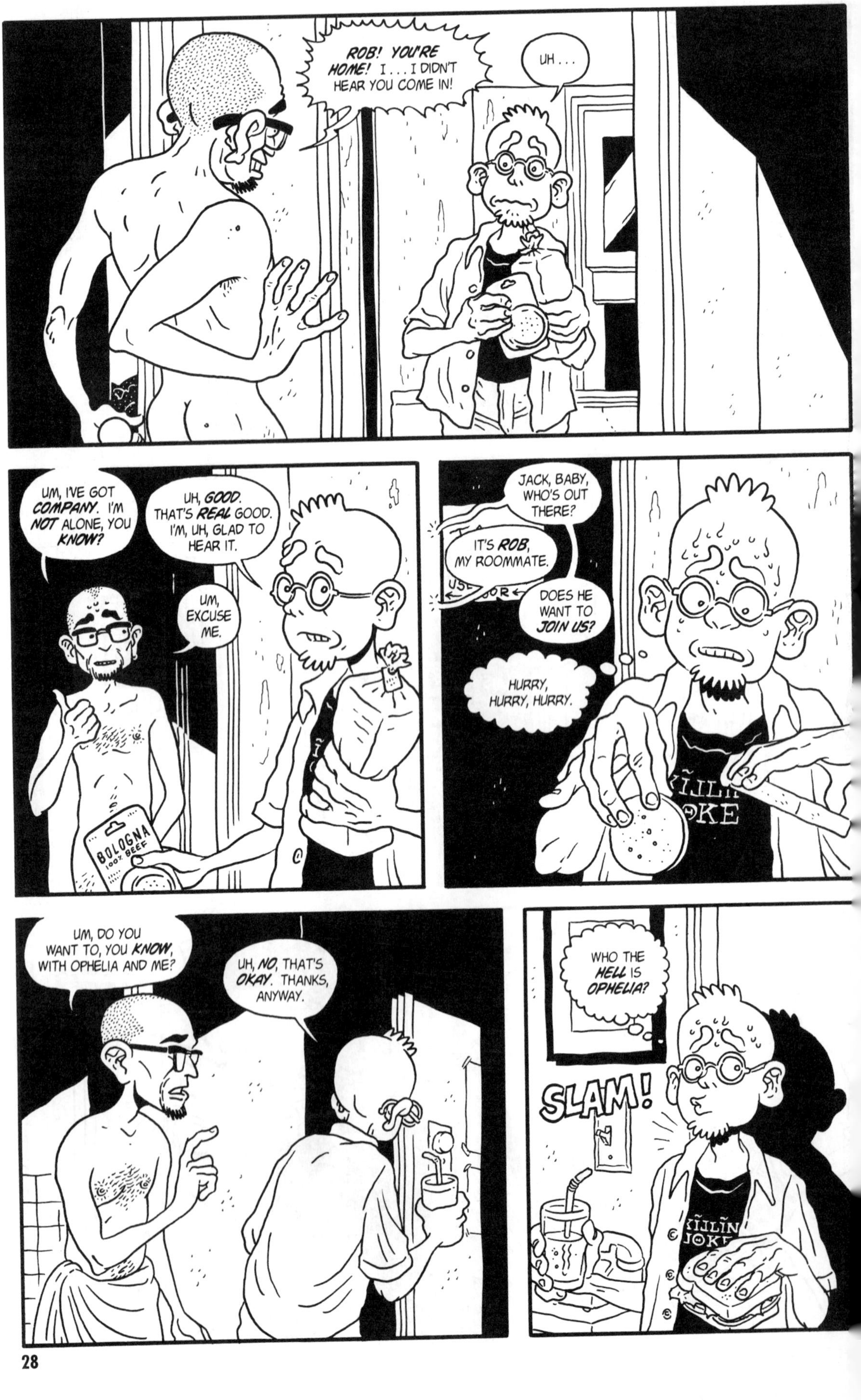
ROB! YOU'RE HOME! I . . . I DIDN'T HEAR YOU COME IN!
UH . . .
UM, I'VE GOT COMPANY. I'M NOT ALONE, YOU KNOW?
UH, GOOD. THAT'S REAL GOOD. I'M, UH, GLAD TO HEAR IT.
UM, EXCUSE ME.
BOLOGNA 100% BEEF
JACK, BABY, WHO'S OUT THERE?
IT'S ROB, MY ROOMMATE.
DOES HE WANT TO JOIN US?
HURRY, HURRY, HURRY.
UM, DO YOU WANT TO, YOU KNOW, WITH OPHELIA AND ME?
UH, NO, THAT'S OKAY. THANKS, ANYWAY.
WHO THE HELL IS OPHELIA?
SLAM!

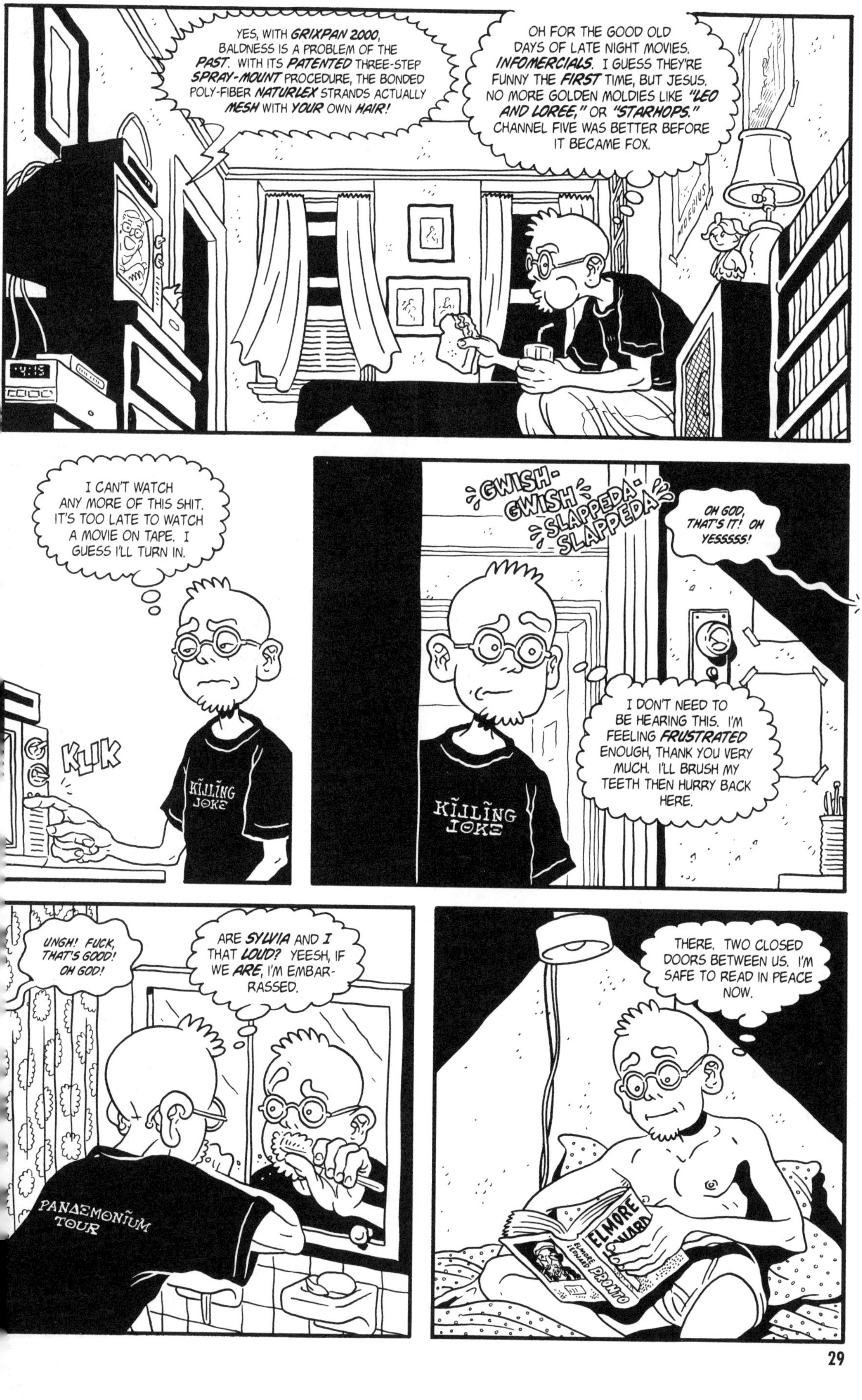
YES, WITH GRIXPAN 2000, BALDNESS IS A PROBLEM OF THE PAST. WITH ITS PATENTED THREE-STEP SPRAY-MOUNT PROCEDURE, THE BONDED POLY-FIBER NATURLEX STRANDS ACTUALLY MESH WITH YOUR OWN HAIR!
OH FOR THE GOOD OLD DAYS OF LATE NIGHT MOVIES. INFOMERCIALS. I GUESS THEY'RE FUNNY THE FIRST TIME, BUT JESUS. NO MORE GOLDEN MOLDIES LIKE "LEO AND LOREE," OR "STARHOPS." CHANNEL FIVE WAS BETTER BEFORE IT BECAME FOX.
MOEBIUS
I CAN'T WATCH ANY MORE OF THIS SHIT. IT'S TOO LATE TO WATCH A MOVIE ON TAPE. I GUESS I'LL TURN IN.
KLIK
KILLING JOKE
GWISH-GWISH SLAPPEDA-SLAPPEDA
OH GOD, THAT'S IT! OH YESSSSS!
I DON'T NEED TO BE HEARING THIS. I'M FEELING FRUSTRATED ENOUGH, THANK YOU VERY MUCH. I'LL BRUSH MY TEETH THEN HURRY BACK HERE.
KILLING JOKE
UNGH! FUCK, THAT'S GOOD! OH GOD!
ARE SYLVIA AND I THAT LOUD? YEESH, IF WE ARE, I'M EMBARRASSED.
PANDEMONIUM TOUR
THERE. TWO CLOSED DOORS BETWEEN US. I'M SAFE TO READ IN PEACE NOW.
ELMORE LEONARD
ELMORE LEONARD PRONTO

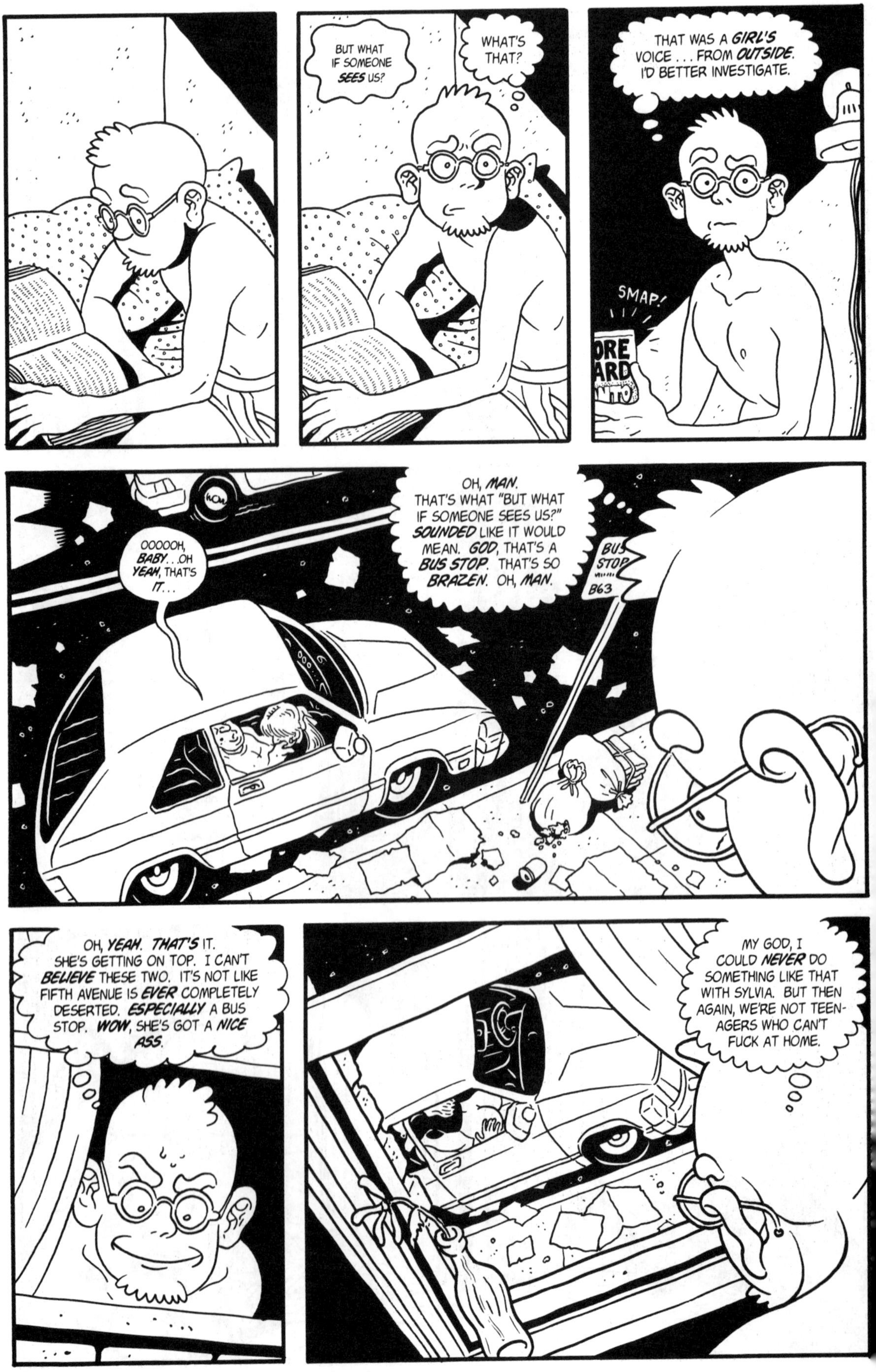
BUT WHAT IF SOMEONE SEES US?
WHAT'S THAT?
THAT WAS A GIRL'S VOICE . . . FROM OUTSIDE. I'D BETTER INVESTIGATE.
SMAP!
OOOOOH, BABY. . .OH YEAH, THAT'S IT. . .
OH, MAN. THAT'S WHAT "BUT WHAT IF SOMEONE SEES US?" SOUNDED LIKE IT WOULD MEAN. GOD, THAT'S A BUS STOP. THAT'S SO BRAZEN. OH, MAN.
BUS STOP
B63
OH, YEAH. THAT'S IT. SHE'S GETTING ON TOP. I CAN'T BELIEVE THESE TWO. IT'S NOT LIKE FIFTH AVENUE IS EVER COMPLETELY DESERTED. ESPECIALLY A BUS STOP. WOW, SHE'S GOT A NICE ASS.
MY GOD, I COULD NEVER DO SOMETHING LIKE THAT WITH SYLVIA. BUT THEN AGAIN, WE'RE NOT TEEN-AGERS WHO CAN'T FUCK AT HOME.

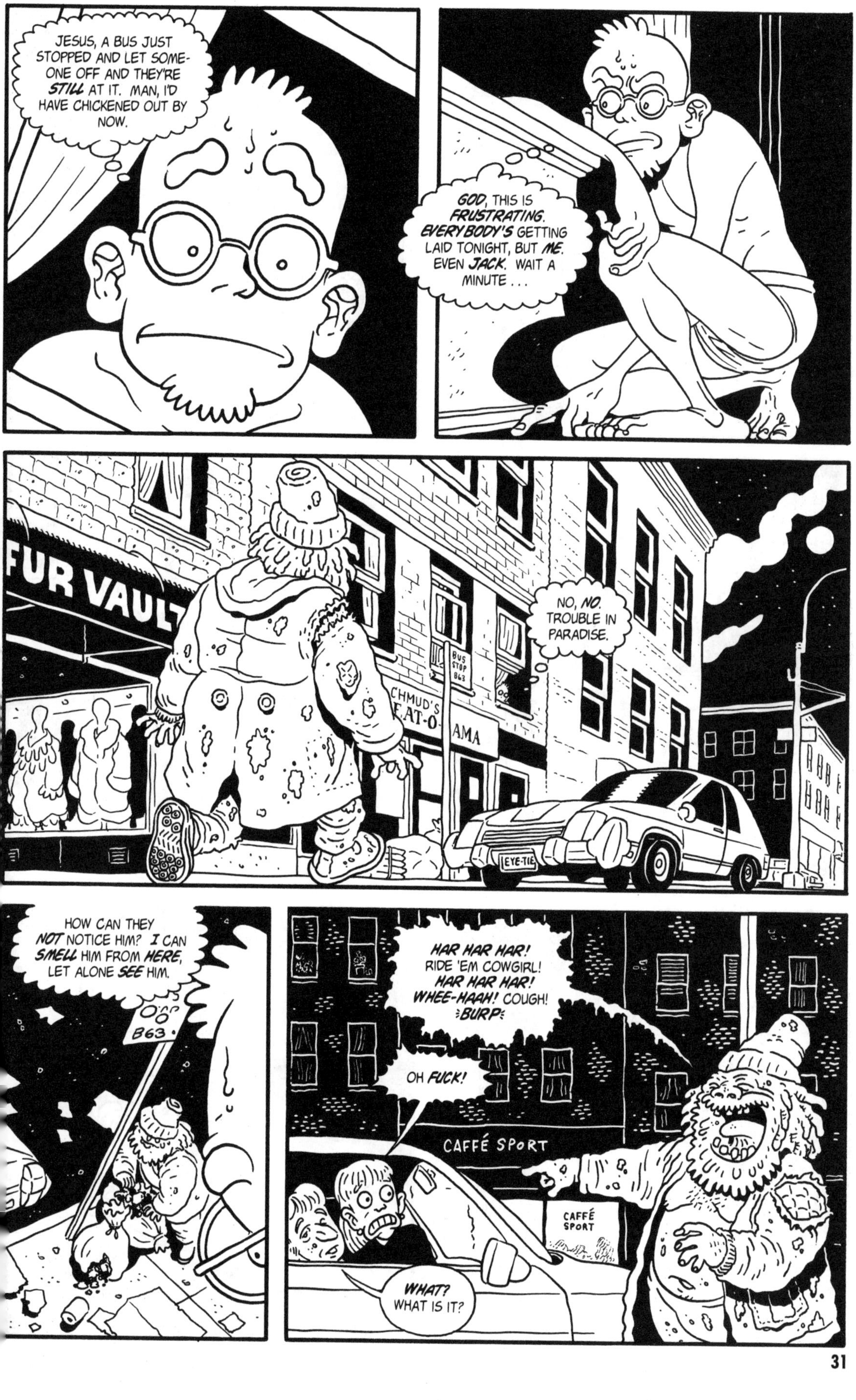
JESUS, A BUS JUST STOPPED AND LET SOME-ONE OFF AND THEY'RE STILL AT IT. MAN, I'D HAVE CHICKENED OUT BY NOW.
GOD, THIS IS FRUSTRATING. EVERYBODY'S GETTING LAID TONIGHT, BUT ME. EVEN JACK. WAIT A MINUTE . . .
FUR VAULT
BUS STOP B63
CHMUD'S
EAT-O
AMA
NO, NO. TROUBLE IN PARADISE.
EYE-TIE
HOW CAN THEY NOT NOTICE HIM? I CAN SMELL HIM FROM HERE, LET ALONE SEE HIM.
B63
HAR HAR HAR! RIDE 'EM COWGIRL! HAR HAR HAR! WHEE-HAAH! COUGH! BURP
OH FUCK!
CAFFÉ SPORT
CAFFÉ SPORT
WHAT? WHAT IS IT?

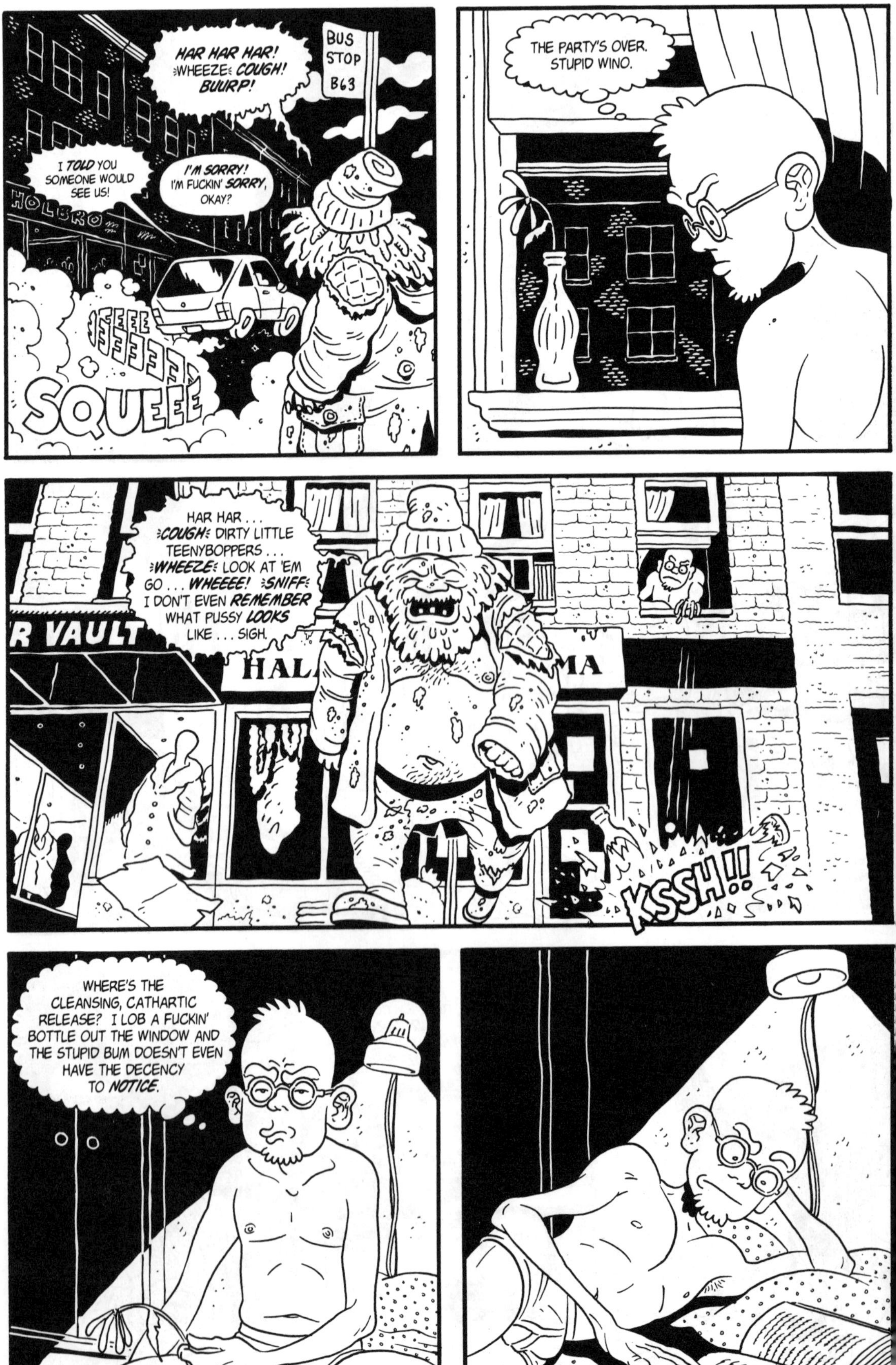
BUS STOP B63
HAR HAR HAR! ≈WHEEZE≈ COUGH! BUURP!
I TOLD YOU SOMEONE WOULD SEE US!
I'M SORRY! I'M FUCKIN' SORRY, OKAY?
HOLBRO
SQUEEE EEEEEEE EEEE
THE PARTY'S OVER. STUPID WINO.
HAR HAR . . . ≈COUGH≈ DIRTY LITTLE TEENYBOPPERS . . . ≈WHEEZE≈ LOOK AT 'EM GO . . . WHEEEE! ≈SNIFF≈ I DON'T EVEN REMEMBER WHAT PUSSY LOOKS LIKE . . . SIGH.
R VAULT
HAL
MA
KSSH!!
WHERE'S THE CLEANSING, CATHARTIC RELEASE? I LOB A FUCKIN' BOTTLE OUT THE WINDOW AND THE STUPID BUM DOESN'T EVEN HAVE THE DECENCY TO NOTICE.

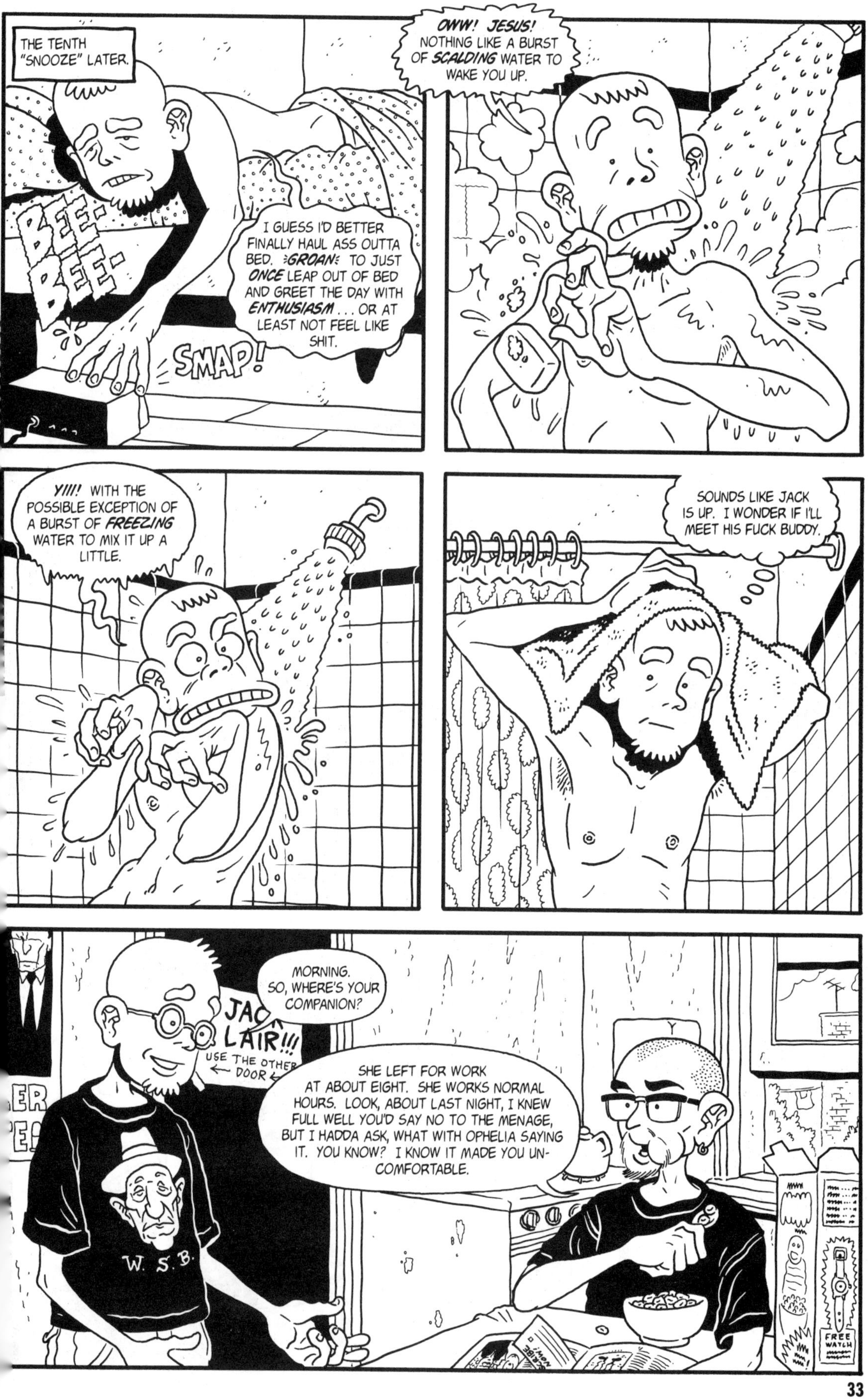
THE TENTH "SNOOZE" LATER.
BEE-BEE-
I GUESS I'D BETTER FINALLY HAUL ASS OUTTA BED. GROAN TO JUST ONCE LEAP OUT OF BED AND GREET THE DAY WITH ENTHUSIASM . . . OR AT LEAST NOT FEEL LIKE SHIT.
SMAP!
OWW! JESUS! NOTHING LIKE A BURST OF SCALDING WATER TO WAKE YOU UP.
YIII! WITH THE POSSIBLE EXCEPTION OF A BURST OF FREEZING WATER TO MIX IT UP A LITTLE.
SOUNDS LIKE JACK IS UP. I WONDER IF I'LL MEET HIS FUCK BUDDY.
MORNING. SO, WHERE'S YOUR COMPANION?
JACK LAIR!!!
USE THE OTHER DOOR
W. S. B.
SHE LEFT FOR WORK AT ABOUT EIGHT. SHE WORKS NORMAL HOURS. LOOK, ABOUT LAST NIGHT, I KNEW FULL WELL YOU'D SAY NO TO THE MENAGE, BUT I HADDA ASK, WHAT WITH OPHELIA SAYING IT. YOU KNOW? I KNOW IT MADE YOU UNCOMFORTABLE.
FREE WATCH

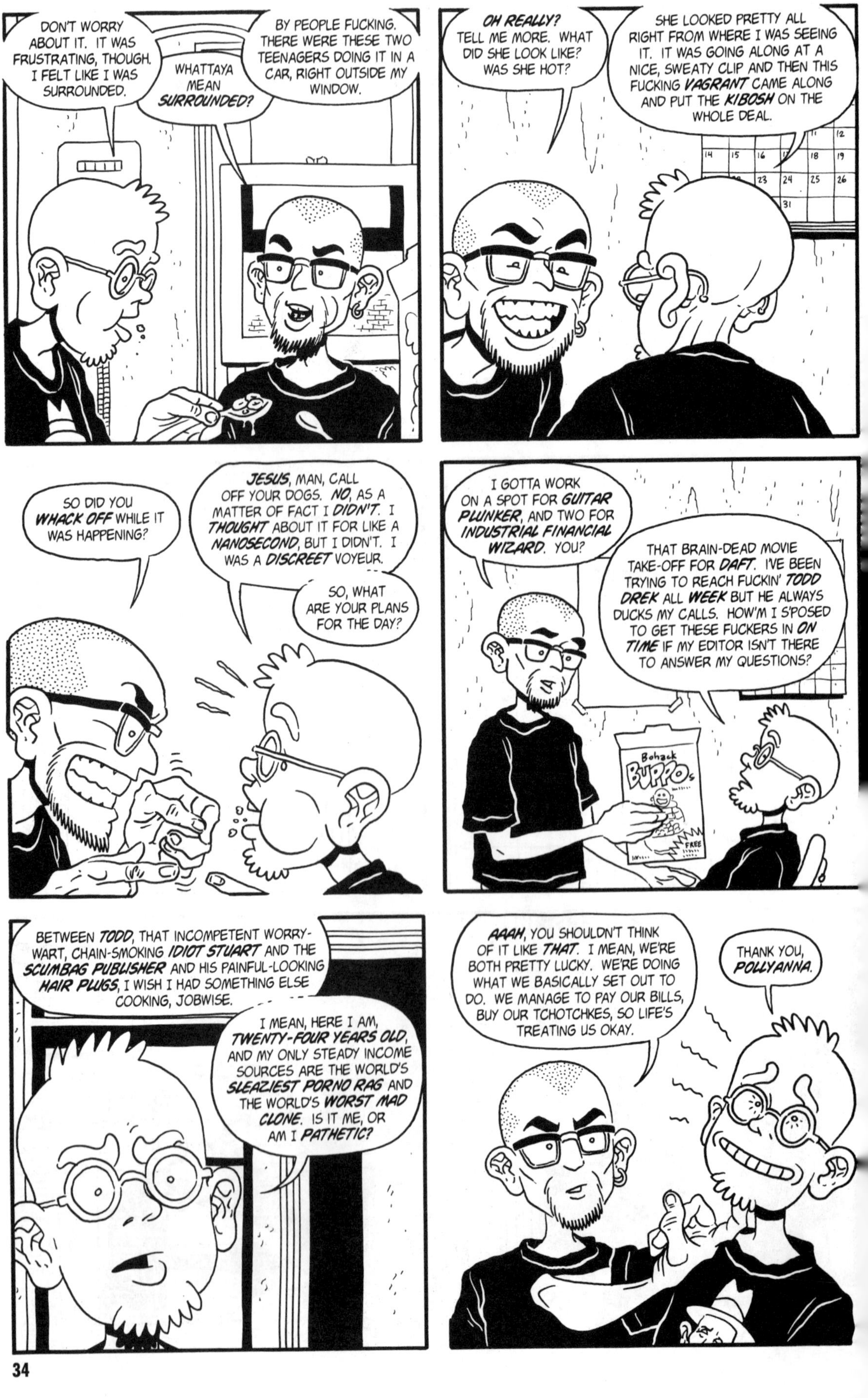
DON'T WORRY ABOUT IT. IT WAS FRUSTRATING, THOUGH. I FELT LIKE I WAS SURROUNDED.
WHATTAYA MEAN SURROUNDED?
BY PEOPLE FUCKING. THERE WERE THESE TWO TEENAGERS DOING IT IN A CAR, RIGHT OUTSIDE MY WINDOW.
OH REALLY? TELL ME MORE. WHAT DID SHE LOOK LIKE? WAS SHE HOT?
SHE LOOKED PRETTY ALL RIGHT FROM WHERE I WAS SEEING IT. IT WAS GOING ALONG AT A NICE, SWEATY CLIP AND THEN THIS FUCKING VAGRANT CAME ALONG AND PUT THE KIBOSH ON THE WHOLE DEAL.
SO DID YOU WHACK OFF WHILE IT WAS HAPPENING?
JESUS, MAN, CALL OFF YOUR DOGS. NO, AS A MATTER OF FACT I DIDN'T. I THOUGHT ABOUT IT FOR LIKE A NANOSECOND, BUT I DIDN'T. I WAS A DISCREET VOYEUR.
SO, WHAT ARE YOUR PLANS FOR THE DAY?
I GOTTA WORK ON A SPOT FOR GUITAR PLUNKER, AND TWO FOR INDUSTRIAL FINANCIAL WIZARD. YOU?
THAT BRAIN-DEAD MOVIE TAKE-OFF FOR DAFT. I'VE BEEN TRYING TO REACH FUCKIN' TODD DREK ALL WEEK BUT HE ALWAYS DUCKS MY CALLS. HOW'M I S'POSED TO GET THESE FUCKERS IN ON TIME IF MY EDITOR ISN'T THERE TO ANSWER MY QUESTIONS?
Bohack BUPPOs
FREE
BETWEEN TODD, THAT INCOMPETENT WORRY-WART, CHAIN-SMOKING IDIOT STUART AND THE SCUMBAG PUBLISHER AND HIS PAINFUL-LOOKING HAIR PLUGS, I WISH I HAD SOMETHING ELSE COOKING, JOBWISE.
I MEAN, HERE I AM, TWENTY-FOUR YEARS OLD, AND MY ONLY STEADY INCOME SOURCES ARE THE WORLD'S SLEAZIEST PORNO RAG AND THE WORLD'S WORST MAD CLONE. IS IT ME, OR AM I PATHETIC?
AAAH, YOU SHOULDN'T THINK OF IT LIKE THAT. I MEAN, WE'RE BOTH PRETTY LUCKY. WE'RE DOING WHAT WE BASICALLY SET OUT TO DO. WE MANAGE TO PAY OUR BILLS, BUY OUR TCHOTCHKES, SO LIFE'S TREATING US OKAY.
THANK YOU, POLLYANNA.

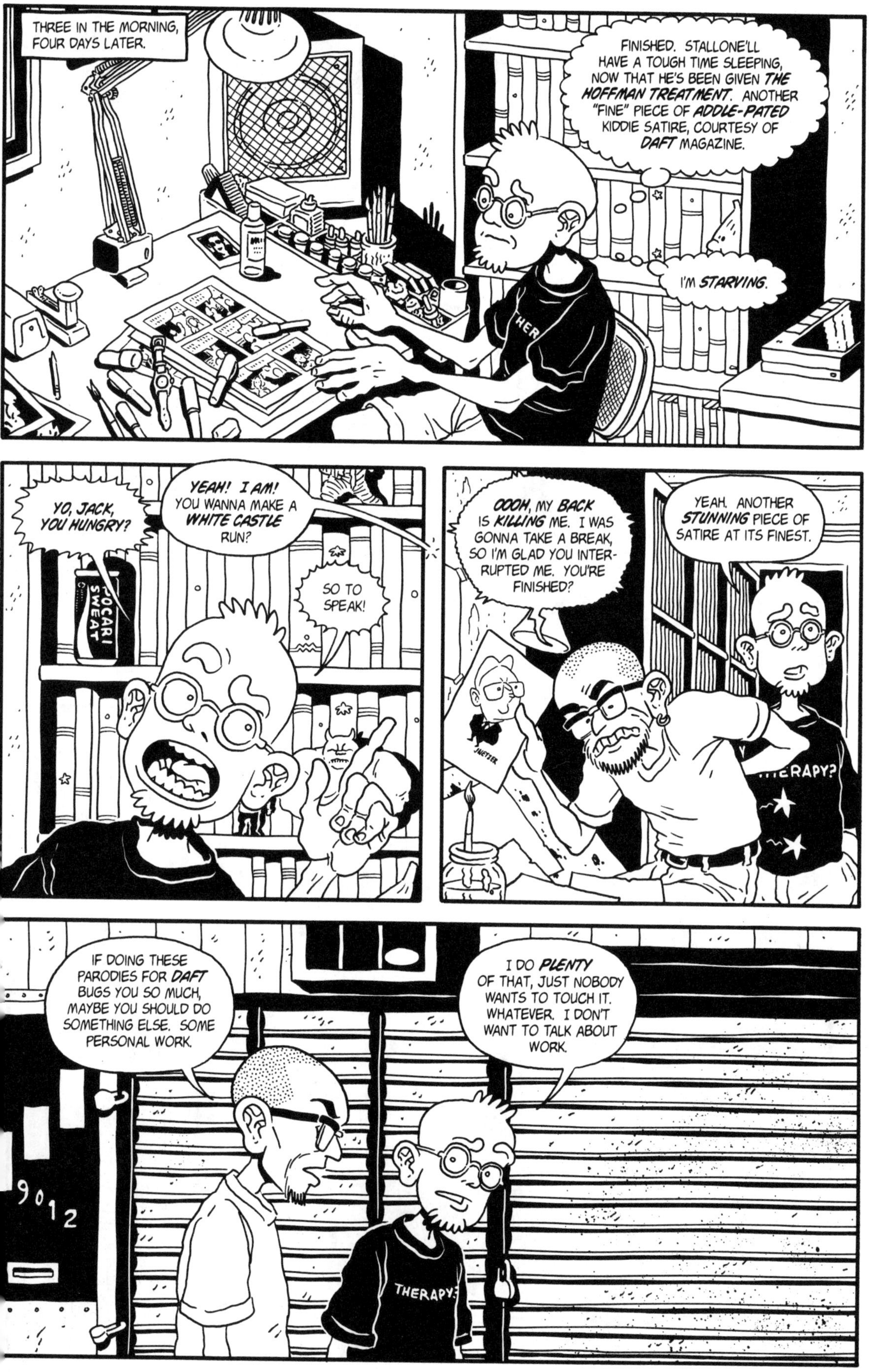
THREE IN THE MORNING, FOUR DAYS LATER.
FINISHED. STALLONE'LL HAVE A TOUGH TIME SLEEPING, NOW THAT HE'S BEEN GIVEN THE HOFFMAN TREATMENT. ANOTHER "FINE" PIECE OF ADDLE-PATED KIDDIE SATIRE, COURTESY OF DAFT MAGAZINE.
I'M STARVING.
YO, JACK, YOU HUNGRY?
YEAH! I AM! YOU WANNA MAKE A WHITE CASTLE RUN?
SO TO SPEAK!
POCARI SWEAT
OOOH, MY BACK IS KILLING ME. I WAS GONNA TAKE A BREAK, SO I'M GLAD YOU INTERRUPTED ME. YOU'RE FINISHED?
YEAH. ANOTHER STUNNING PIECE OF SATIRE AT ITS FINEST.
THERAPY?
IF DOING THESE PARODIES FOR DAFT BUGS YOU SO MUCH, MAYBE YOU SHOULD DO SOMETHING ELSE. SOME PERSONAL WORK.
I DO PLENTY OF THAT, JUST NOBODY WANTS TO TOUCH IT. WHATEVER. I DON'T WANT TO TALK ABOUT WORK.
9012
THERAPY?

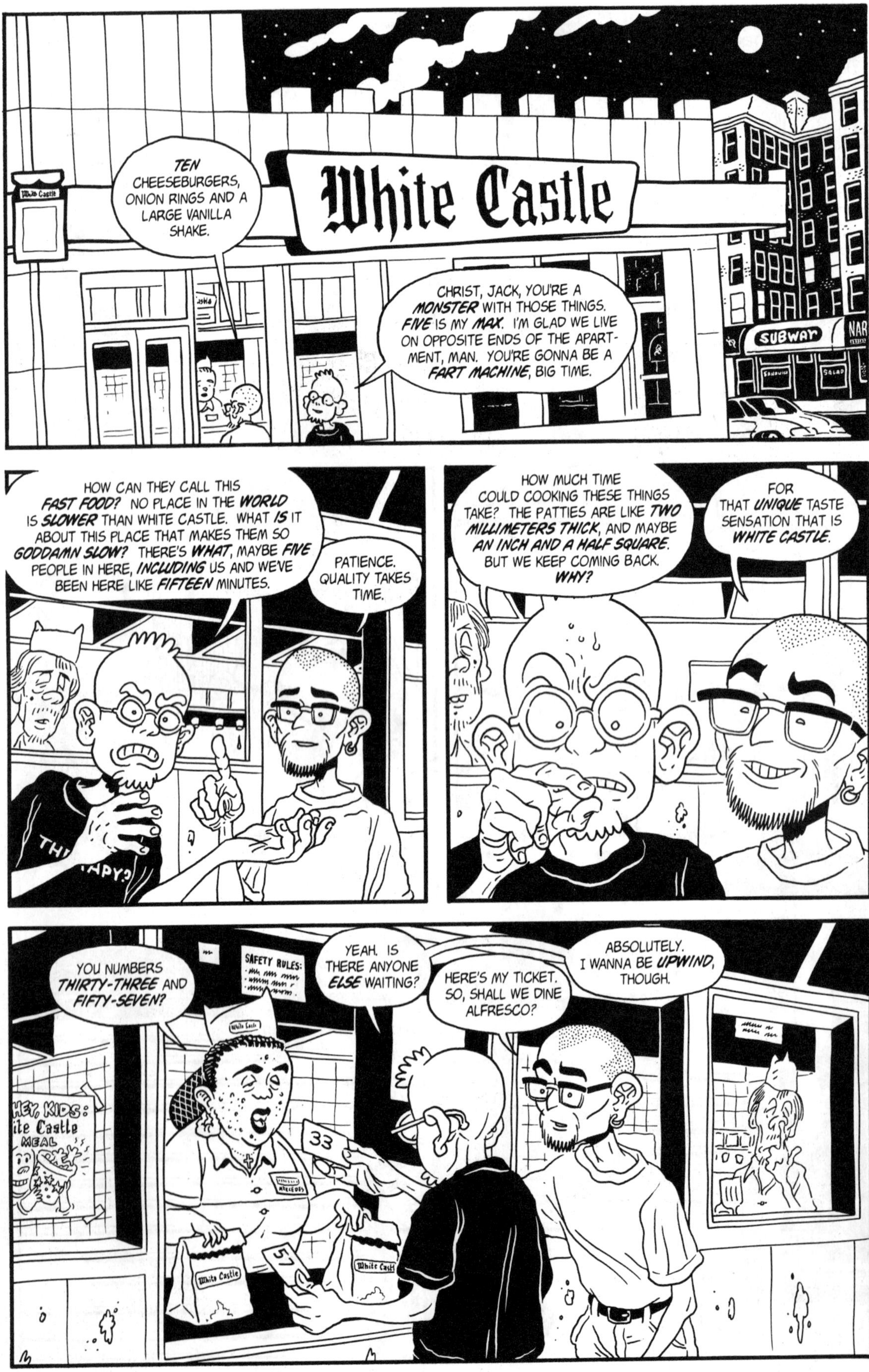
White Castle
TEN CHEESEBURGERS, ONION RINGS AND A LARGE VANILLA SHAKE.
CHRIST, JACK, YOU'RE A MONSTER WITH THOSE THINGS. FIVE IS MY MAX. I'M GLAD WE LIVE ON OPPOSITE ENDS OF THE APARTMENT, MAN. YOU'RE GONNA BE A FART MACHINE, BIG TIME.
SUBWAY
HOW CAN THEY CALL THIS FAST FOOD? NO PLACE IN THE WORLD IS SLOWER THAN WHITE CASTLE. WHAT IS IT ABOUT THIS PLACE THAT MAKES THEM SO GODDAMN SLOW? THERE'S WHAT, MAYBE FIVE PEOPLE IN HERE, INCLUDING US AND WE'VE BEEN HERE LIKE FIFTEEN MINUTES.
PATIENCE. QUALITY TAKES TIME.
HOW MUCH TIME COULD COOKING THESE THINGS TAKE? THE PATTIES ARE LIKE TWO MILLIMETERS THICK, AND MAYBE AN INCH AND A HALF SQUARE. BUT WE KEEP COMING BACK. WHY?
FOR THAT UNIQUE TASTE SENSATION THAT IS WHITE CASTLE.
YOU NUMBERS THIRTY-THREE AND FIFTY-SEVEN?
SAFETY RULES:
YEAH. IS THERE ANYONE ELSE WAITING?
HERE'S MY TICKET. SO, SHALL WE DINE ALFRESCO?
ABSOLUTELY. I WANNA BE UPWIND, THOUGH.
33
57
White Castle
White Castle

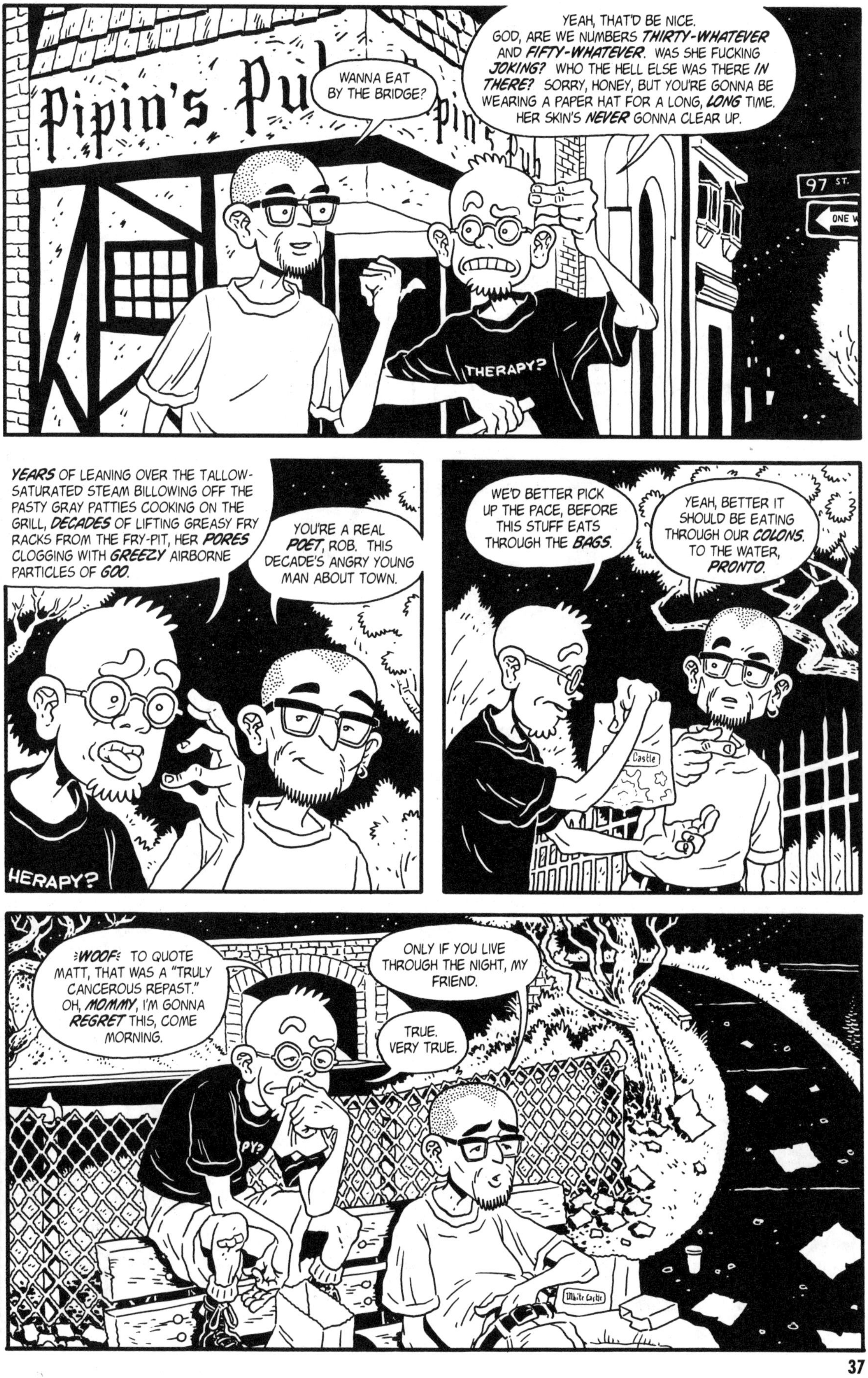
Pipin's Pub
WANNA EAT BY THE BRIDGE?
YEAH, THAT'D BE NICE. GOD, ARE WE NUMBERS THIRTY-WHATEVER AND FIFTY-WHATEVER. WAS SHE FUCKING JOKING? WHO THE HELL ELSE WAS THERE IN THERE? SORRY, HONEY, BUT YOU'RE GONNA BE WEARING A PAPER HAT FOR A LONG, LONG TIME. HER SKIN'S NEVER GONNA CLEAR UP.
THERAPY?
97 ST.
YEARS OF LEANING OVER THE TALLOW-SATURATED STEAM BILLOWING OFF THE PASTY GRAY PATTIES COOKING ON THE GRILL, DECADES OF LIFTING GREASY FRY RACKS FROM THE FRY-PIT, HER PORES CLOGGING WITH GREEZY AIRBORNE PARTICLES OF GOO.
YOU'RE A REAL POET, ROB. THIS DECADE'S ANGRY YOUNG MAN ABOUT TOWN.
HERAPY?
WE'D BETTER PICK UP THE PACE, BEFORE THIS STUFF EATS THROUGH THE BAGS.
YEAH, BETTER IT SHOULD BE EATING THROUGH OUR COLONS. TO THE WATER, PRONTO.
WOOF TO QUOTE MATT, THAT WAS A "TRULY CANCEROUS REPAST." OH, MOMMY, I'M GONNA REGRET THIS, COME MORNING.
ONLY IF YOU LIVE THROUGH THE NIGHT, MY FRIEND.
TRUE. VERY TRUE.
White Castle

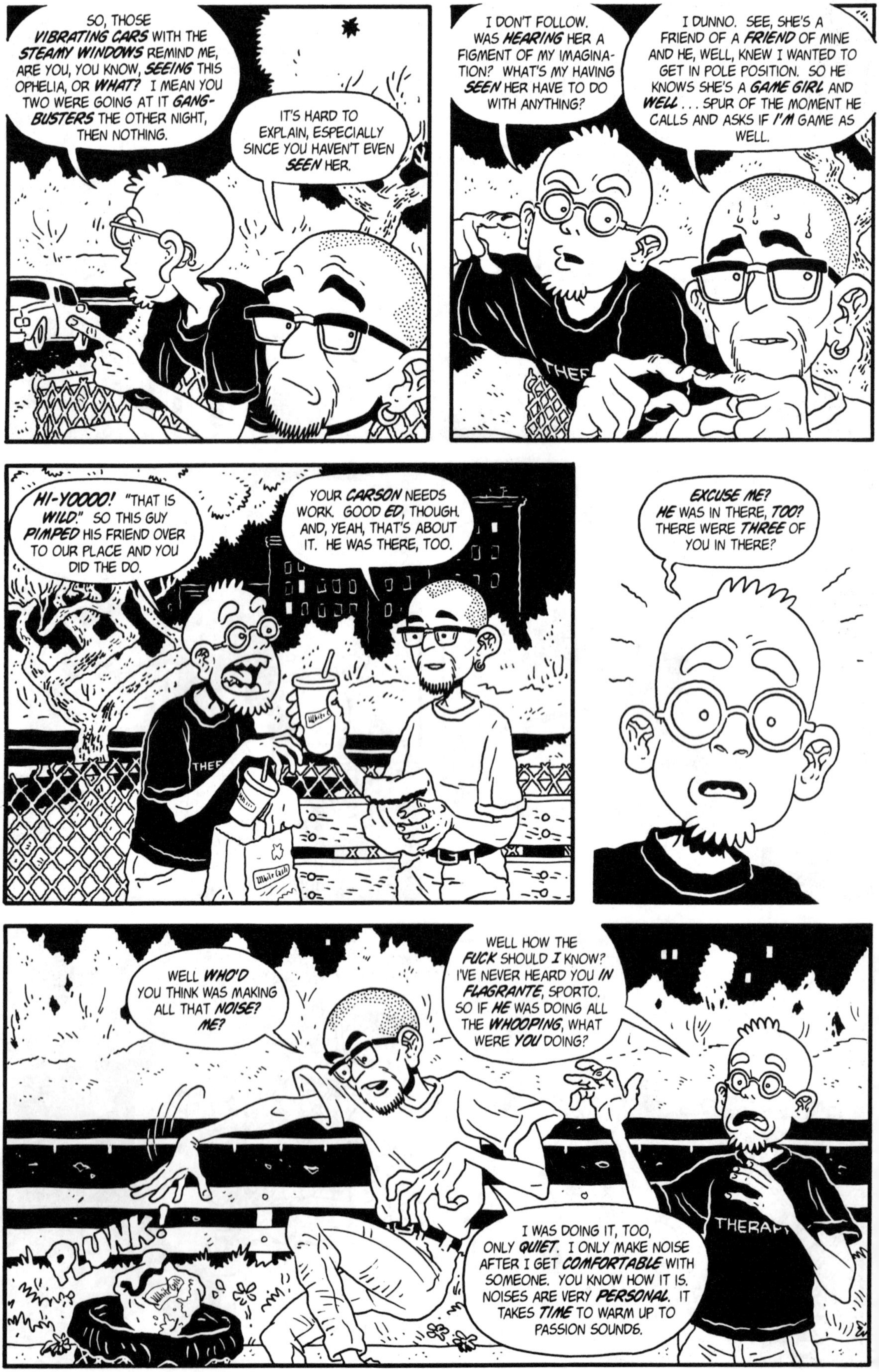

SO, THOSE VIBRATING CARS WITH THE STEAMY WINDOWS REMIND ME, ARE YOU, YOU KNOW, SEEING THIS OPHELIA, OR WHAT? I MEAN YOU TWO WERE GOING AT IT GANGBUSTERS THE OTHER NIGHT, THEN NOTHING.
IT'S HARD TO EXPLAIN, ESPECIALLY SINCE YOU HAVEN'T EVEN SEEN HER.
I DON'T FOLLOW. WAS HEARING HER A FIGMENT OF MY IMAGINATION? WHAT'S MY HAVING SEEN HER HAVE TO DO WITH ANYTHING?
I DUNNO. SEE, SHE'S A FRIEND OF A FRIEND OF MINE AND HE, WELL, KNEW I WANTED TO GET IN POLE POSITION. SO HE KNOWS SHE'S A GAME GIRL AND WELL . . . SPUR OF THE MOMENT HE CALLS AND ASKS IF I'M GAME AS WELL.
HI-YOOOO! "THAT IS WILD." SO THIS GUY PIMPED HIS FRIEND OVER TO OUR PLACE AND YOU DID THE DO.
YOUR CARSON NEEDS WORK. GOOD ED, THOUGH. AND, YEAH, THAT'S ABOUT IT. HE WAS THERE, TOO.
EXCUSE ME? HE WAS IN THERE, TOO? THERE WERE THREE OF YOU IN THERE?
WELL WHO'D YOU THINK WAS MAKING ALL THAT NOISE? ME?
WELL HOW THE FUCK SHOULD I KNOW? I'VE NEVER HEARD YOU IN FLAGRANTE, SPORTO. SO IF HE WAS DOING ALL THE WHOOPING, WHAT WERE YOU DOING?
PLUNK!
I WAS DOING IT, TOO, ONLY QUIET. I ONLY MAKE NOISE AFTER I GET COMFORTABLE WITH SOMEONE. YOU KNOW HOW IT IS. NOISES ARE VERY PERSONAL. IT TAKES TIME TO WARM UP TO PASSION SOUNDS.

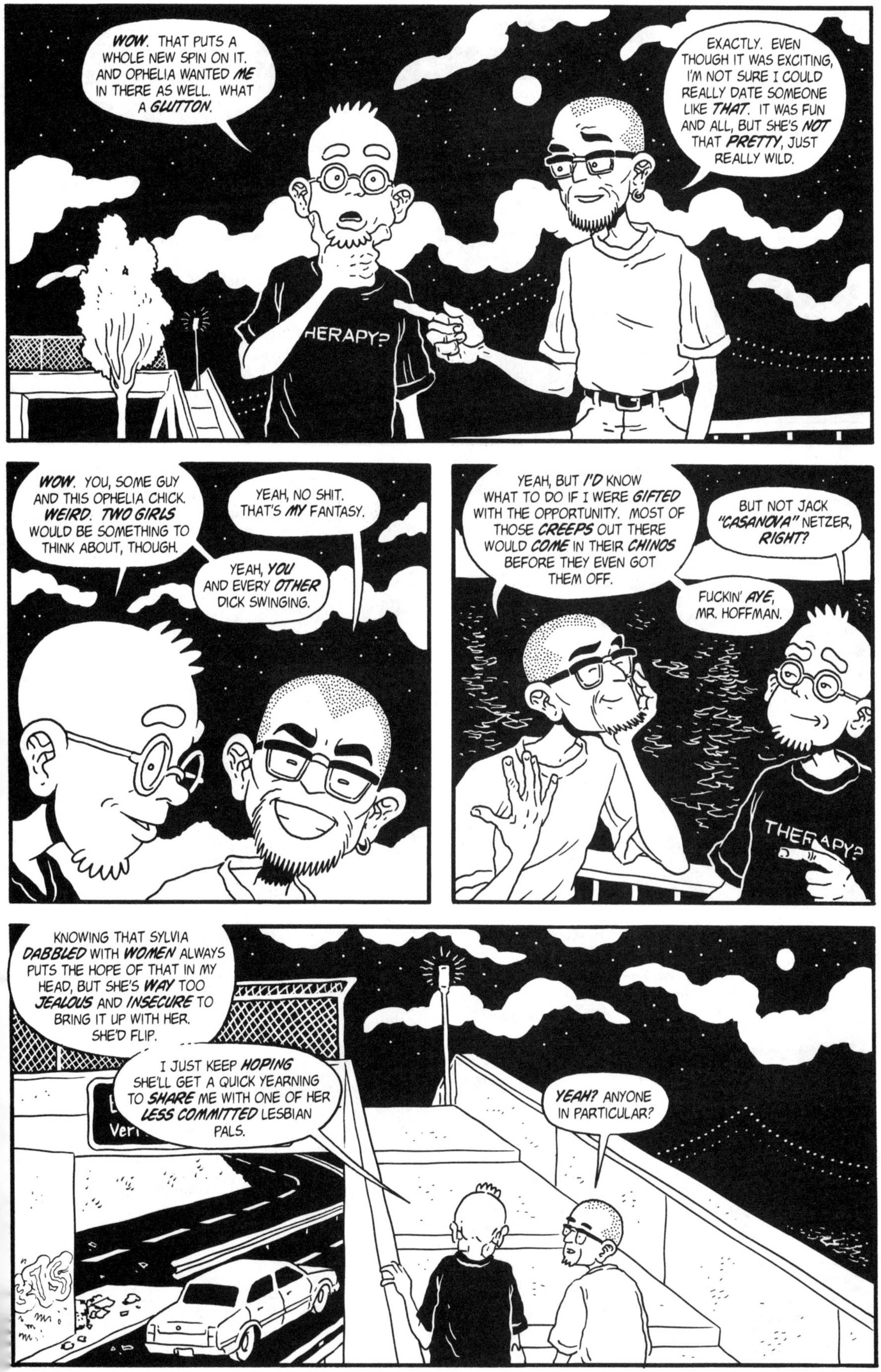
WOW. THAT PUTS A WHOLE NEW SPIN ON IT. AND OPHELIA WANTED ME IN THERE AS WELL. WHAT A GLUTTON.
EXACTLY. EVEN THOUGH IT WAS EXCITING, I'M NOT SURE I COULD REALLY DATE SOMEONE LIKE THAT. IT WAS FUN AND ALL, BUT SHE'S NOT THAT PRETTY, JUST REALLY WILD.
THERAPY?
WOW. YOU, SOME GUY AND THIS OPHELIA CHICK. WEIRD. TWO GIRLS WOULD BE SOMETHING TO THINK ABOUT, THOUGH.
YEAH, NO SHIT. THAT'S MY FANTASY.
YEAH, YOU AND EVERY OTHER DICK SWINGING.
YEAH, BUT I'D KNOW WHAT TO DO IF I WERE GIFTED WITH THE OPPORTUNITY. MOST OF THOSE CREEPS OUT THERE WOULD COME IN THEIR CHINOS BEFORE THEY EVEN GOT THEM OFF.
BUT NOT JACK "CASANOVA" NETZER, RIGHT?
FUCKIN' AYE, MR. HOFFMAN.
THERAPY?
KNOWING THAT SYLVIA DABBLED WITH WOMEN ALWAYS PUTS THE HOPE OF THAT IN MY HEAD, BUT SHE'S WAY TOO JEALOUS AND INSECURE TO BRING IT UP WITH HER. SHE'D FLIP.
I JUST KEEP HOPING SHE'LL GET A QUICK YEARNING TO SHARE ME WITH ONE OF HER LESS COMMITTED LESBIAN PALS.
YEAH? ANYONE IN PARTICULAR?

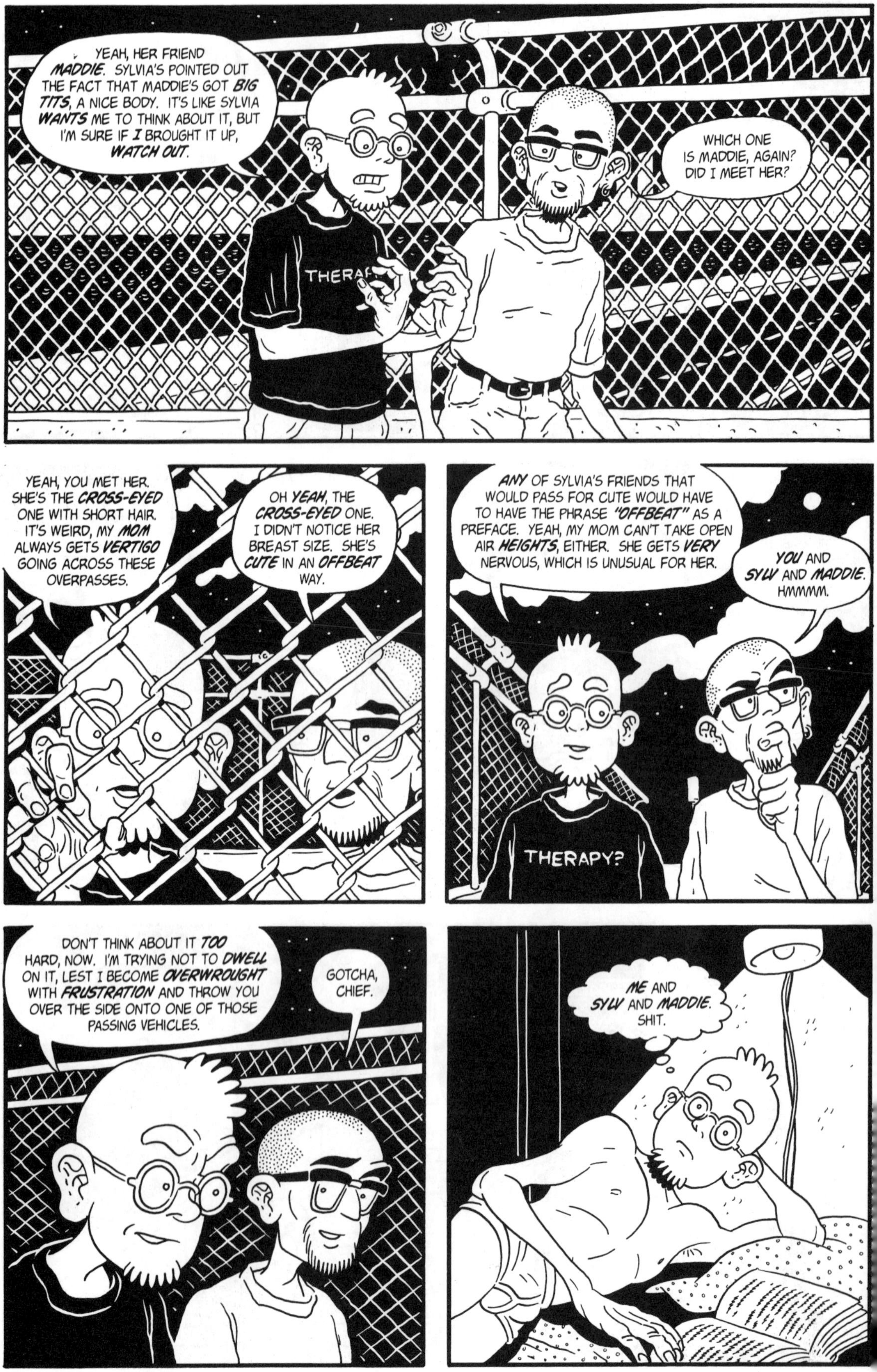
YEAH, HER FRIEND MADDIE. SYLVIA'S POINTED OUT THE FACT THAT MADDIE'S GOT BIG TITS, A NICE BODY. IT'S LIKE SYLVIA WANTS ME TO THINK ABOUT IT, BUT I'M SURE IF I BROUGHT IT UP, WATCH OUT.
WHICH ONE IS MADDIE, AGAIN? DID I MEET HER?
THERAP
YEAH, YOU MET HER. SHE'S THE CROSS-EYED ONE WITH SHORT HAIR. IT'S WEIRD, MY MOM ALWAYS GETS VERTIGO GOING ACROSS THESE OVERPASSES.
OH YEAH, THE CROSS-EYED ONE. I DIDN'T NOTICE HER BREAST SIZE. SHE'S CUTE IN AN OFFBEAT WAY.
ANY OF SYLVIA'S FRIENDS THAT WOULD PASS FOR CUTE WOULD HAVE TO HAVE THE PHRASE "OFFBEAT" AS A PREFACE. YEAH, MY MOM CAN'T TAKE OPEN AIR HEIGHTS, EITHER. SHE GETS VERY NERVOUS, WHICH IS UNUSUAL FOR HER.
YOU AND SYLV AND MADDIE. HMMMM.
THERAPY?
DON'T THINK ABOUT IT TOO HARD, NOW. I'M TRYING NOT TO DWELL ON IT, LEST I BECOME OVERWROUGHT WITH FRUSTRATION AND THROW YOU OVER THE SIDE ONTO ONE OF THOSE PASSING VEHICLES.
GOTCHA, CHIEF.
ME AND SYLV AND MADDIE. SHIT.

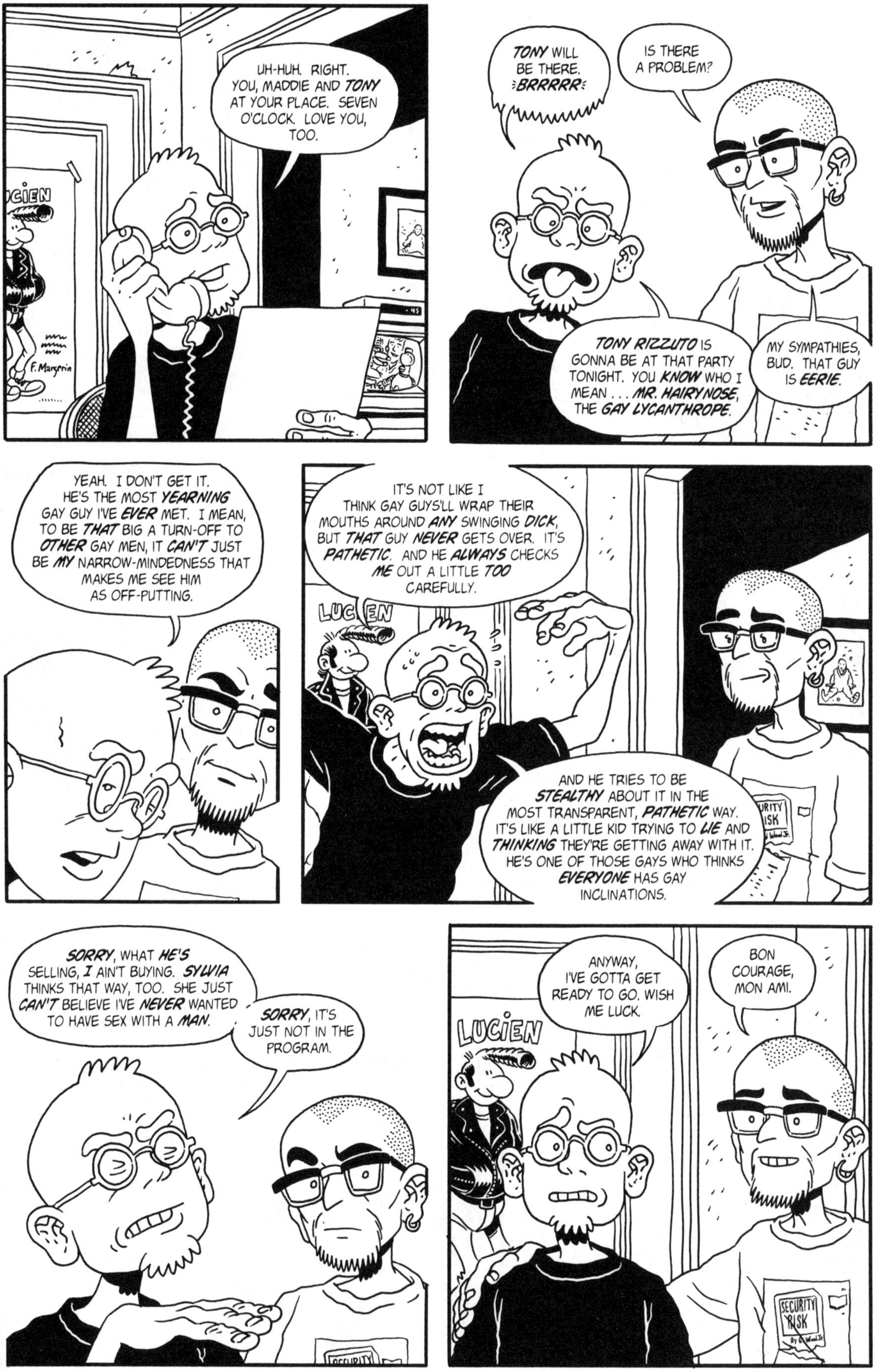
UH-HUH. RIGHT. YOU, MADDIE AND TONY AT YOUR PLACE. SEVEN O'CLOCK. LOVE YOU, TOO.
LUCIEN
F. Margerin
TONY WILL BE THERE. BRRRRR
IS THERE A PROBLEM?
TONY RIZZUTO IS GONNA BE AT THAT PARTY TONIGHT. YOU KNOW WHO I MEAN . . . MR. HAIRYNOSE, THE GAY LYCANTHROPE.
MY SYMPATHIES, BUD. THAT GUY IS EERIE.
YEAH. I DON'T GET IT. HE'S THE MOST YEARNING GAY GUY I'VE EVER MET. I MEAN, TO BE THAT BIG A TURN-OFF TO OTHER GAY MEN, IT CAN'T JUST BE MY NARROW-MINDEDNESS THAT MAKES ME SEE HIM AS OFF-PUTTING.
IT'S NOT LIKE I THINK GAY GUYS'LL WRAP THEIR MOUTHS AROUND ANY SWINGING DICK, BUT THAT GUY NEVER GETS OVER. IT'S PATHETIC. AND HE ALWAYS CHECKS ME OUT A LITTLE TOO CAREFULLY.
AND HE TRIES TO BE STEALTHY ABOUT IT IN THE MOST TRANSPARENT, PATHETIC WAY. IT'S LIKE A LITTLE KID TRYING TO LIE AND THINKING THEY'RE GETTING AWAY WITH IT. HE'S ONE OF THOSE GAYS WHO THINKS EVERYONE HAS GAY INCLINATIONS.
SORRY, WHAT HE'S SELLING, I AIN'T BUYING. SYLVIA THINKS THAT WAY, TOO. SHE JUST CAN'T BELIEVE I'VE NEVER WANTED TO HAVE SEX WITH A MAN.
SORRY, IT'S JUST NOT IN THE PROGRAM.
ANYWAY, I'VE GOTTA GET READY TO GO. WISH ME LUCK.
BON COURAGE, MON AMI.
LUCIEN
SECURITY RISK

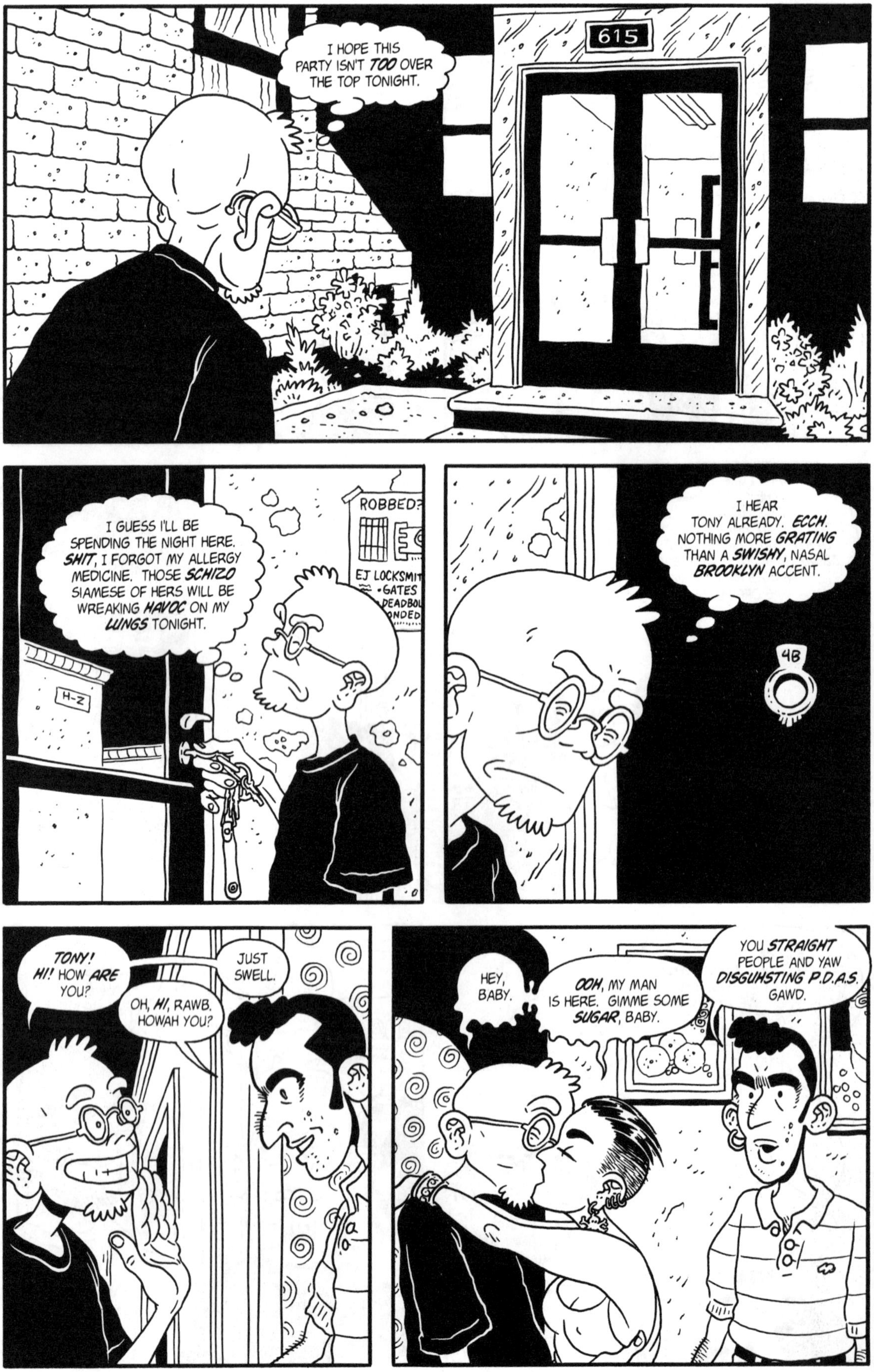
615
I HOPE THIS PARTY ISN'T *TOO* OVER THE TOP TONIGHT.
I GUESS I'LL BE SPENDING THE NIGHT HERE. *SHIT*, I FORGOT MY ALLERGY MEDICINE. THOSE *SCHIZO* SIAMESE OF HERS WILL BE WREAKING *HAVOC* ON MY *LUNGS* TONIGHT.
ROBBED?
EJ LOCKSMIT
•GATES
DEADBOL
ONDED
H–Z
I HEAR TONY ALREADY. *ECCH*. NOTHING MORE *GRATING* THAN A *SWISHY*, NASAL *BROOKLYN* ACCENT.
4B
TONY! HI! HOW *ARE* YOU?
JUST SWELL.
OH, *HI*, RAWB. HOWAH YOU?
HEY, BABY.
OOH, MY MAN IS HERE. GIMME SOME *SUGAR*, BABY.
YOU *STRAIGHT* PEOPLE AND YAW *DISGUHSTING P.D.A.S.* GAWD.

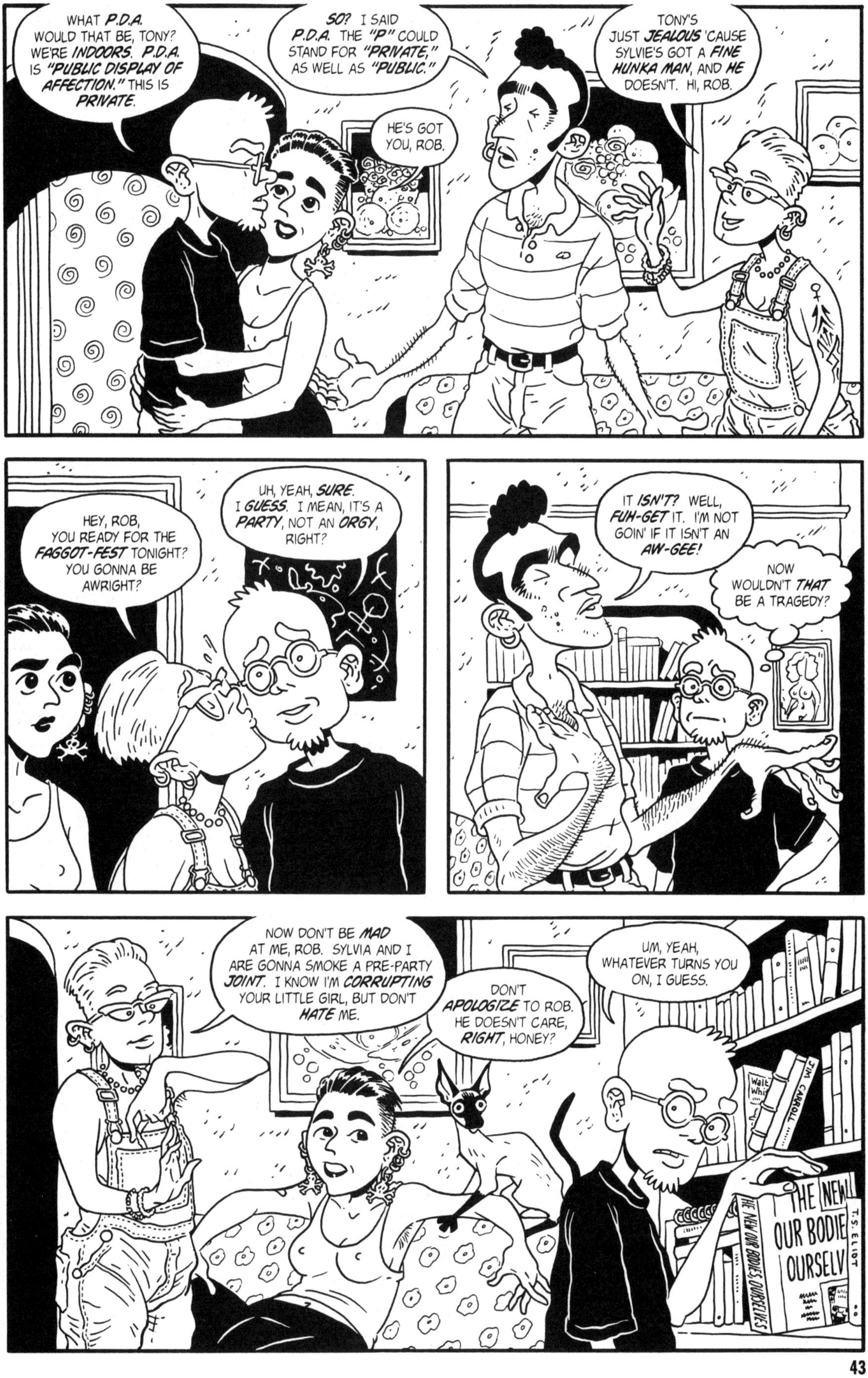
WHAT P.D.A. WOULD THAT BE, TONY? WE'RE INDOORS. P.D.A. IS "PUBLIC DISPLAY OF AFFECTION." THIS IS PRIVATE.
SO? I SAID P.D.A. THE "P" COULD STAND FOR "PRIVATE," AS WELL AS "PUBLIC."
HE'S GOT YOU, ROB.
TONY'S JUST JEALOUS 'CAUSE SYLVIE'S GOT A FINE HUNKA MAN, AND HE DOESN'T. HI, ROB.
HEY, ROB, YOU READY FOR THE FAGGOT-FEST TONIGHT? YOU GONNA BE AWRIGHT?
UH, YEAH, SURE. I GUESS. I MEAN, IT'S A PARTY, NOT AN ORGY, RIGHT?
IT ISN'T? WELL, FUH-GET IT. I'M NOT GOIN' IF IT ISN'T AN AW-GEE!
NOW WOULDN'T THAT BE A TRAGEDY?
NOW DON'T BE MAD AT ME, ROB. SYLVIA AND I ARE GONNA SMOKE A PRE-PARTY JOINT. I KNOW I'M CORRUPTING YOUR LITTLE GIRL, BUT DON'T HATE ME.
DON'T APOLOGIZE TO ROB. HE DOESN'T CARE, RIGHT, HONEY?
UM, YEAH, WHATEVER TURNS YOU ON, I GUESS.
JIM CARROLL
THE NEW OUR BODIES OURSELVES
T.S. ELIOT

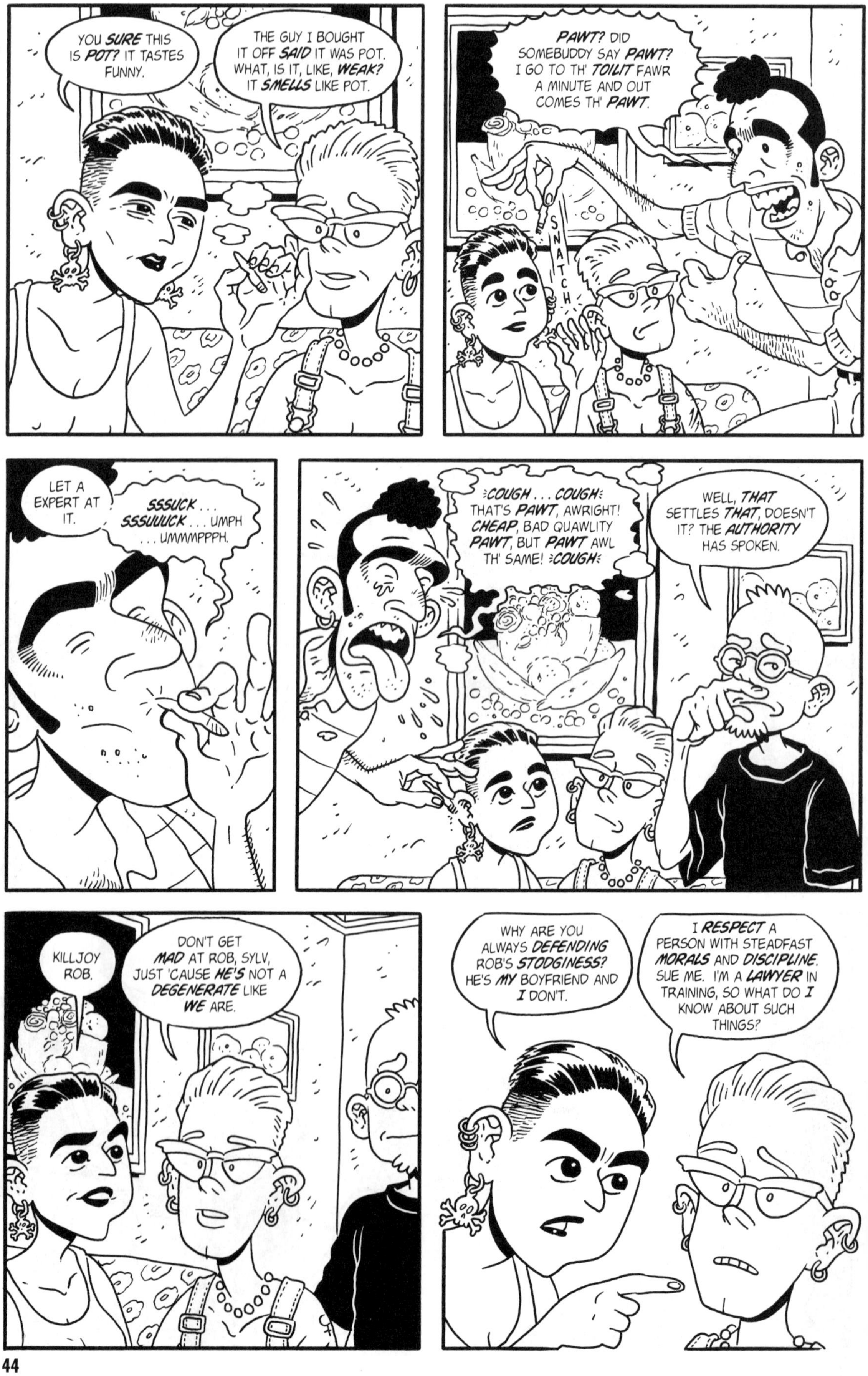
YOU SURE THIS IS POT? IT TASTES FUNNY.
THE GUY I BOUGHT IT OFF SAID IT WAS POT. WHAT, IS IT, LIKE, WEAK? IT SMELLS LIKE POT.
PAWT? DID SOMEBUDDY SAY PAWT? I GO TO TH' TOILIT FAWR A MINUTE AND OUT COMES TH' PAWT.
SNATCH
LET A EXPERT AT IT.
SSSUCK . . . SSSUUUCK . . . UMPH . . . UMMMPPPH.
COUGH . . . COUGH THAT'S PAWT, AWRIGHT! CHEAP, BAD QUAWLITY PAWT, BUT PAWT AWL TH' SAME! COUGH
WELL, THAT SETTLES THAT, DOESN'T IT? THE AUTHORITY HAS SPOKEN.
KILLJOY ROB.
DON'T GET MAD AT ROB, SYLV, JUST 'CAUSE HE'S NOT A DEGENERATE LIKE WE ARE.
WHY ARE YOU ALWAYS DEFENDING ROB'S STODGINESS? HE'S MY BOYFRIEND AND I DON'T.
I RESPECT A PERSON WITH STEADFAST MORALS AND DISCIPLINE. SUE ME. I'M A LAWYER IN TRAINING, SO WHAT DO I KNOW ABOUT SUCH THINGS?

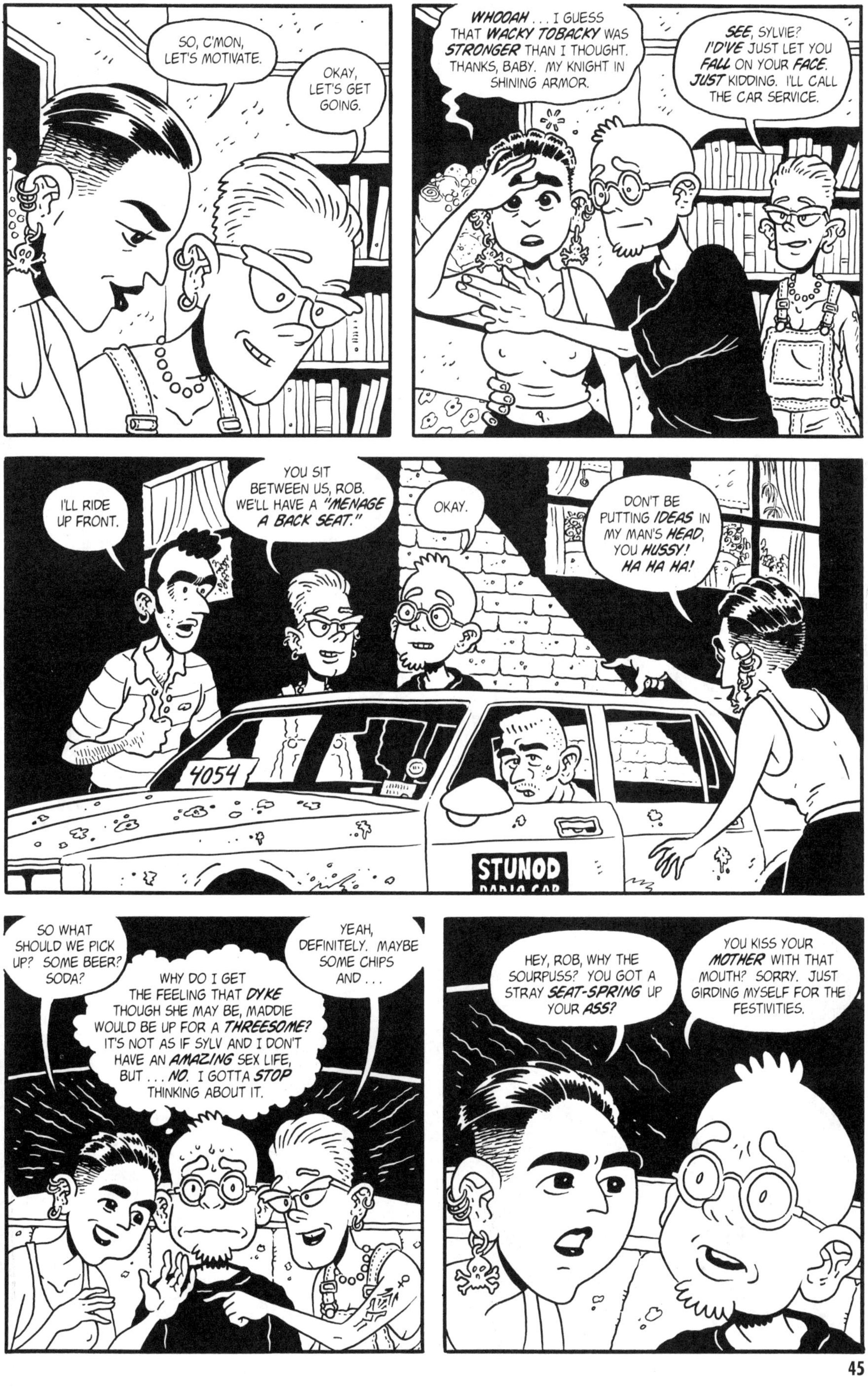
SO, C'MON, LET'S MOTIVATE.
OKAY, LET'S GET GOING.
WHOOAH . . . I GUESS THAT WACKY TOBACKY WAS STRONGER THAN I THOUGHT. THANKS, BABY. MY KNIGHT IN SHINING ARMOR.
SEE, SYLVIE? I'D'VE JUST LET YOU FALL ON YOUR FACE. JUST KIDDING. I'LL CALL THE CAR SERVICE.
I'LL RIDE UP FRONT.
YOU SIT BETWEEN US, ROB. WE'LL HAVE A "MENAGE A BACK SEAT."
OKAY.
DON'T BE PUTTING IDEAS IN MY MAN'S HEAD, YOU HUSSY! HA HA HA!
4054
STUNOD
SO WHAT SHOULD WE PICK UP? SOME BEER? SODA?
WHY DO I GET THE FEELING THAT DYKE THOUGH SHE MAY BE, MADDIE WOULD BE UP FOR A THREESOME? IT'S NOT AS IF SYLV AND I DON'T HAVE AN AMAZING SEX LIFE, BUT . . . NO. I GOTTA STOP THINKING ABOUT IT.
YEAH, DEFINITELY. MAYBE SOME CHIPS AND . . .
HEY, ROB, WHY THE SOURPUSS? YOU GOT A STRAY SEAT-SPRING UP YOUR ASS?
YOU KISS YOUR MOTHER WITH THAT MOUTH? SORRY. JUST GIRDING MYSELF FOR THE FESTIVITIES.

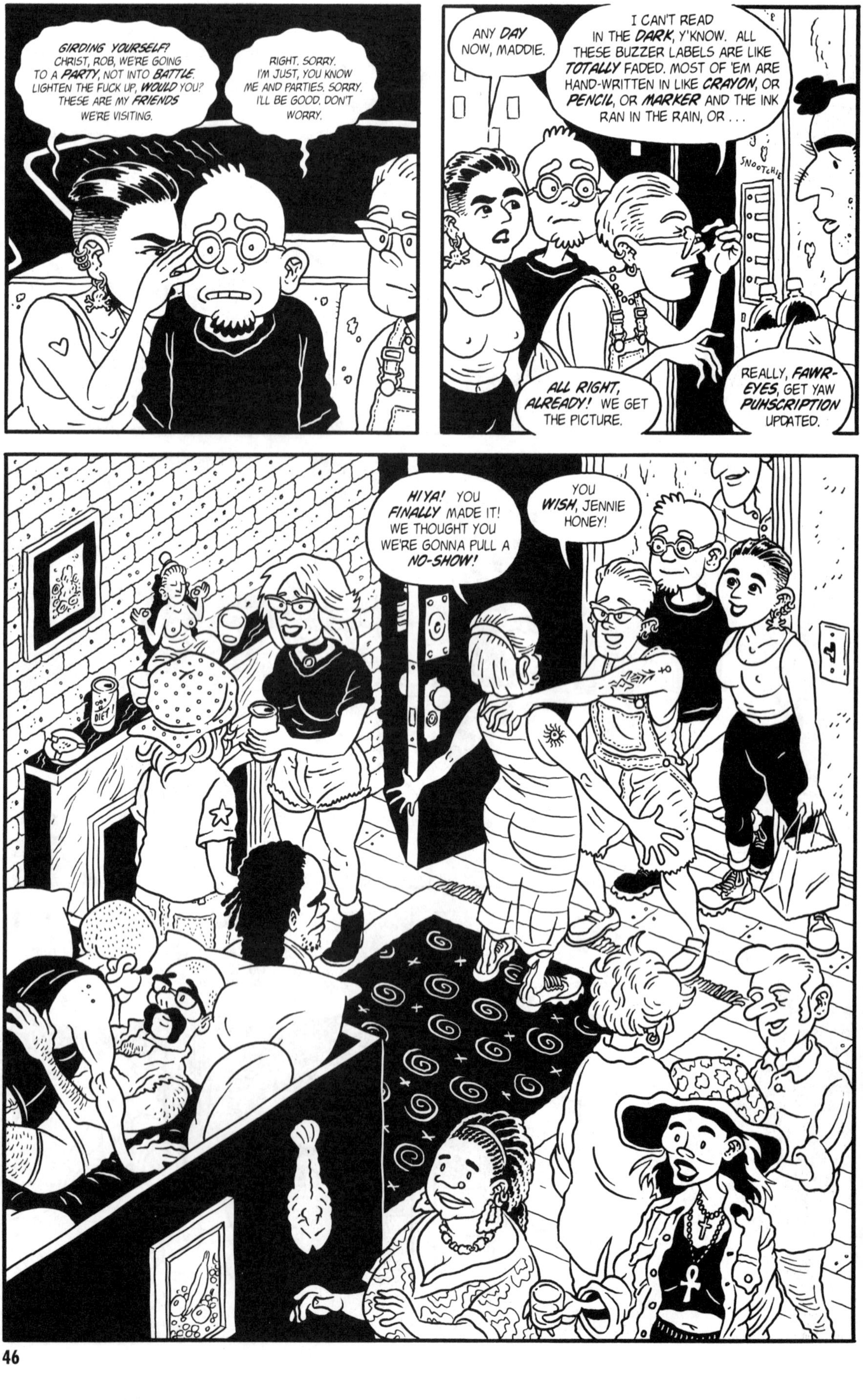
GIRDING YOURSELF? CHRIST, ROB, WE'RE GOING TO A PARTY, NOT INTO BATTLE. LIGHTEN THE FUCK UP, WOULD YOU? THESE ARE MY FRIENDS WE'RE VISITING.
RIGHT. SORRY. I'M JUST, YOU KNOW ME AND PARTIES. SORRY. I'LL BE GOOD. DON'T WORRY.
ANY DAY NOW, MADDIE.
I CAN'T READ IN THE DARK, Y'KNOW. ALL THESE BUZZER LABELS ARE LIKE TOTALLY FADED. MOST OF 'EM ARE HAND-WRITTEN IN LIKE CRAYON, OR PENCIL, OR MARKER AND THE INK RAN IN THE RAIN, OR . . .
SNOOTCHIE
ALL RIGHT, ALREADY! WE GET THE PICTURE.
REALLY, FAWR-EYES, GET YAW PUHSCRIPTION UPDATED.
HIYA! YOU FINALLY MADE IT! WE THOUGHT YOU WE'RE GONNA PULL A NO-SHOW!
YOU WISH, JENNIE HONEY!
DIET

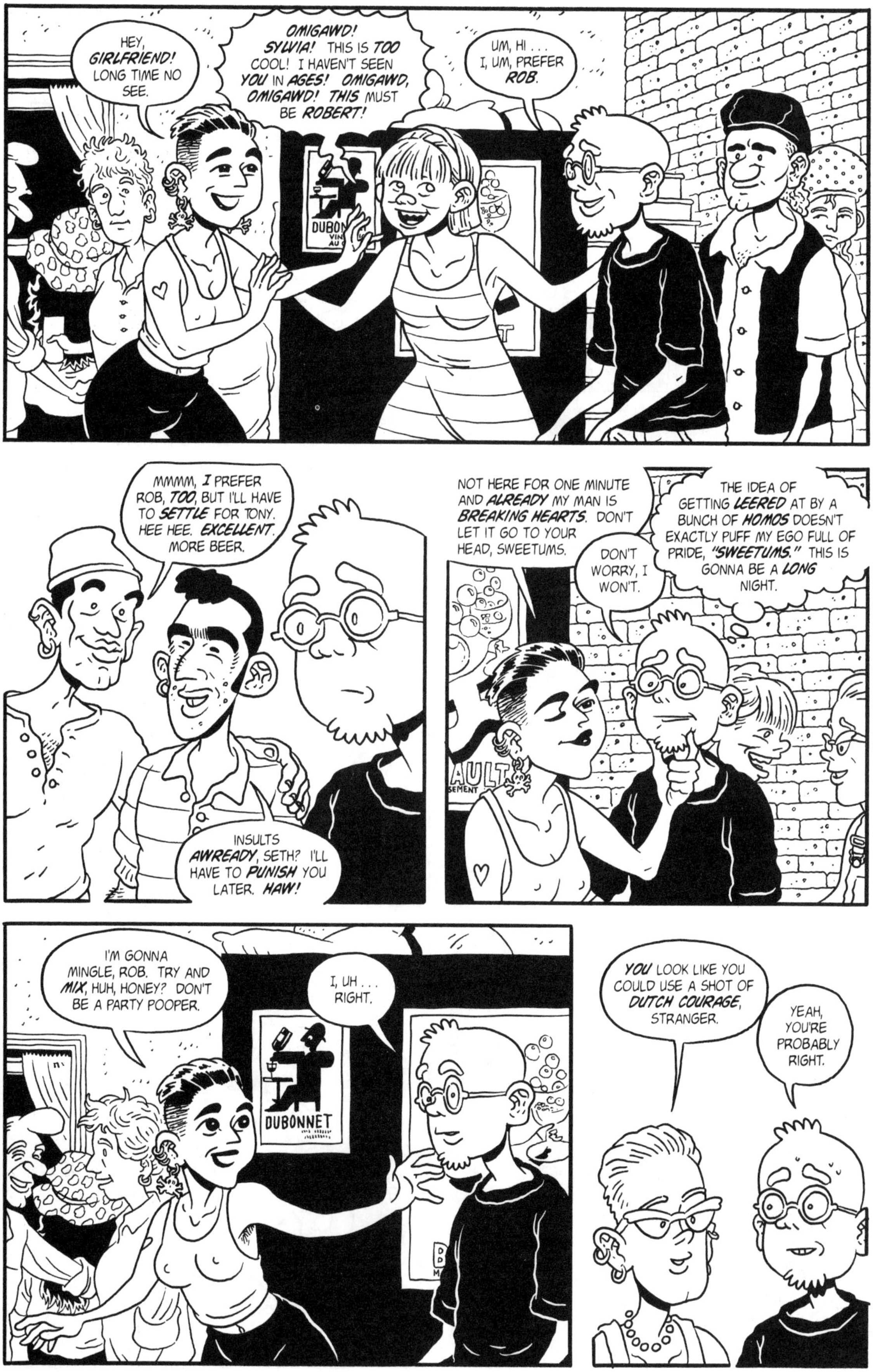
HEY, GIRLFRIEND! LONG TIME NO SEE.
OMIGAWD! SYLVIA! THIS IS TOO COOL! I HAVEN'T SEEN YOU IN AGES! OMIGAWD, OMIGAWD! THIS MUST BE ROBERT!
UM, HI . . . I, UM, PREFER ROB.
DUBONNET
MMMM, I PREFER ROB, TOO, BUT I'LL HAVE TO SETTLE FOR TONY. HEE HEE. EXCELLENT. MORE BEER.
INSULTS AWREADY, SETH? I'LL HAVE TO PUNISH YOU LATER. HAW!
NOT HERE FOR ONE MINUTE AND ALREADY MY MAN IS BREAKING HEARTS. DON'T LET IT GO TO YOUR HEAD, SWEETUMS.
DON'T WORRY, I WON'T.
THE IDEA OF GETTING LEERED AT BY A BUNCH OF HOMOS DOESN'T EXACTLY PUFF MY EGO FULL OF PRIDE, "SWEETUMS." THIS IS GONNA BE A LONG NIGHT.
I'M GONNA MINGLE, ROB. TRY AND MIX, HUH, HONEY? DON'T BE A PARTY POOPER.
I, UH . . . RIGHT.
DUBONNET
YOU LOOK LIKE YOU COULD USE A SHOT OF DUTCH COURAGE, STRANGER.
YEAH, YOU'RE PROBABLY RIGHT.

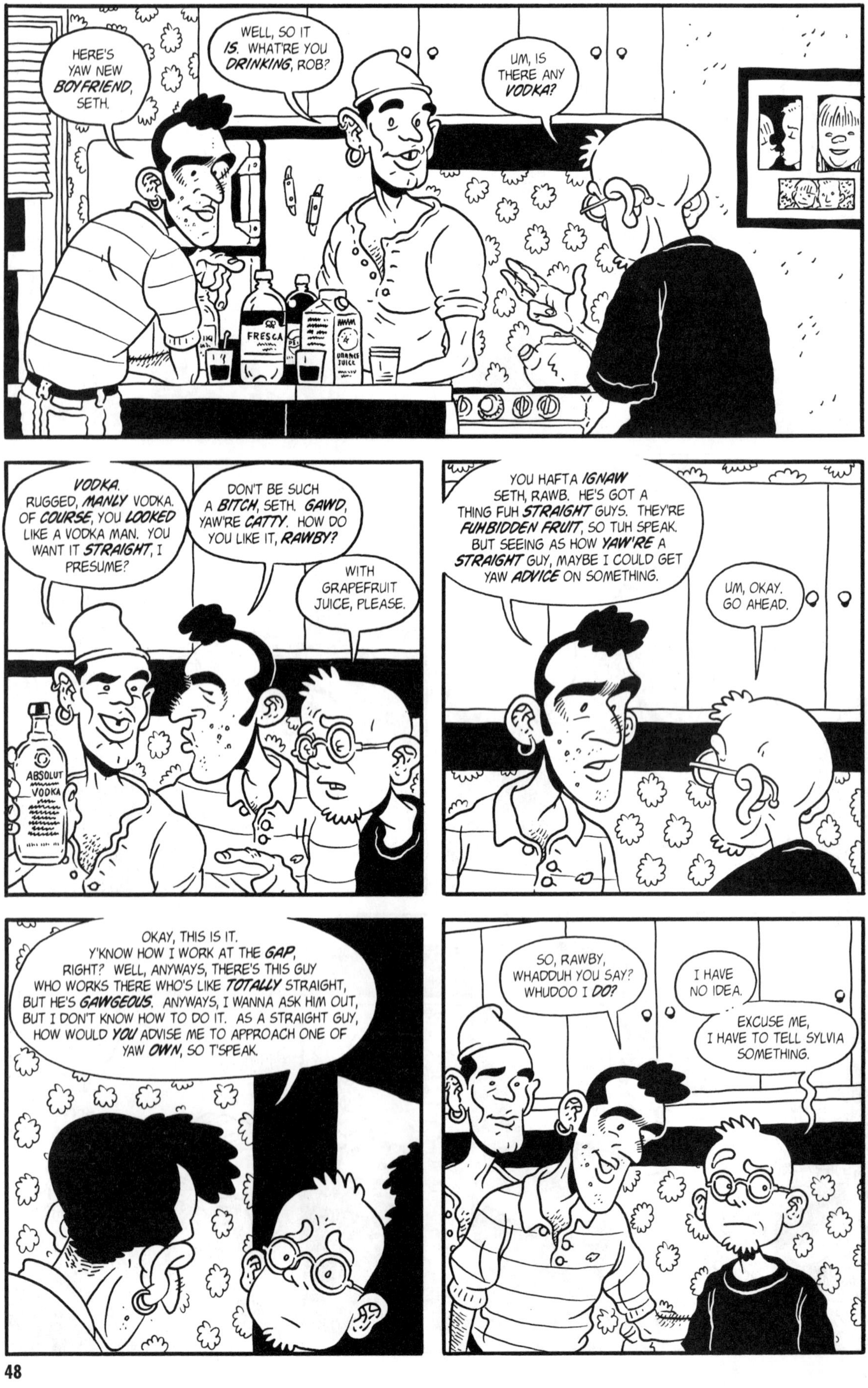
HERE'S YAW NEW BOYFRIEND, SETH.
WELL, SO IT IS. WHAT'RE YOU DRINKING, ROB?
UM, IS THERE ANY VODKA?
FRESCA
ORANGE JUICE
VODKA. RUGGED, MANLY VODKA. OF COURSE, YOU LOOKED LIKE A VODKA MAN. YOU WANT IT STRAIGHT, I PRESUME?
DON'T BE SUCH A BITCH, SETH. GAWD, YAW'RE CATTY. HOW DO YOU LIKE IT, RAWBY?
WITH GRAPEFRUIT JUICE, PLEASE.
ABSOLUT VODKA
YOU HAFTA IGNAW SETH, RAWB. HE'S GOT A THING FUH STRAIGHT GUYS. THEY'RE FUHBIDDEN FRUIT, SO TUH SPEAK. BUT SEEING AS HOW YAW'RE A STRAIGHT GUY, MAYBE I COULD GET YAW ADVICE ON SOMETHING.
UM, OKAY. GO AHEAD.
OKAY, THIS IS IT. Y'KNOW HOW I WORK AT THE GAP, RIGHT? WELL, ANYWAYS, THERE'S THIS GUY WHO WORKS THERE WHO'S LIKE TOTALLY STRAIGHT, BUT HE'S GAWGEOUS. ANYWAYS, I WANNA ASK HIM OUT, BUT I DON'T KNOW HOW TO DO IT. AS A STRAIGHT GUY, HOW WOULD YOU ADVISE ME TO APPROACH ONE OF YAW OWN, SO T'SPEAK.
SO, RAWBY, WHADDUH YOU SAY? WHUDOO I DO?
I HAVE NO IDEA.
EXCUSE ME, I HAVE TO TELL SYLVIA SOMETHING.

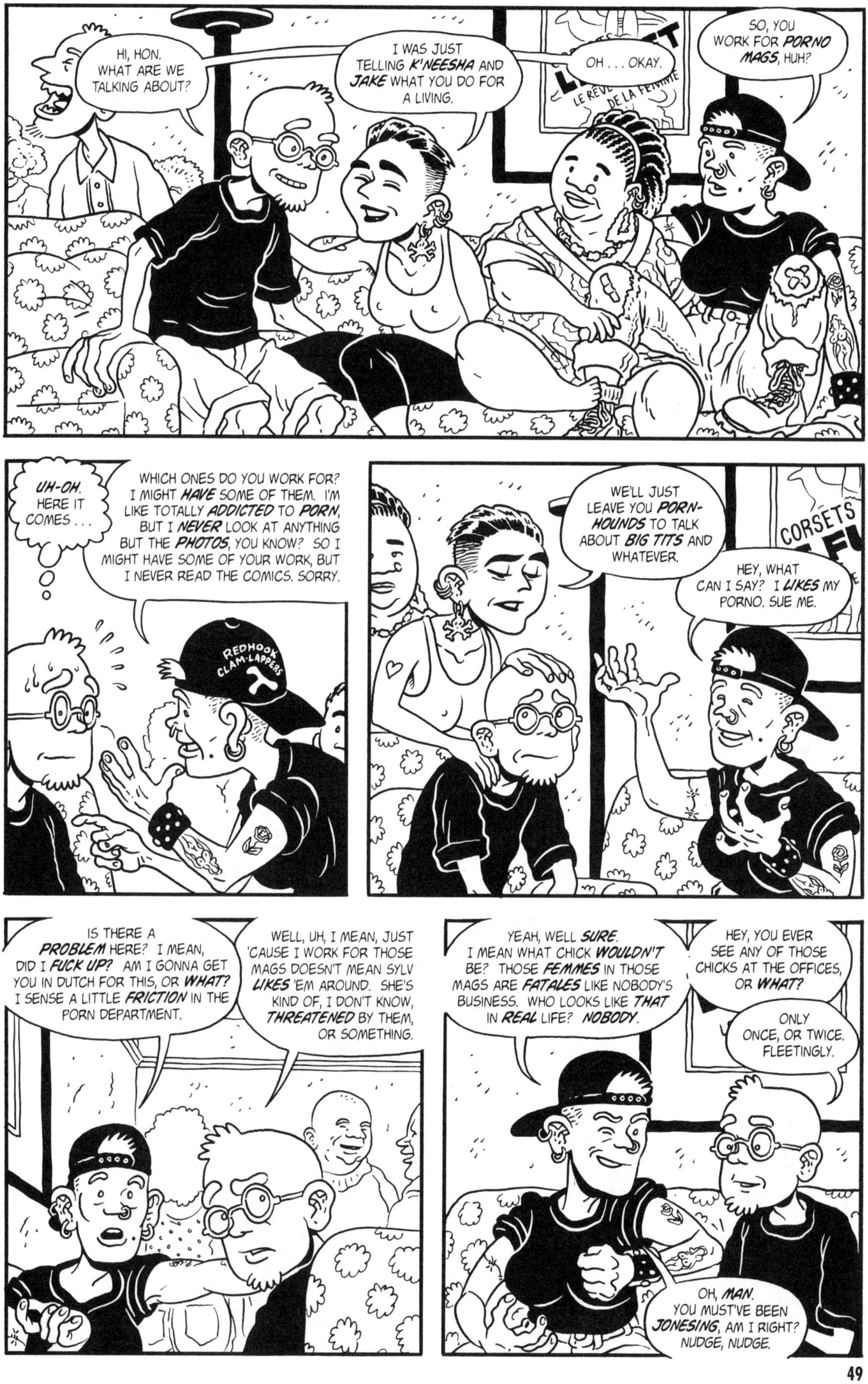
HI, HON. WHAT ARE WE TALKING ABOUT?
I WAS JUST TELLING K'NEESHA AND JAKE WHAT YOU DO FOR A LIVING.
OH . . . OKAY.
SO, YOU WORK FOR PORNO MAGS, HUH?
UH-OH. HERE IT COMES . . .
WHICH ONES DO YOU WORK FOR? I MIGHT HAVE SOME OF THEM. I'M LIKE TOTALLY ADDICTED TO PORN, BUT I NEVER LOOK AT ANYTHING BUT THE PHOTOS, YOU KNOW? SO I MIGHT HAVE SOME OF YOUR WORK, BUT I NEVER READ THE COMICS. SORRY.
REDHOOK CLAM-LAPPERS
WE'LL JUST LEAVE YOU PORN-HOUNDS TO TALK ABOUT BIG TITS AND WHATEVER.
CORSETS
HEY, WHAT CAN I SAY? I LIKES MY PORNO. SUE ME.
IS THERE A PROBLEM HERE? I MEAN, DID I FUCK UP? AM I GONNA GET YOU IN DUTCH FOR THIS, OR WHAT? I SENSE A LITTLE FRICTION IN THE PORN DEPARTMENT.
WELL, UH, I MEAN, JUST 'CAUSE I WORK FOR THOSE MAGS DOESN'T MEAN SYLV LIKES 'EM AROUND. SHE'S KIND OF, I DON'T KNOW, THREATENED BY THEM, OR SOMETHING.
YEAH, WELL SURE. I MEAN WHAT CHICK WOULDN'T BE? THOSE FEMMES IN THOSE MAGS ARE FATALES LIKE NOBODY'S BUSINESS. WHO LOOKS LIKE THAT IN REAL LIFE? NOBODY.
HEY, YOU EVER SEE ANY OF THOSE CHICKS AT THE OFFICES, OR WHAT?
ONLY ONCE, OR TWICE. FLEETINGLY.
OH, MAN. YOU MUST'VE BEEN JONESING, AM I RIGHT? NUDGE, NUDGE.

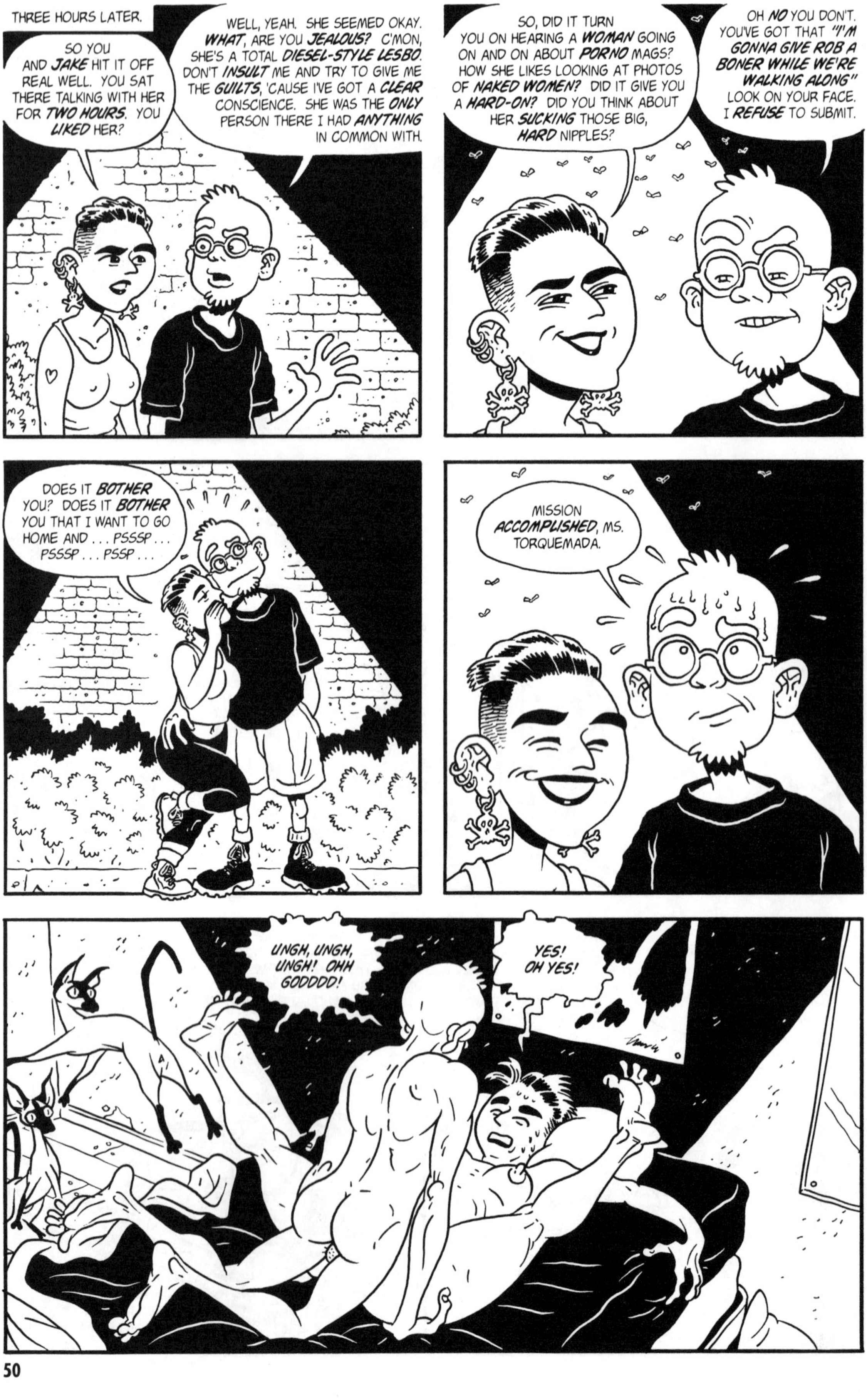
THREE HOURS LATER.
SO YOU AND JAKE HIT IT OFF REAL WELL. YOU SAT THERE TALKING WITH HER FOR TWO HOURS. YOU LIKED HER?
WELL, YEAH. SHE SEEMED OKAY. WHAT, ARE YOU JEALOUS? C'MON, SHE'S A TOTAL DIESEL-STYLE LESBO. DON'T INSULT ME AND TRY TO GIVE ME THE GUILTS, 'CAUSE I'VE GOT A CLEAR CONSCIENCE. SHE WAS THE ONLY PERSON THERE I HAD ANYTHING IN COMMON WITH.
SO, DID IT TURN YOU ON HEARING A WOMAN GOING ON AND ON ABOUT PORNO MAGS? HOW SHE LIKES LOOKING AT PHOTOS OF NAKED WOMEN? DID IT GIVE YOU A HARD-ON? DID YOU THINK ABOUT HER SUCKING THOSE BIG, HARD NIPPLES?
OH NO YOU DON'T. YOU'VE GOT THAT "I'M GONNA GIVE ROB A BONER WHILE WE'RE WALKING ALONG" LOOK ON YOUR FACE. I REFUSE TO SUBMIT.
DOES IT BOTHER YOU? DOES IT BOTHER YOU THAT I WANT TO GO HOME AND . . . PSSSP . . . PSSSP . . . PSSP . . .
MISSION ACCOMPLISHED, MS. TORQUEMADA.
UNGH, UNGH, UNGH! OHH GODDDD!
YES! OH YES!

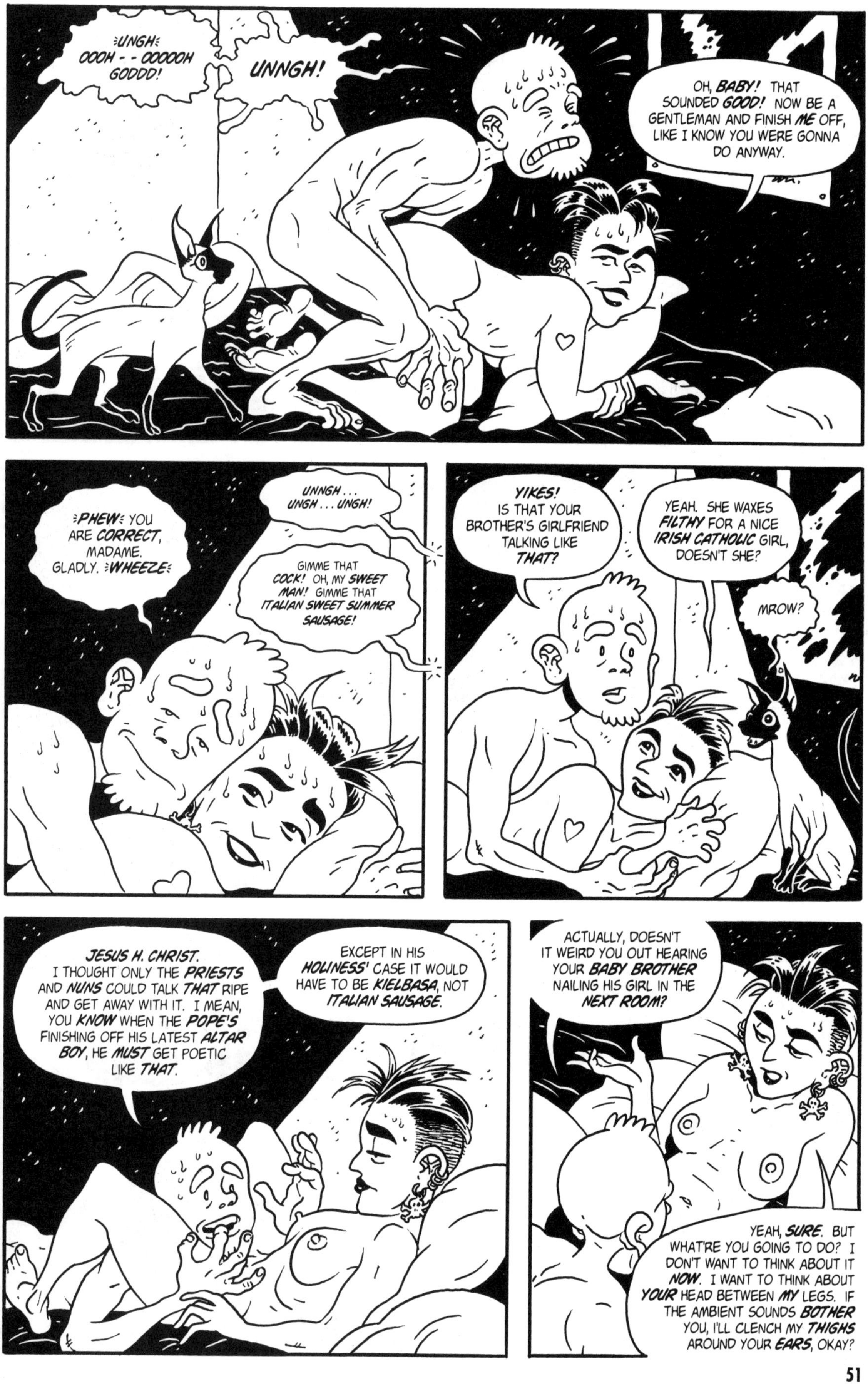
UNGH OOOH - - OOOOOH GODDD!
UNNGH!
OH, BABY! THAT SOUNDED GOOD! NOW BE A GENTLEMAN AND FINISH ME OFF, LIKE I KNOW YOU WERE GONNA DO ANYWAY.
PHEW YOU ARE CORRECT, MADAME. GLADLY. WHEEZE
UNNGH . . . UNGH . . . UNGH!
GIMME THAT COCK! OH, MY SWEET MAN! GIMME THAT ITALIAN SWEET SUMMER SAUSAGE!
YIKES! IS THAT YOUR BROTHER'S GIRLFRIEND TALKING LIKE THAT?
YEAH. SHE WAXES FILTHY FOR A NICE IRISH CATHOLIC GIRL, DOESN'T SHE?
MROW?
JESUS H. CHRIST. I THOUGHT ONLY THE PRIESTS AND NUNS COULD TALK THAT RIPE AND GET AWAY WITH IT. I MEAN, YOU KNOW WHEN THE POPE'S FINISHING OFF HIS LATEST ALTAR BOY, HE MUST GET POETIC LIKE THAT.
EXCEPT IN HIS HOLINESS' CASE IT WOULD HAVE TO BE KIELBASA, NOT ITALIAN SAUSAGE.
ACTUALLY, DOESN'T IT WEIRD YOU OUT HEARING YOUR BABY BROTHER NAILING HIS GIRL IN THE NEXT ROOM?
YEAH, SURE. BUT WHAT'RE YOU GOING TO DO? I DON'T WANT TO THINK ABOUT IT NOW. I WANT TO THINK ABOUT YOUR HEAD BETWEEN MY LEGS. IF THE AMBIENT SOUNDS BOTHER YOU, I'LL CLENCH MY THIGHS AROUND YOUR EARS, OKAY?

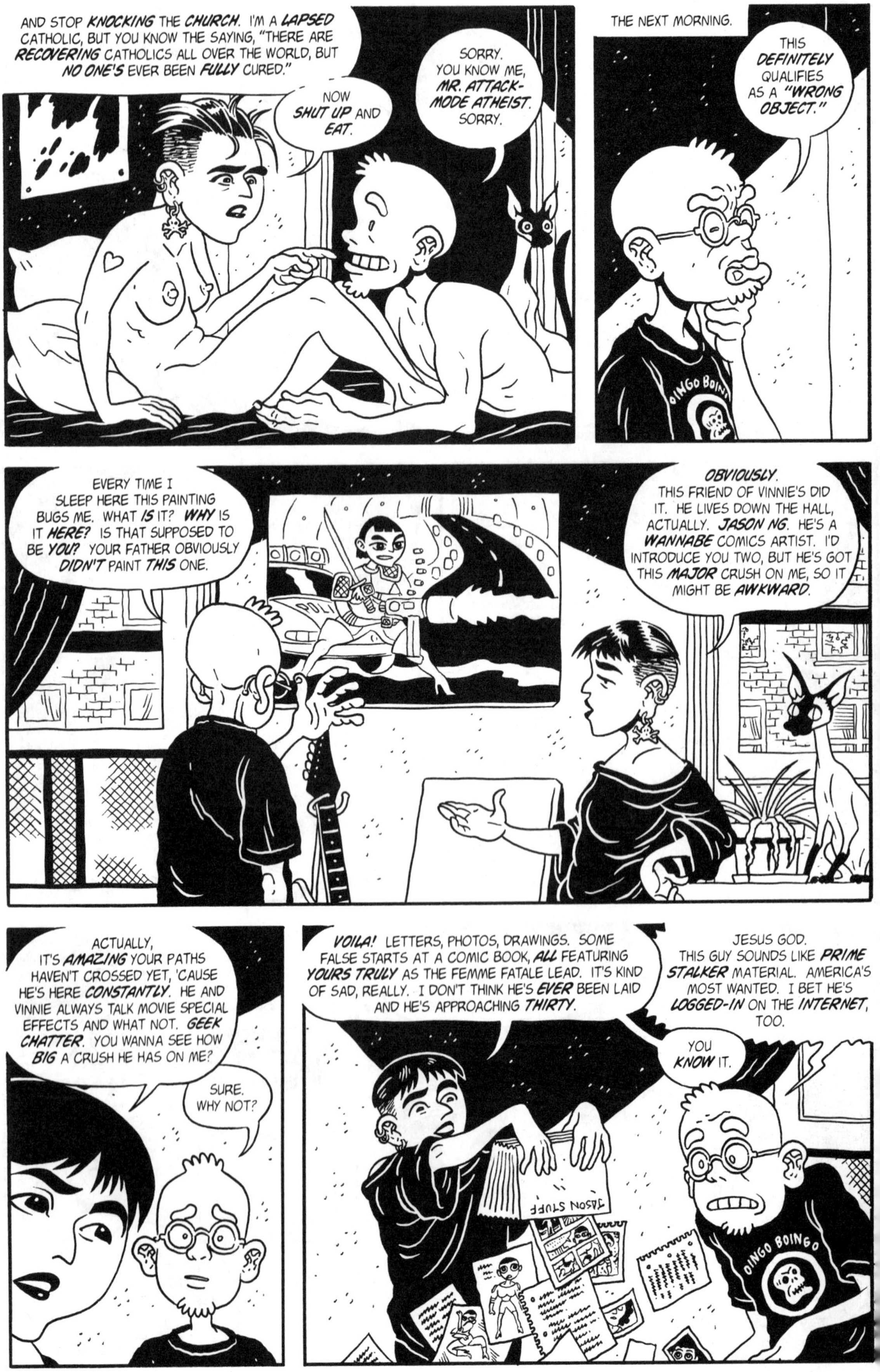
AND STOP KNOCKING THE CHURCH. I'M A LAPSED CATHOLIC, BUT YOU KNOW THE SAYING, "THERE ARE RECOVERING CATHOLICS ALL OVER THE WORLD, BUT NO ONE'S EVER BEEN FULLY CURED."
NOW SHUT UP AND EAT.
SORRY. YOU KNOW ME, MR. ATTACK-MODE ATHEIST. SORRY.
THE NEXT MORNING.
THIS DEFINITELY QUALIFIES AS A "WRONG OBJECT."
OINGO BOINGO
EVERY TIME I SLEEP HERE THIS PAINTING BUGS ME. WHAT IS IT? WHY IS IT HERE? IS THAT SUPPOSED TO BE YOU? YOUR FATHER OBVIOUSLY DIDN'T PAINT THIS ONE.
OBVIOUSLY. THIS FRIEND OF VINNIE'S DID IT. HE LIVES DOWN THE HALL, ACTUALLY. JASON NG. HE'S A WANNABE COMICS ARTIST. I'D INTRODUCE YOU TWO, BUT HE'S GOT THIS MAJOR CRUSH ON ME, SO IT MIGHT BE AWKWARD.
ACTUALLY, IT'S AMAZING YOUR PATHS HAVEN'T CROSSED YET, 'CAUSE HE'S HERE CONSTANTLY. HE AND VINNIE ALWAYS TALK MOVIE SPECIAL EFFECTS AND WHAT NOT. GEEK CHATTER. YOU WANNA SEE HOW BIG A CRUSH HE HAS ON ME?
SURE. WHY NOT?
VOILA! LETTERS, PHOTOS, DRAWINGS. SOME FALSE STARTS AT A COMIC BOOK, ALL FEATURING YOURS TRULY AS THE FEMME FATALE LEAD. IT'S KIND OF SAD, REALLY. I DON'T THINK HE'S EVER BEEN LAID AND HE'S APPROACHING THIRTY.
JASON STUFF
JESUS GOD. THIS GUY SOUNDS LIKE PRIME STALKER MATERIAL. AMERICA'S MOST WANTED. I BET HE'S LOGGED-IN ON THE INTERNET, TOO.
YOU KNOW IT.
OINGO BOINGO

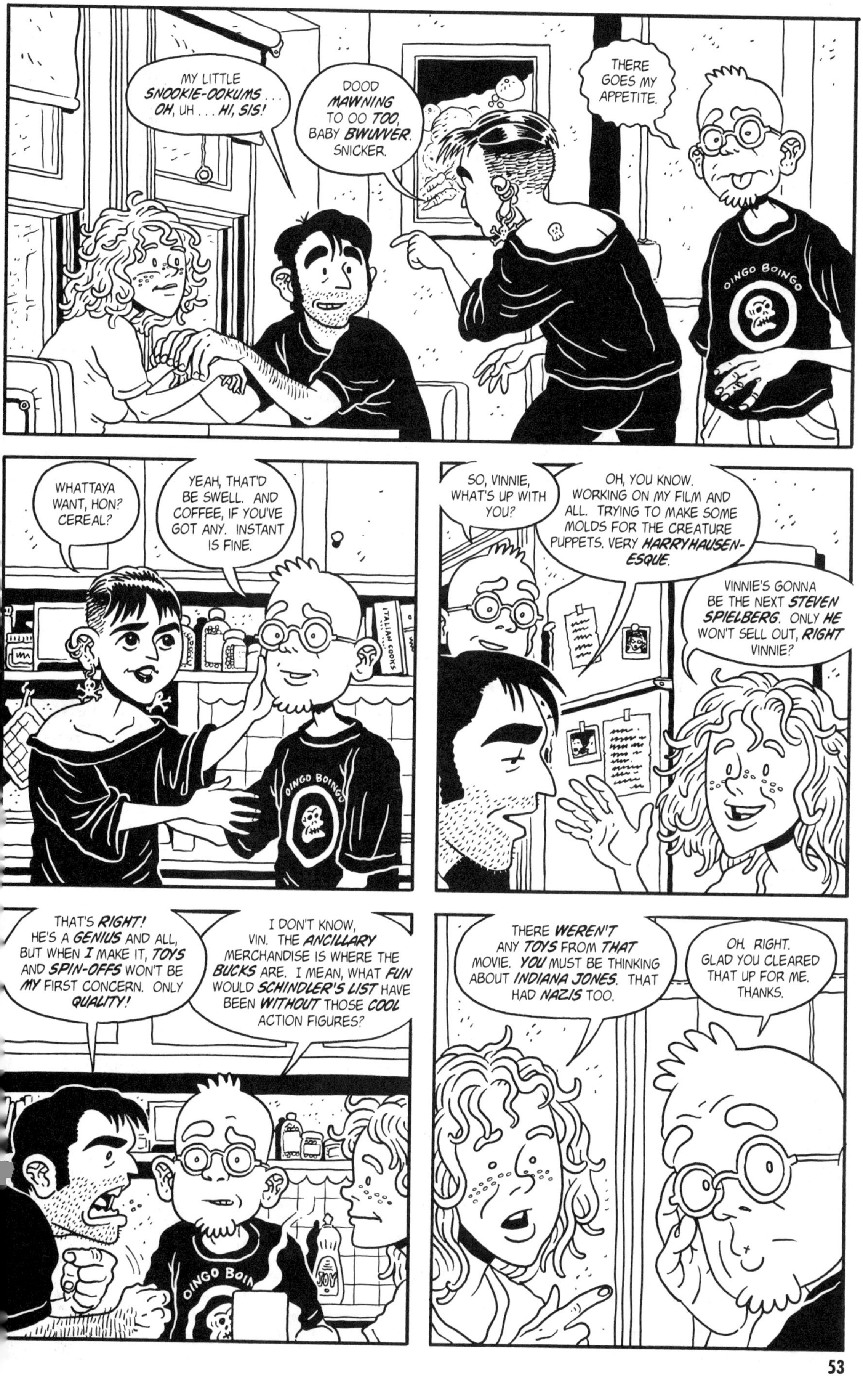

MY LITTLE SNOOKIE-OOKUMS... OH, UH... HI, SIS!
DOOD MAWNING TO OO TOO, BABY BWUVVER. SNICKER.
THERE GOES MY APPETITE.
WHATTAYA WANT, HON? CEREAL?
YEAH, THAT'D BE SWELL. AND COFFEE, IF YOU'VE GOT ANY. INSTANT IS FINE.
ITALIAN COOKS
OINGO BOINGO
SO, VINNIE, WHAT'S UP WITH YOU?
OH, YOU KNOW. WORKING ON MY FILM AND ALL. TRYING TO MAKE SOME MOLDS FOR THE CREATURE PUPPETS. VERY HARRYHAUSEN-ESQUE.
VINNIE'S GONNA BE THE NEXT STEVEN SPIELBERG. ONLY HE WON'T SELL OUT, RIGHT VINNIE?
THAT'S RIGHT! HE'S A GENIUS AND ALL, BUT WHEN I MAKE IT, TOYS AND SPIN-OFFS WON'T BE MY FIRST CONCERN. ONLY QUALITY!
I DON'T KNOW, VIN. THE ANCILLARY MERCHANDISE IS WHERE THE BUCKS ARE. I MEAN, WHAT FUN WOULD SCHINDLER'S LIST HAVE BEEN WITHOUT THOSE COOL ACTION FIGURES?
JOY
THERE WEREN'T ANY TOYS FROM THAT MOVIE. YOU MUST BE THINKING ABOUT INDIANA JONES. THAT HAD NAZIS TOO.
OH. RIGHT. GLAD YOU CLEARED THAT UP FOR ME. THANKS.

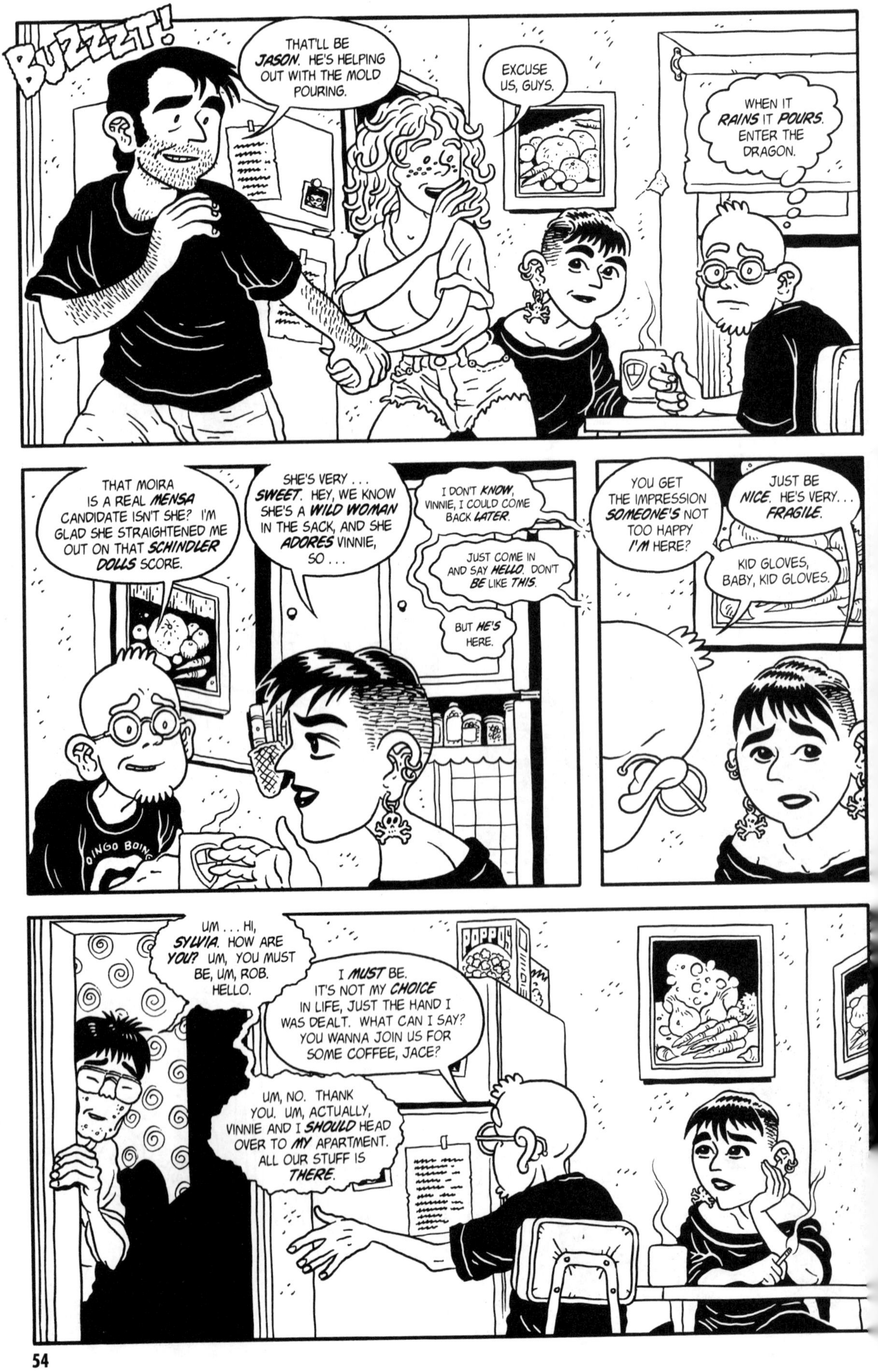
BUZZZT!
THAT'LL BE JASON. HE'S HELPING OUT WITH THE MOLD POURING.
EXCUSE US, GUYS.
WHEN IT RAINS IT POURS. ENTER THE DRAGON.
THAT MOIRA IS A REAL MENSA CANDIDATE ISN'T SHE? I'M GLAD SHE STRAIGHTENED ME OUT ON THAT SCHINDLER DOLLS SCORE.
SHE'S VERY . . . SWEET. HEY, WE KNOW SHE'S A WILD WOMAN IN THE SACK, AND SHE ADORES VINNIE, SO . . .
I DON'T KNOW, VINNIE, I COULD COME BACK LATER.
JUST COME IN AND SAY HELLO. DON'T BE LIKE THIS.
BUT HE'S HERE.
OINGO BOING
YOU GET THE IMPRESSION SOMEONE'S NOT TOO HAPPY I'M HERE?
JUST BE NICE. HE'S VERY . . . FRAGILE.
KID GLOVES, BABY, KID GLOVES.
UM . . . HI, SYLVIA. HOW ARE YOU? UM, YOU MUST BE, UM, ROB. HELLO.
POPPOS
I MUST BE. IT'S NOT MY CHOICE IN LIFE, JUST THE HAND I WAS DEALT. WHAT CAN I SAY? YOU WANNA JOIN US FOR SOME COFFEE, JACE?
UM, NO. THANK YOU. UM, ACTUALLY, VINNIE AND I SHOULD HEAD OVER TO MY APARTMENT. ALL OUR STUFF IS THERE.

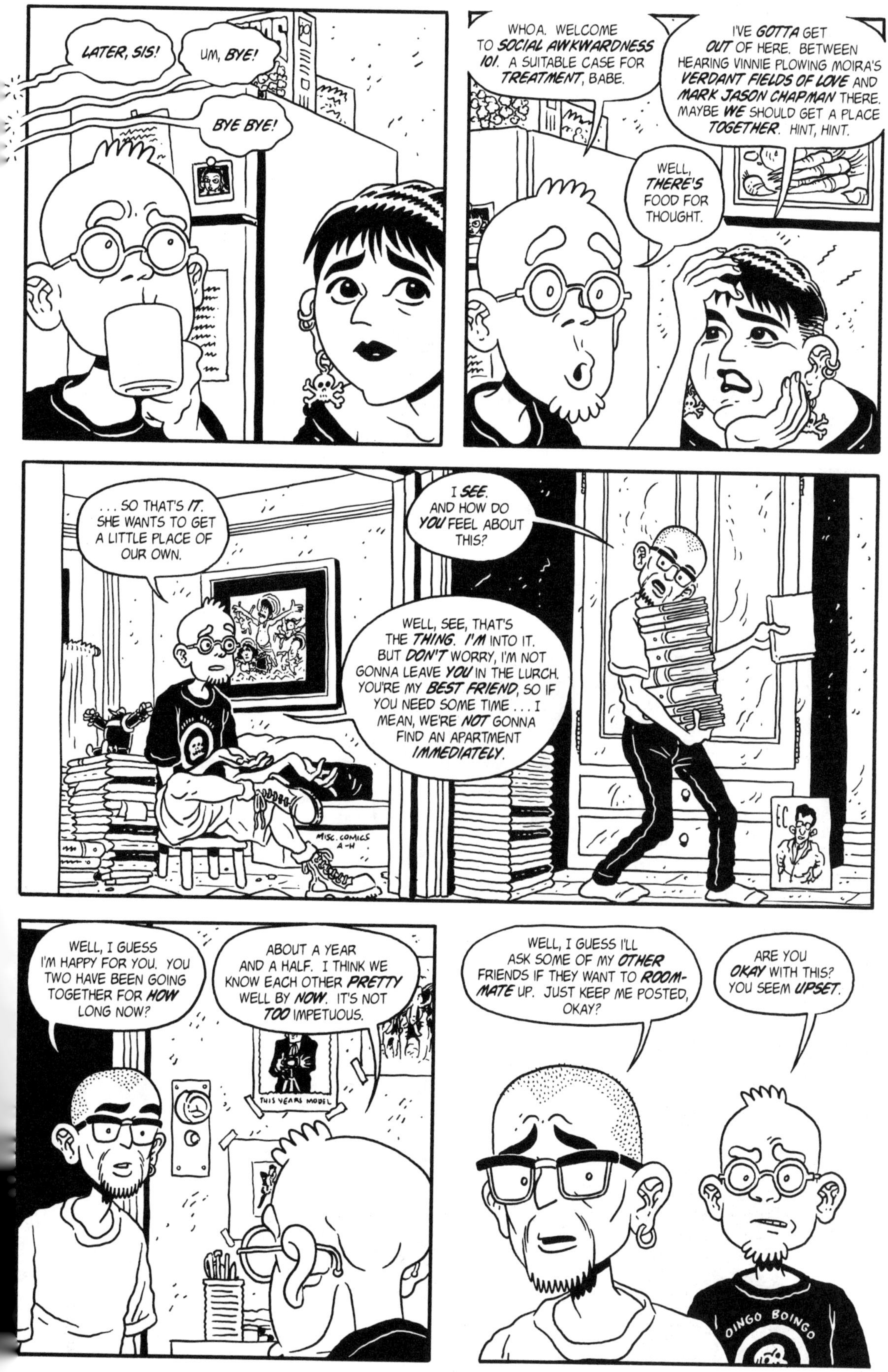
LATER, SIS!
UM, BYE!
BYE BYE!
WHOA. WELCOME TO SOCIAL AWKWARDNESS 101. A SUITABLE CASE FOR TREATMENT, BABE.
I'VE GOTTA GET OUT OF HERE. BETWEEN HEARING VINNIE PLOWING MOIRA'S VERDANT FIELDS OF LOVE AND MARK JASON CHAPMAN THERE. MAYBE WE SHOULD GET A PLACE TOGETHER. HINT, HINT.
WELL, THERE'S FOOD FOR THOUGHT.
. . . SO THAT'S IT. SHE WANTS TO GET A LITTLE PLACE OF OUR OWN.
I SEE. AND HOW DO YOU FEEL ABOUT THIS?
WELL, SEE, THAT'S THE THING. I'M INTO IT. BUT DON'T WORRY, I'M NOT GONNA LEAVE YOU IN THE LURCH. YOU'RE MY BEST FRIEND, SO IF YOU NEED SOME TIME . . . I MEAN, WE'RE NOT GONNA FIND AN APARTMENT IMMEDIATELY.
MISC. COMICS A-H
EC
WELL, I GUESS I'M HAPPY FOR YOU. YOU TWO HAVE BEEN GOING TOGETHER FOR HOW LONG NOW?
ABOUT A YEAR AND A HALF. I THINK WE KNOW EACH OTHER PRETTY WELL BY NOW. IT'S NOT TOO IMPETUOUS.
THIS YEARS MODEL
WELL, I GUESS I'LL ASK SOME OF MY OTHER FRIENDS IF THEY WANT TO ROOM-MATE UP. JUST KEEP ME POSTED, OKAY?
ARE YOU OKAY WITH THIS? YOU SEEM UPSET.
OINGO BOINGO

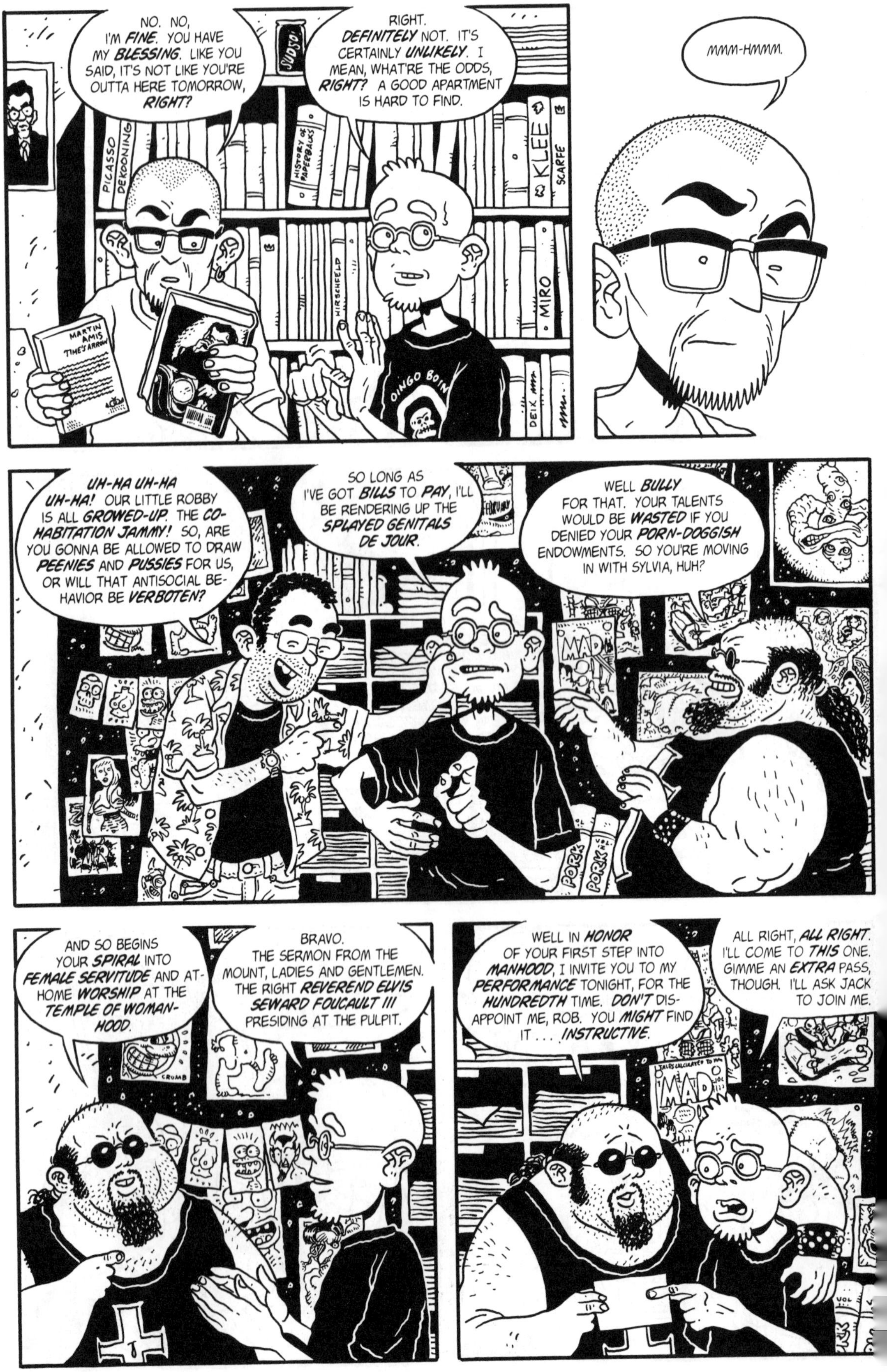
NO. NO, I'M FINE. YOU HAVE MY BLESSING. LIKE YOU SAID, IT'S NOT LIKE YOU'RE OUTTA HERE TOMORROW, RIGHT?
RIGHT. DEFINITELY NOT. IT'S CERTAINLY UNLIKELY. I MEAN, WHAT'RE THE ODDS, RIGHT? A GOOD APARTMENT IS HARD TO FIND.
MMM-HMMM.
UH-HA UH-HA UH-HA! OUR LITTLE ROBBY IS ALL GROWED-UP. THE CO-HABITATION JAMMY! SO, ARE YOU GONNA BE ALLOWED TO DRAW PEENIES AND PUSSIES FOR US, OR WILL THAT ANTISOCIAL BE-HAVIOR BE VERBOTEN?
SO LONG AS I'VE GOT BILLS TO PAY, I'LL BE RENDERING UP THE SPLAYED GENITALS DE JOUR.
WELL BULLY FOR THAT. YOUR TALENTS WOULD BE WASTED IF YOU DENIED YOUR PORN-DOGGISH ENDOWMENTS. SO YOU'RE MOVING IN WITH SYLVIA, HUH?
AND SO BEGINS YOUR SPIRAL INTO FEMALE SERVITUDE AND AT-HOME WORSHIP AT THE TEMPLE OF WOMAN-HOOD.
BRAVO. THE SERMON FROM THE MOUNT, LADIES AND GENTLEMEN. THE RIGHT REVEREND ELVIS SEWARD FOUCAULT III PRESIDING AT THE PULPIT.
WELL IN HONOR OF YOUR FIRST STEP INTO MANHOOD, I INVITE YOU TO MY PERFORMANCE TONIGHT, FOR THE HUNDREDTH TIME. DON'T DIS-APPOINT ME, ROB. YOU MIGHT FIND IT . . . INSTRUCTIVE.
ALL RIGHT, ALL RIGHT. I'LL COME TO THIS ONE. GIMME AN EXTRA PASS, THOUGH. I'LL ASK JACK TO JOIN ME.

THIS IS THE PLACE. I'M GLAD WE MET HERE, INSTEAD OF ARRIVING *TOGETHER*. *GOD*, I'M *SO* FUCKING *EMBARRASSED* BY YOUR *GET-UP*, MAN. WHAT KIND OF MAN HAS A PAIR OF *THIGH-HIGH PATENT LEATHER BOOTS* JUST *RARING* TO GO IN HIS WARDROBE?

YEAH, WELL, *MAYBE*. BUT *YOU*, MY FRIEND, ARE GONNA SEEM MORE OUT OF PLACE THAN *ME*. WHEN IN *ROME*, I ALWAYS SAY.

WELCOME, *OBVIOUS NEOPHYTES*, TO *THE OSSUARY*. STEP INTO THE *VOID*.

the OSSUARY

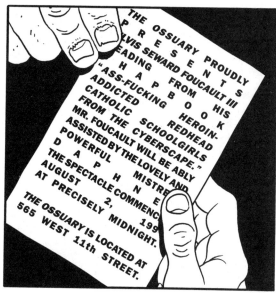

THE OSSUARY PROUDLY PRESENTS ELVIS SEWARD FOUCAULT III READING FROM HIS *CHAPBOOK* "ASS-FUCKING ADDICTED CATHOLIC REDHEAD FROM THE CYBERSCAPE." MR. FOUCAULT WILL BE ABLY ASSISTED BY THE LOVELY AND POWERFUL MISTRESS DAPHNE. THE SPECTACLE COMMENCES AUGUST 2, 199— AT PRECISELY MIDNIGHT. THE OSSUARY IS LOCATED AT 565 WEST 11th STREET.

YOU KNOW WHAT I FEEL LIKE? I FEEL LIKE I'M IN *INVASION OF THE BODY SNATCHERS* AND SOMEONE'S GONNA SPOT ME AND START SOUNDING THE ALARM.

OR THAT OLD *STAR TREK* WHERE EVERYONE BELONGED TO THIS ANCIENT ORDER. YOU KNOW, "IT'S THE WILL OF *LANDRU*." THEY'RE GONNA SPOT ME AND START SAYING, "HE'S *NOT* OF THE *BODY*."

YEAH, WELL KEEP TALKING *CLASSIC TREK* AND IT'LL BE A *SELF-FULFILLING PROPHECY*, MATEY.

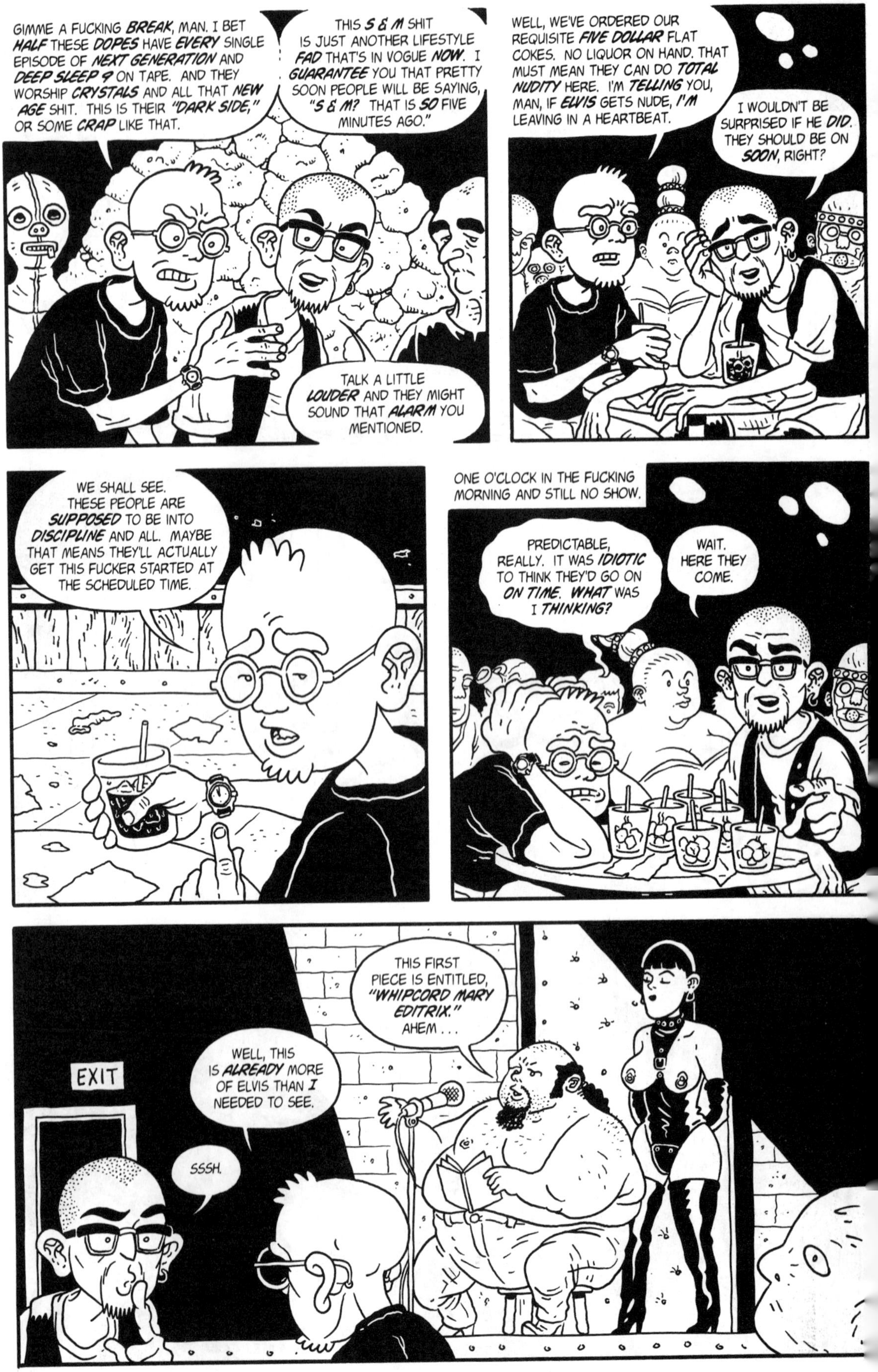
GIMME A FUCKING BREAK, MAN. I BET HALF THESE DOPES HAVE EVERY SINGLE EPISODE OF NEXT GENERATION AND DEEP SLEEP 9 ON TAPE. AND THEY WORSHIP CRYSTALS AND ALL THAT NEW AGE SHIT. THIS IS THEIR "DARK SIDE," OR SOME CRAP LIKE THAT.
THIS S & M SHIT IS JUST ANOTHER LIFESTYLE FAD THAT'S IN VOGUE NOW. I GUARANTEE YOU THAT PRETTY SOON PEOPLE WILL BE SAYING, "S & M? THAT IS SO FIVE MINUTES AGO."
TALK A LITTLE LOUDER AND THEY MIGHT SOUND THAT ALARM YOU MENTIONED.
WELL, WE'VE ORDERED OUR REQUISITE FIVE DOLLAR FLAT COKES. NO LIQUOR ON HAND. THAT MUST MEAN THEY CAN DO TOTAL NUDITY HERE. I'M TELLING YOU, MAN, IF ELVIS GETS NUDE, I'M LEAVING IN A HEARTBEAT.
I WOULDN'T BE SURPRISED IF HE DID. THEY SHOULD BE ON SOON, RIGHT?
WE SHALL SEE. THESE PEOPLE ARE SUPPOSED TO BE INTO DISCIPLINE AND ALL. MAYBE THAT MEANS THEY'LL ACTUALLY GET THIS FUCKER STARTED AT THE SCHEDULED TIME.
ONE O'CLOCK IN THE FUCKING MORNING AND STILL NO SHOW.
PREDICTABLE, REALLY. IT WAS IDIOTIC TO THINK THEY'D GO ON ON TIME. WHAT WAS I THINKING?
WAIT. HERE THEY COME.
EXIT
WELL, THIS IS ALREADY MORE OF ELVIS THAN I NEEDED TO SEE.
THIS FIRST PIECE IS ENTITLED, "WHIPCORD MARY EDITRIX." AHEM . . .
SSSH.

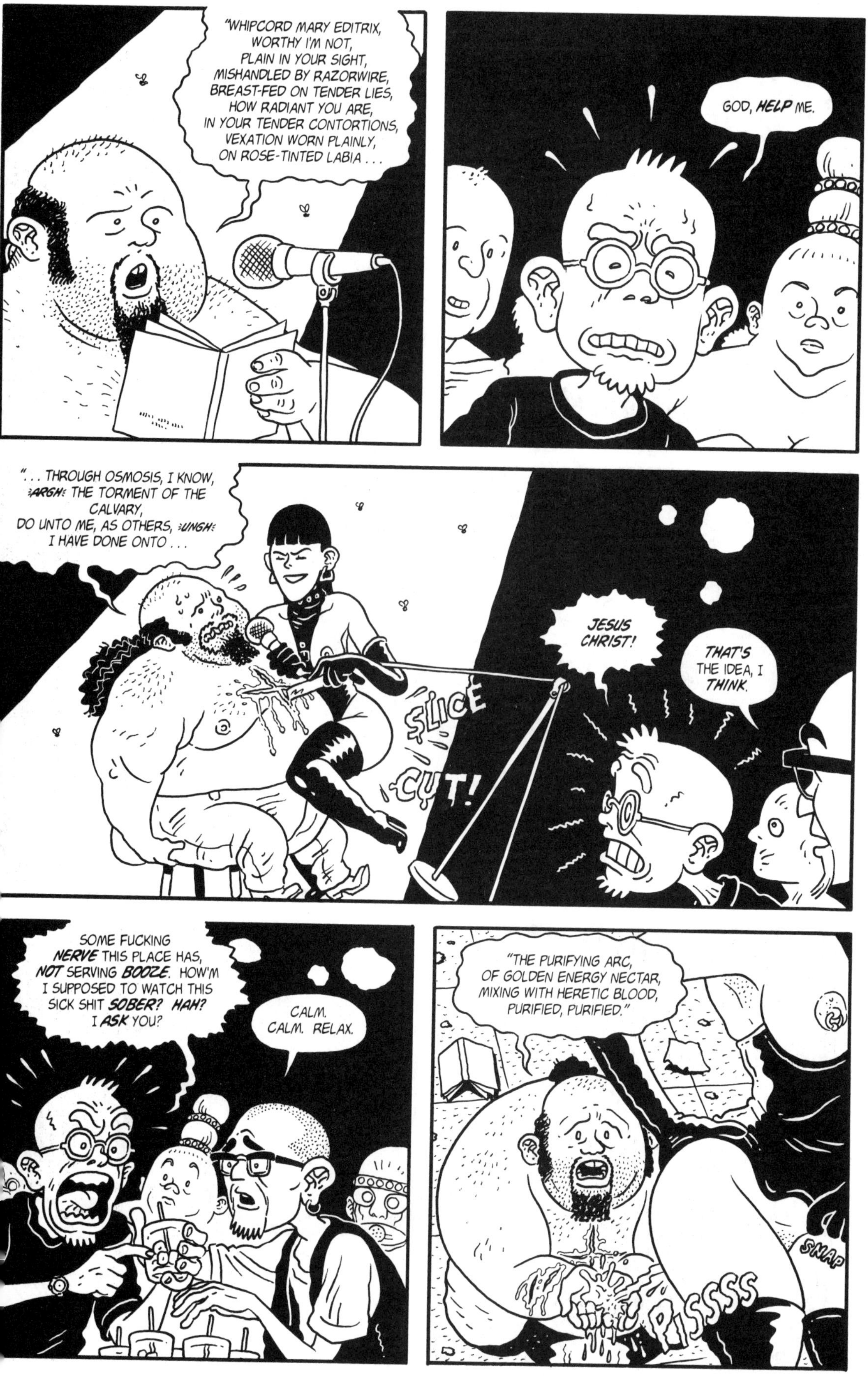
"WHIPCORD MARY EDITRIX, WORTHY I'M NOT, PLAIN IN YOUR SIGHT, MISHANDLED BY RAZORWIRE, BREAST-FED ON TENDER LIES, HOW RADIANT YOU ARE, IN YOUR TENDER CONTORTIONS, VEXATION WORN PLAINLY, ON ROSE-TINTED LABIA . . .
GOD, HELP ME.
". . . THROUGH OSMOSIS, I KNOW, ARGH THE TORMENT OF THE CALVARY, DO UNTO ME, AS OTHERS, UNGH I HAVE DONE ONTO . . .
SLICE
CUT!
JESUS CHRIST!
THAT'S THE IDEA, I THINK.
SOME FUCKING NERVE THIS PLACE HAS, NOT SERVING BOOZE. HOW'M I SUPPOSED TO WATCH THIS SICK SHIT SOBER? HAH? I ASK YOU?
CALM. CALM. RELAX.
"THE PURIFYING ARC, OF GOLDEN ENERGY NECTAR, MIXING WITH HERETIC BLOOD, PURIFIED, PURIFIED."
SNAP
PISSSS

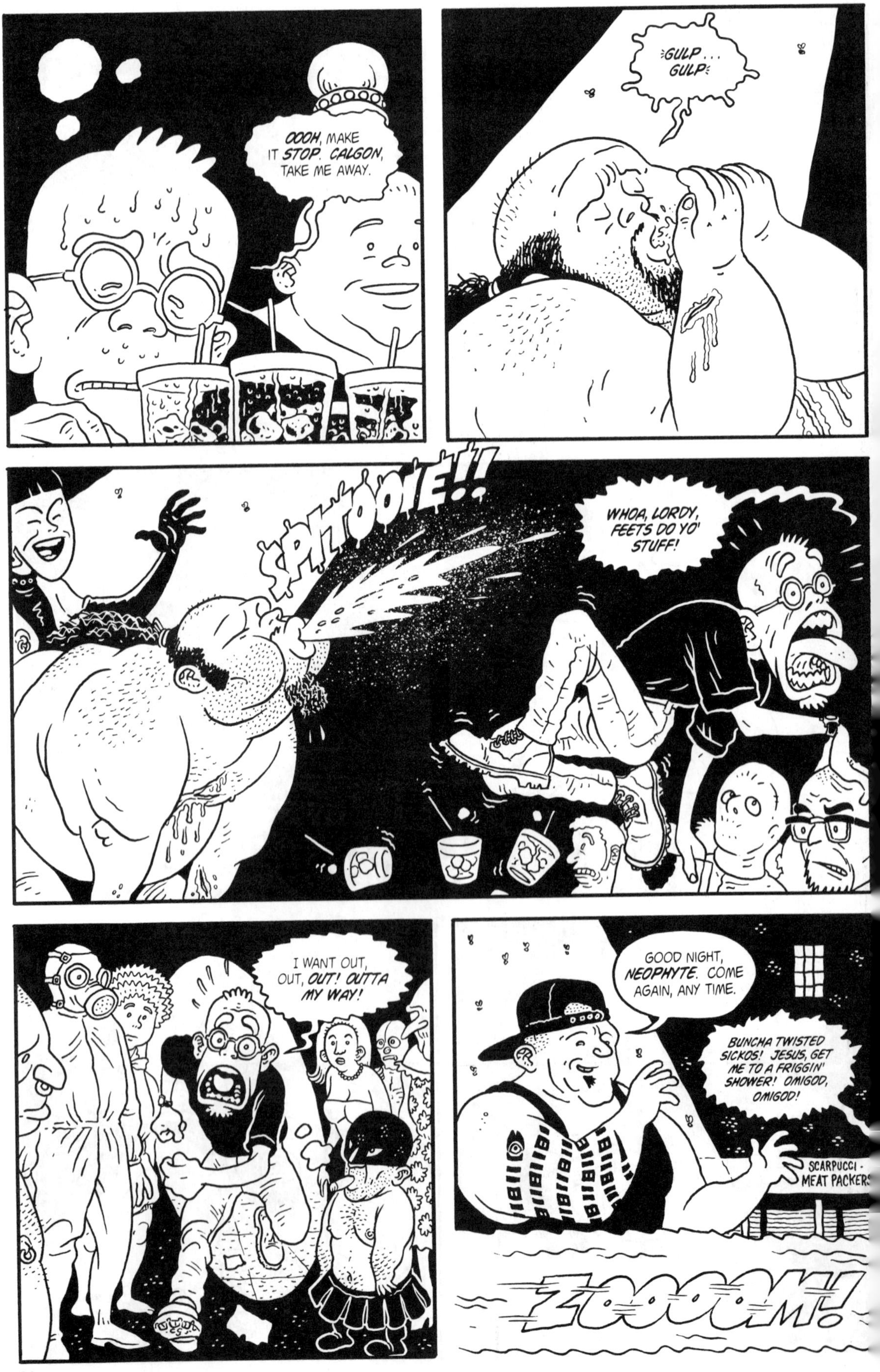
OOOH, MAKE IT STOP. CALGON, TAKE ME AWAY.
GULP... GULP
SPHTOOIE!!
WHOA, LORDY, FEETS DO YO' STUFF!
I WANT OUT, OUT, OUT! OUTTA MY WAY!
GOOD NIGHT, NEOPHYTE. COME AGAIN, ANY TIME.
BUNCHA TWISTED SICKOS! JESUS, GET ME TO A FRIGGIN' SHOWER! OMIGOD, OMIGOD!
SCARPUCCI - MEAT PACKERS
ZOOOOM!

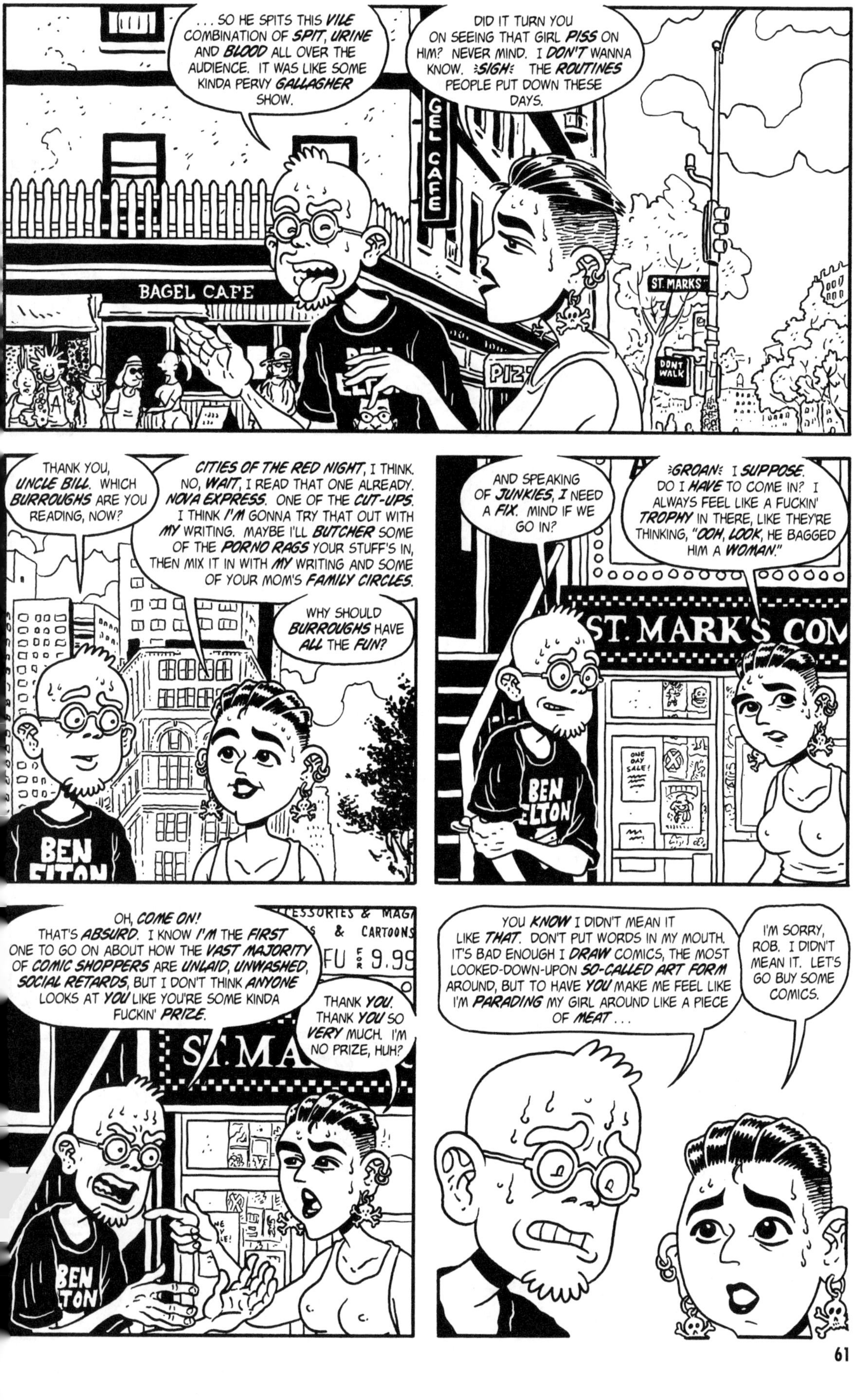
. . . SO HE SPITS THIS VILE COMBINATION OF SPIT, URINE AND BLOOD ALL OVER THE AUDIENCE. IT WAS LIKE SOME KINDA PERVY GALLAGHER SHOW.
DID IT TURN YOU ON SEEING THAT GIRL PISS ON HIM? NEVER MIND. I DON'T WANNA KNOW. SIGH THE ROUTINES PEOPLE PUT DOWN THESE DAYS.
GEL CAFE
BAGEL CAFE
ST. MARKS
DONT WALK
THANK YOU, UNCLE BILL. WHICH BURROUGHS ARE YOU READING, NOW?
CITIES OF THE RED NIGHT, I THINK. NO, WAIT, I READ THAT ONE ALREADY. NOVA EXPRESS. ONE OF THE CUT-UPS. I THINK I'M GONNA TRY THAT OUT WITH MY WRITING. MAYBE I'LL BUTCHER SOME OF THE PORNO RAGS YOUR STUFF'S IN, THEN MIX IT IN WITH MY WRITING AND SOME OF YOUR MOM'S FAMILY CIRCLES.
WHY SHOULD BURROUGHS HAVE ALL THE FUN?
BEN ELTON
AND SPEAKING OF JUNKIES, I NEED A FIX. MIND IF WE GO IN?
GROAN I SUPPOSE. DO I HAVE TO COME IN? I ALWAYS FEEL LIKE A FUCKIN' TROPHY IN THERE, LIKE THEY'RE THINKING, "OOH, LOOK, HE BAGGED HIM A WOMAN."
ST. MARK'S COM
ONE DAY SALE!
BEN ELTON
OH, COME ON! THAT'S ABSURD. I KNOW I'M THE FIRST ONE TO GO ON ABOUT HOW THE VAST MAJORITY OF COMIC SHOPPERS ARE UNLAID, UNWASHED, SOCIAL RETARDS, BUT I DON'T THINK ANYONE LOOKS AT YOU LIKE YOU'RE SOME KINDA FUCKIN' PRIZE.
THANK YOU. THANK YOU SO VERY MUCH. I'M NO PRIZE, HUH?
& CARTOONS
ST. MA
BEN ELTON
YOU KNOW I DIDN'T MEAN IT LIKE THAT. DON'T PUT WORDS IN MY MOUTH. IT'S BAD ENOUGH I DRAW COMICS, THE MOST LOOKED-DOWN-UPON SO-CALLED ART FORM AROUND, BUT TO HAVE YOU MAKE ME FEEL LIKE I'M PARADING MY GIRL AROUND LIKE A PIECE OF MEAT . . .
I'M SORRY, ROB. I DIDN'T MEAN IT. LET'S GO BUY SOME COMICS.

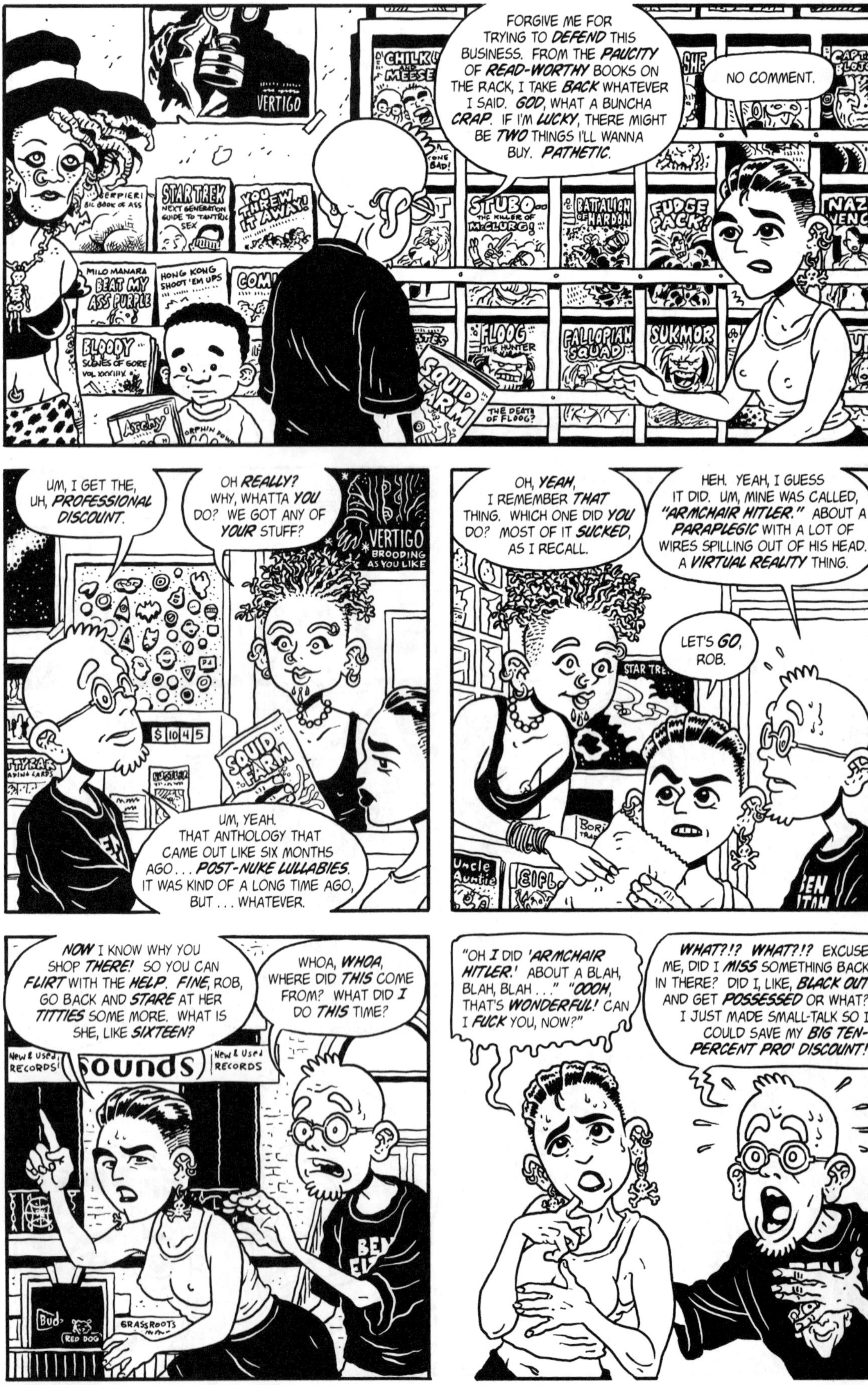
FORGIVE ME FOR TRYING TO DEFEND THIS BUSINESS. FROM THE PAUCITY OF READ-WORTHY BOOKS ON THE RACK, I TAKE BACK WHATEVER I SAID. GOD, WHAT A BUNCHA CRAP. IF I'M LUCKY, THERE MIGHT BE TWO THINGS I'LL WANNA BUY. PATHETIC.
NO COMMENT.
UM, I GET THE, UH, PROFESSIONAL DISCOUNT.
OH REALLY? WHY, WHATTA YOU DO? WE GOT ANY OF YOUR STUFF?
UM, YEAH. THAT ANTHOLOGY THAT CAME OUT LIKE SIX MONTHS AGO... POST-NUKE LULLABIES. IT WAS KIND OF A LONG TIME AGO, BUT... WHATEVER.
OH, YEAH, I REMEMBER THAT THING. WHICH ONE DID YOU DO? MOST OF IT SUCKED, AS I RECALL.
HEH. YEAH, I GUESS IT DID. UM, MINE WAS CALLED, "ARMCHAIR HITLER." ABOUT A PARAPLEGIC WITH A LOT OF WIRES SPILLING OUT OF HIS HEAD. A VIRTUAL REALITY THING.
LET'S GO, ROB.
NOW I KNOW WHY YOU SHOP THERE! SO YOU CAN FLIRT WITH THE HELP. FINE, ROB, GO BACK AND STARE AT HER TITTIES SOME MORE. WHAT IS SHE, LIKE SIXTEEN?
WHOA, WHOA, WHERE DID THIS COME FROM? WHAT DID I DO THIS TIME?
"OH I DID 'ARMCHAIR HITLER.' ABOUT A BLAH, BLAH, BLAH..." "OOOH, THAT'S WONDERFUL! CAN I FUCK YOU, NOW?"
WHAT?!? WHAT?!? EXCUSE ME, DID I MISS SOMETHING BACK IN THERE? DID I, LIKE, BLACK OUT AND GET POSSESSED OR WHAT? I JUST MADE SMALL-TALK SO I COULD SAVE MY BIG TEN-PERCENT PRO' DISCOUNT!

COMMUNITY
CENTER
PRESENTS

COMMUNITY
EDUCATION
FOR THE

BEN
ELTON

OOOGH, MY *GUT*. NOTHING LIKE A LITTLE *CONFRONTATION* TO SET IT OFF.

WHY DO YOU PUT UP WITH A *BITCH* LIKE ME? ≳SNIFF≲ YOU DIDN'T DO *ANYTHING*. I DON'T KNOW *WHAT* GETS INTO ME. ≳SOB≲

BEN
ELTON

NEW YORK

NYC

Don't worr

IT'S OKAY, HONEY. IT'S OKAY.

DRUG free

IT'S *NOT* OKAY. ≳SOB≲ I ACT LIKE SUCH A *JEALOUS ASS* SOMETIMES. IT'S BECAUSE I *LOVE* YOU *SO MUCH.* ≳SNIFFLE≲ I DON'T WANNA *LOSE* YOU TO SOMEONE ELSE, AND I KNOW HOW YOU *GO* FOR THEM *PUNKY* LITTLE CHICKS.

ORIGINAL

NEW Y

GOVERNOR

LEGALIZE I

YOU'RE STUPID!

cool as fuck

BEN
ELTON

YOU'RE THE ONE FOR ME, SYLVIA. NO ONE ELSE. *JUST* YOU. OKAY? I *LOVE* YOU. I'M JUST BAD AT SMALL TALK, *ESPECIALLY* ABOUT MY *WORK.* I ALWAYS FEEL *STUPID* TALKING ABOUT WHAT I DO.

YOU SHOULDN'T. ≳SNIFF≲ YOU'RE AMAZINGLY *TALENTED.* YOU *SHOULD* HAVE A *HUGE EGO.* I'M SORRY. WHY DO YOU PUT UP WITH ME? I'M A *HORRIBLE* PERSON.

ORIGINAL GRUNGE

MANSON

HOWARD
ST RN

GOVERNOR

IN CASE OF EMERGENCY

FRE

RK
UCKIN
ITY

NEW YORK

DAMN THIS *HEAT. THAT'S* WHERE THIS IS COMING FROM. IT'S THE *HEAT* AND *HUMIDITY.* LET'S JUST GO GRAB A BITE TO EAT. I NEED SOMETHING TO SETTLE MY GUT.

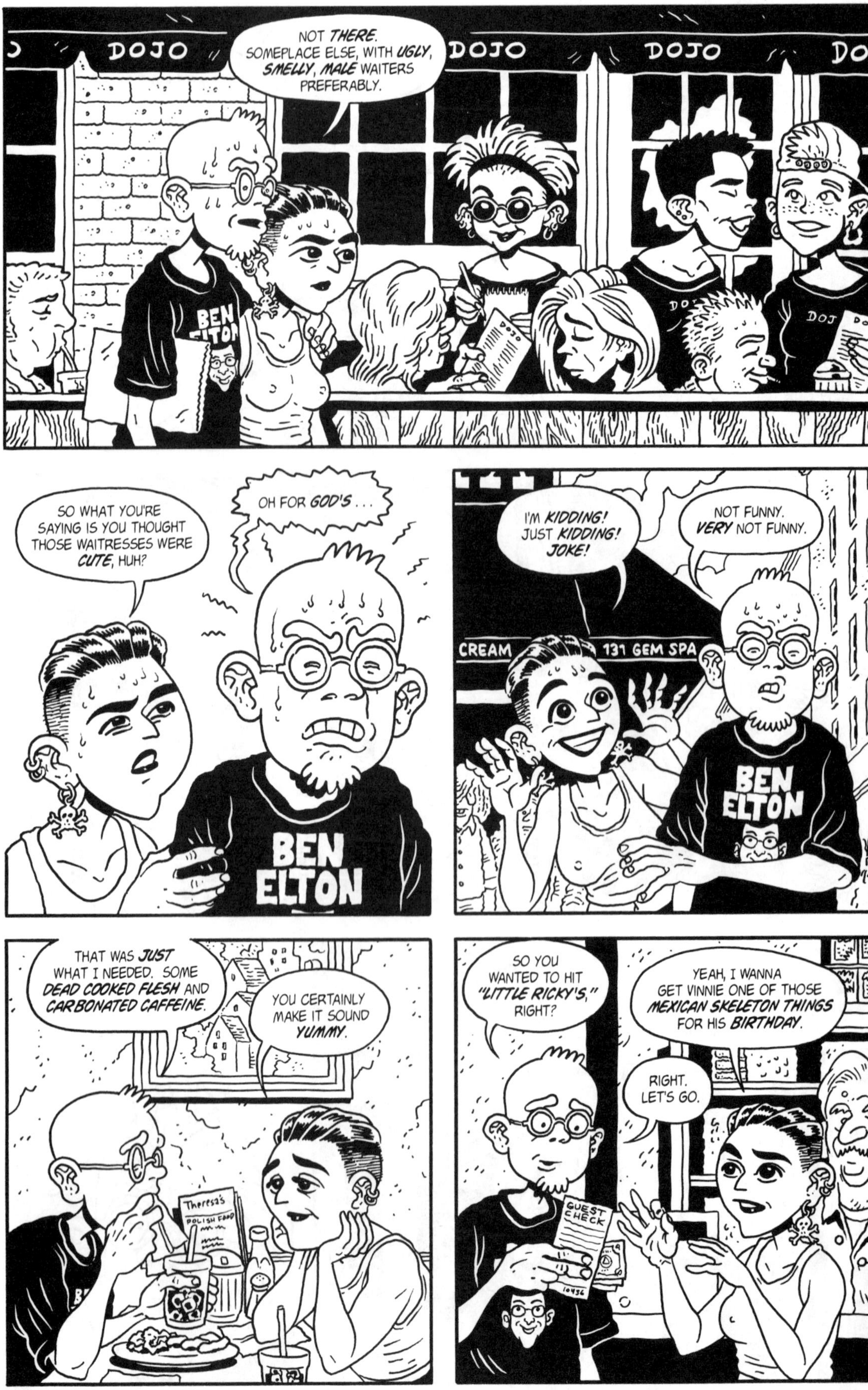
DOJO
NOT THERE. SOMEPLACE ELSE, WITH UGLY, SMELLY, MALE WAITERS PREFERABLY.
DOJO
DOJO
BEN ELTON
SO WHAT YOU'RE SAYING IS YOU THOUGHT THOSE WAITRESSES WERE CUTE, HUH?
OH FOR GOD'S . . .
BEN ELTON
I'M KIDDING! JUST KIDDING! JOKE!
NOT FUNNY. VERY NOT FUNNY.
CREAM
131 GEM SPA
BEN ELTON
THAT WAS JUST WHAT I NEEDED. SOME DEAD COOKED FLESH AND CARBONATED CAFFEINE.
YOU CERTAINLY MAKE IT SOUND YUMMY.
Theresa's
POLISH FOOD
SO YOU WANTED TO HIT "LITTLE RICKY'S," RIGHT?
YEAH, I WANNA GET VINNIE ONE OF THOSE MEXICAN SKELETON THINGS FOR HIS BIRTHDAY.
RIGHT. LET'S GO.
GUEST CHECK

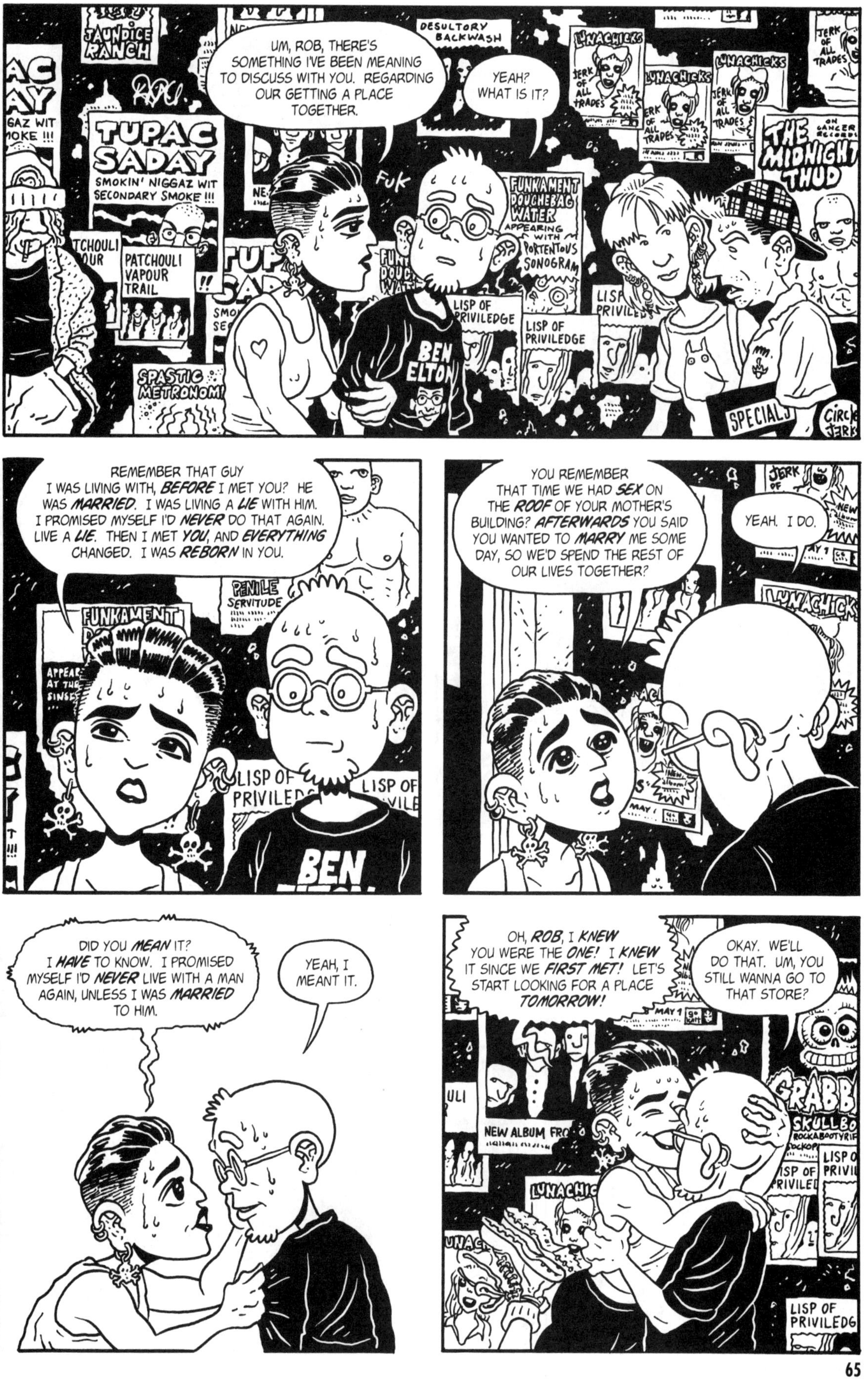
UM, ROB, THERE'S SOMETHING I'VE BEEN MEANING TO DISCUSS WITH YOU. REGARDING OUR GETTING A PLACE TOGETHER.
YEAH? WHAT IS IT?
REMEMBER THAT GUY I WAS LIVING WITH, BEFORE I MET YOU? HE WAS MARRIED. I WAS LIVING A LIE WITH HIM. I PROMISED MYSELF I'D NEVER DO THAT AGAIN. LIVE A LIE. THEN I MET YOU, AND EVERYTHING CHANGED. I WAS REBORN IN YOU.
YOU REMEMBER THAT TIME WE HAD SEX ON THE ROOF OF YOUR MOTHER'S BUILDING? AFTERWARDS YOU SAID YOU WANTED TO MARRY ME SOME DAY, SO WE'D SPEND THE REST OF OUR LIVES TOGETHER?
YEAH. I DO.
DID YOU MEAN IT? I HAVE TO KNOW. I PROMISED MYSELF I'D NEVER LIVE WITH A MAN AGAIN, UNLESS I WAS MARRIED TO HIM.
YEAH, I MEANT IT.
OH, ROB, I KNEW YOU WERE THE ONE! I KNEW IT SINCE WE FIRST MET! LET'S START LOOKING FOR A PLACE TOMORROW!
OKAY. WE'LL DO THAT. UM, YOU STILL WANNA GO TO THAT STORE?

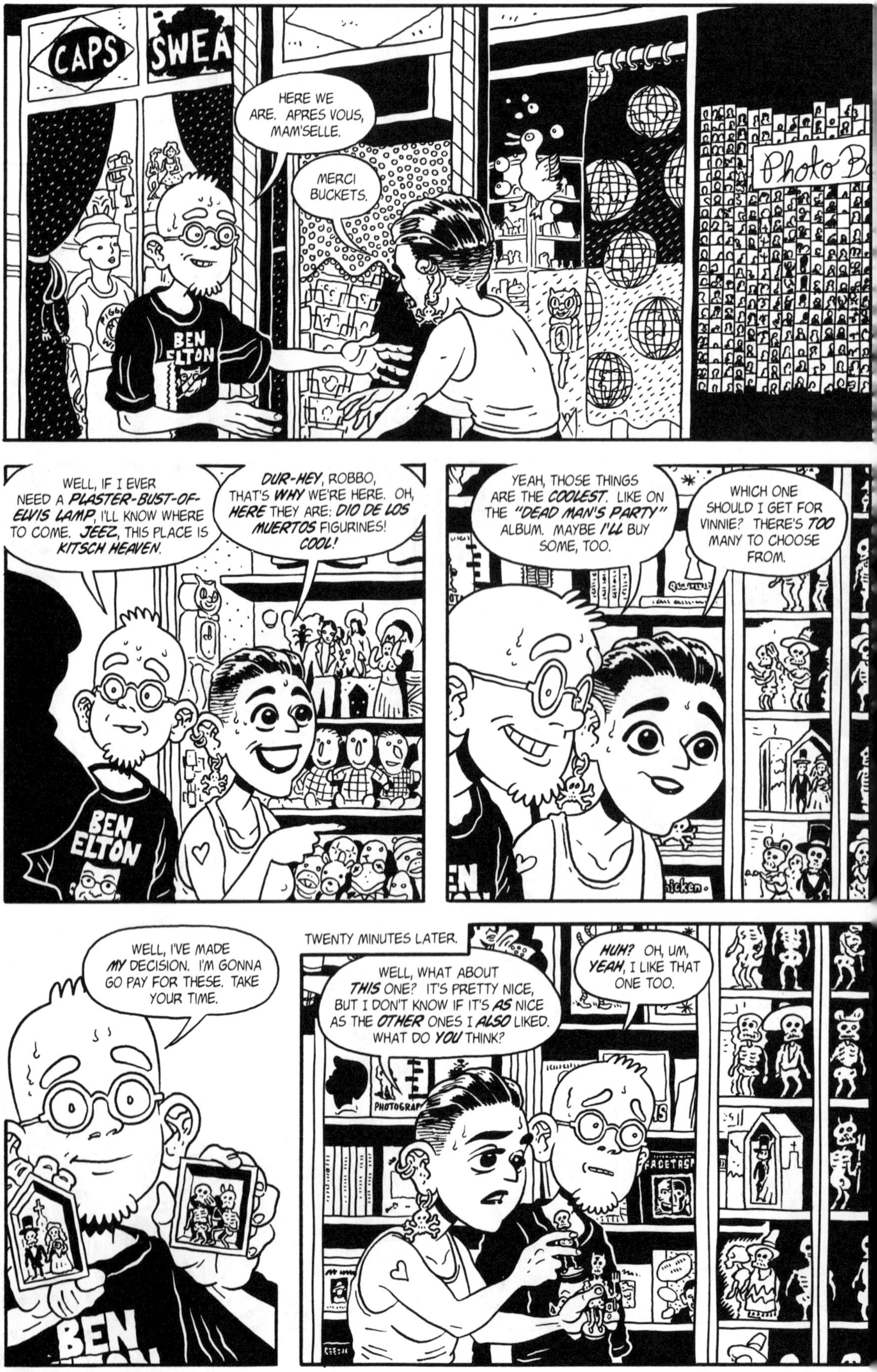
CAPS
SWEA
HERE WE ARE. APRES VOUS, MAM'SELLE.
MERCI BUCKETS.
Photo B
BEN ELTON
WELL, IF I EVER NEED A PLASTER-BUST-OF-ELVIS LAMP, I'LL KNOW WHERE TO COME. JEEZ, THIS PLACE IS KITSCH HEAVEN.
DUR-HEY, ROBBO, THAT'S WHY WE'RE HERE. OH, HERE THEY ARE: DIO DE LOS MUERTOS FIGURINES! COOL!
BEN ELTON
YEAH, THOSE THINGS ARE THE COOLEST. LIKE ON THE "DEAD MAN'S PARTY" ALBUM. MAYBE I'LL BUY SOME, TOO.
WHICH ONE SHOULD I GET FOR VINNIE? THERE'S TOO MANY TO CHOOSE FROM.
WELL, I'VE MADE MY DECISION. I'M GONNA GO PAY FOR THESE. TAKE YOUR TIME.
BEN
TWENTY MINUTES LATER.
WELL, WHAT ABOUT THIS ONE? IT'S PRETTY NICE, BUT I DON'T KNOW IF IT'S AS NICE AS THE OTHER ONES I ALSO LIKED. WHAT DO YOU THINK?
HUH? OH, UM, YEAH, I LIKE THAT ONE TOO.

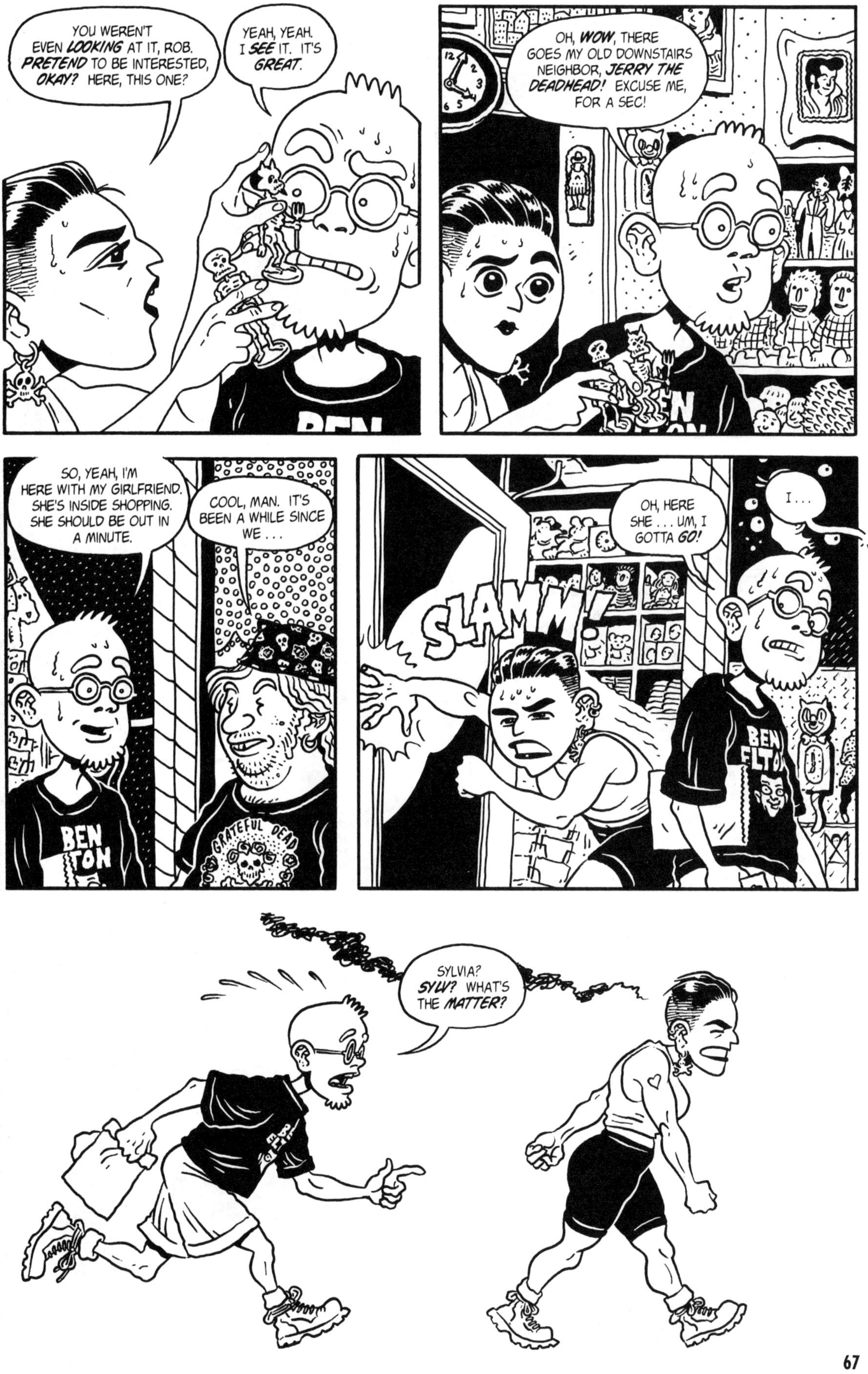
YOU WEREN'T EVEN LOOKING AT IT, ROB. PRETEND TO BE INTERESTED, OKAY? HERE, THIS ONE?
YEAH, YEAH. I SEE IT. IT'S GREAT.
OH, WOW, THERE GOES MY OLD DOWNSTAIRS NEIGHBOR, JERRY THE DEADHEAD! EXCUSE ME, FOR A SEC!
BEN
SO, YEAH, I'M HERE WITH MY GIRLFRIEND. SHE'S INSIDE SHOPPING. SHE SHOULD BE OUT IN A MINUTE.
COOL, MAN. IT'S BEEN A WHILE SINCE WE . . .
BEN TON
GRATEFUL DEAD
OH, HERE SHE . . . UM, I GOTTA GO!
I . . .
SLAMM!
SYLVIA? SYLV? WHAT'S THE MATTER?

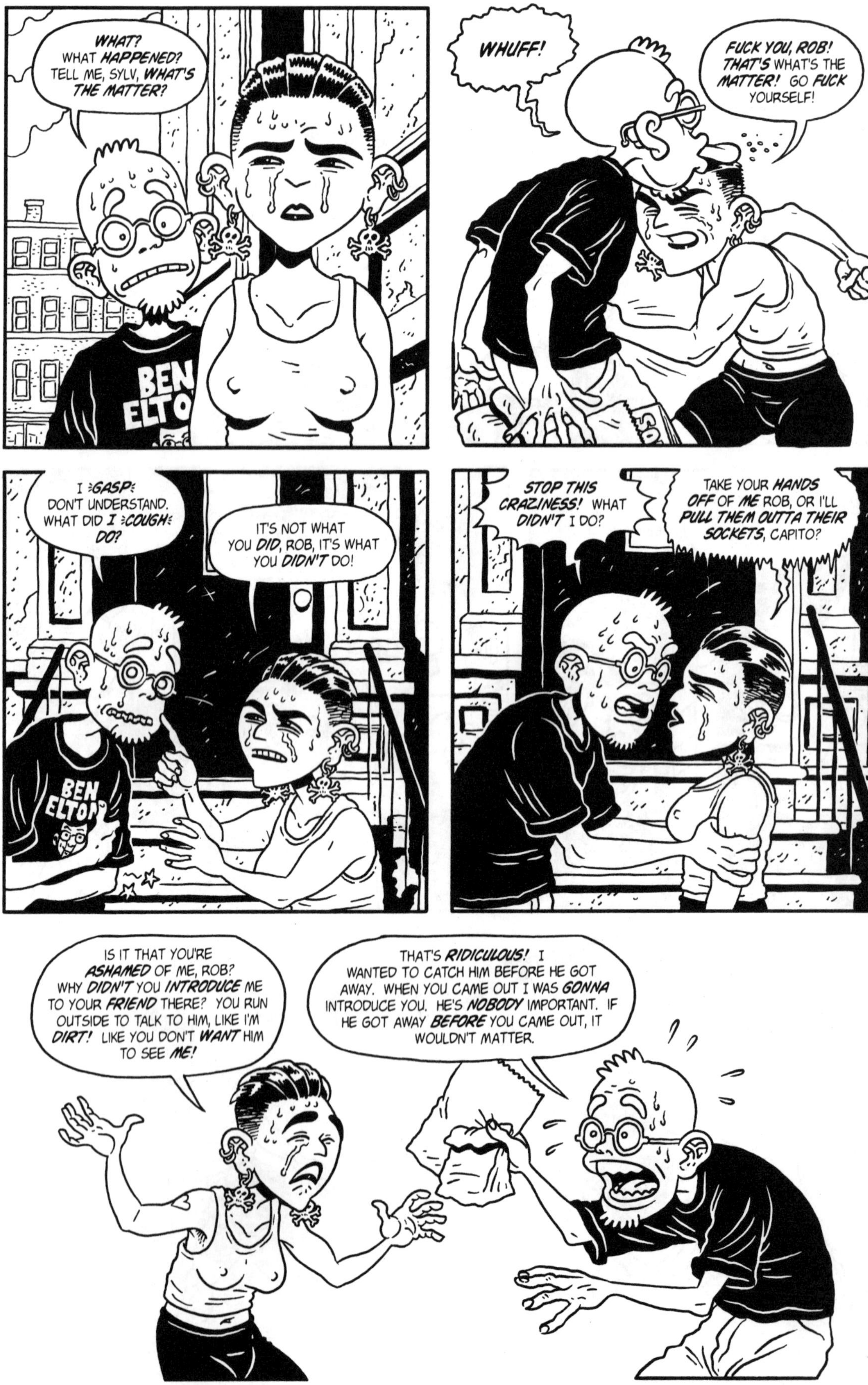
WHAT? WHAT HAPPENED? TELL ME, SYLV, WHAT'S THE MATTER?
BEN ELTON
WHUFF!
FUCK YOU, ROB! THAT'S WHAT'S THE MATTER! GO FUCK YOURSELF!
I *GASP* DON'T UNDERSTAND. WHAT DID I *COUGH* DO?
IT'S NOT WHAT YOU DID, ROB, IT'S WHAT YOU DIDN'T DO!
BEN ELTON
STOP THIS CRAZINESS! WHAT DIDN'T I DO?
TAKE YOUR HANDS OFF OF ME ROB, OR I'LL PULL THEM OUTTA THEIR SOCKETS, CAPITO?
IS IT THAT YOU'RE ASHAMED OF ME, ROB? WHY DIDN'T YOU INTRODUCE ME TO YOUR FRIEND THERE? YOU RUN OUTSIDE TO TALK TO HIM, LIKE I'M DIRT! LIKE YOU DON'T WANT HIM TO SEE ME!
THAT'S RIDICULOUS! I WANTED TO CATCH HIM BEFORE HE GOT AWAY. WHEN YOU CAME OUT I WAS GONNA INTRODUCE YOU. HE'S NOBODY IMPORTANT. IF HE GOT AWAY BEFORE YOU CAME OUT, IT WOULDN'T MATTER.

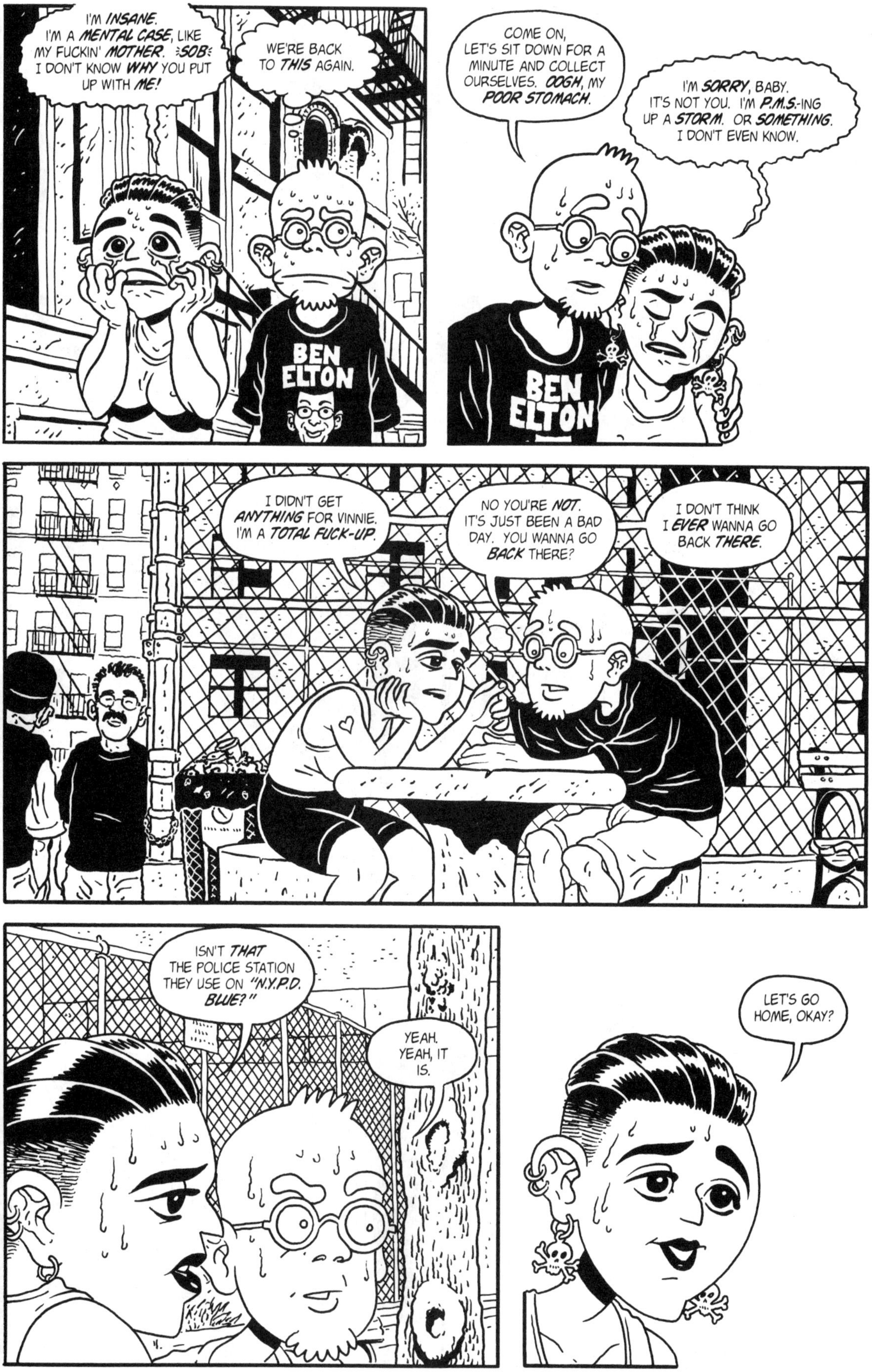

I'M INSANE. I'M A MENTAL CASE, LIKE MY FUCKIN' MOTHER. SOB I DON'T KNOW WHY YOU PUT UP WITH ME!
WE'RE BACK TO THIS AGAIN.
BEN ELTON
COME ON, LET'S SIT DOWN FOR A MINUTE AND COLLECT OURSELVES. OOGH, MY POOR STOMACH.
I'M SORRY, BABY. IT'S NOT YOU. I'M P.M.S.-ING UP A STORM. OR SOMETHING. I DON'T EVEN KNOW.
BEN ELTON
I DIDN'T GET ANYTHING FOR VINNIE. I'M A TOTAL FUCK-UP.
NO YOU'RE NOT. IT'S JUST BEEN A BAD DAY. YOU WANNA GO BACK THERE?
I DON'T THINK I EVER WANNA GO BACK THERE.
ISN'T THAT THE POLICE STATION THEY USE ON "N.Y.P.D. BLUE?"
YEAH. YEAH, IT IS.
LET'S GO HOME, OKAY?

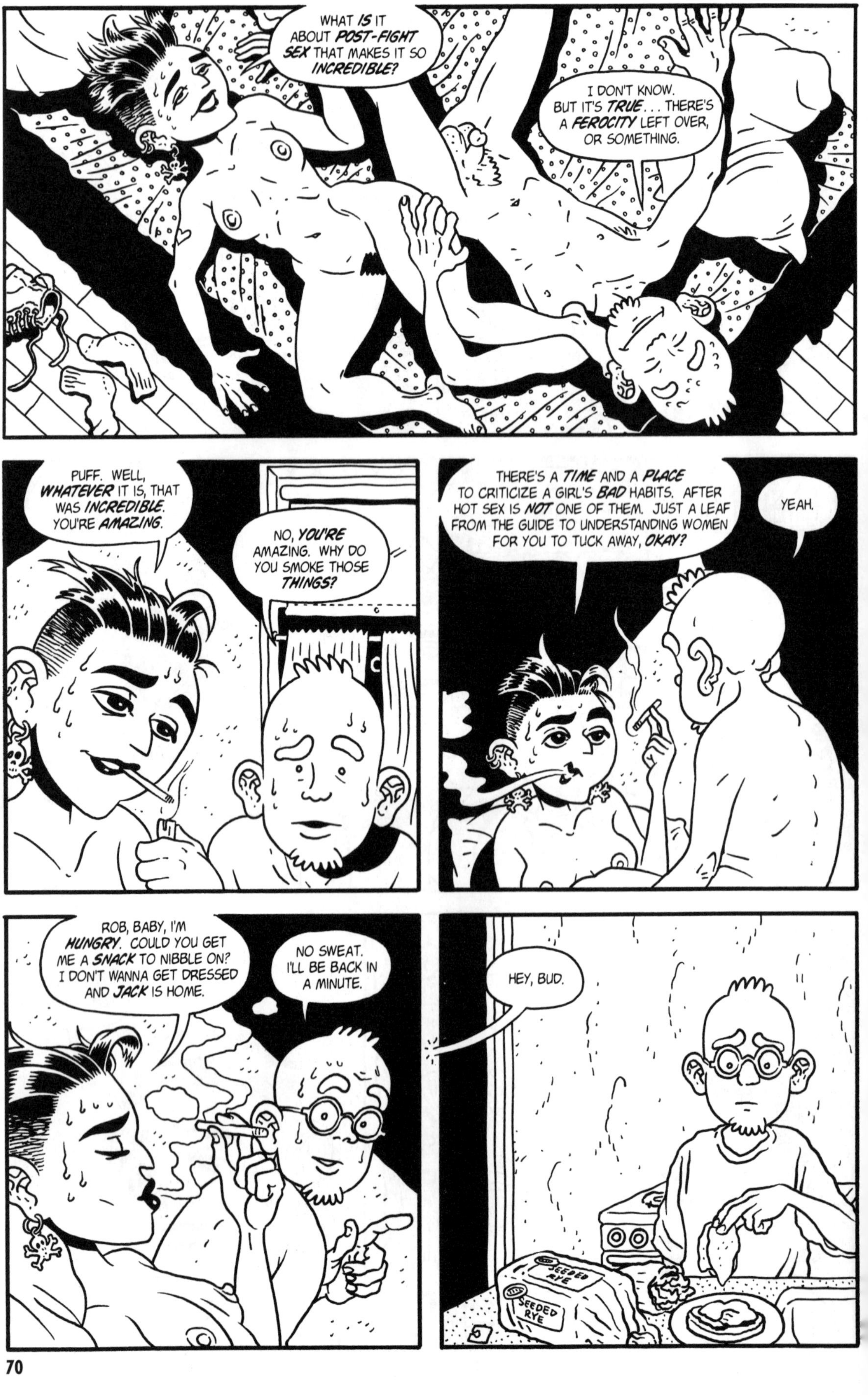

WHAT IS IT ABOUT POST-FIGHT SEX THAT MAKES IT SO INCREDIBLE?
I DON'T KNOW. BUT IT'S TRUE. . . THERE'S A FEROCITY LEFT OVER, OR SOMETHING.
PUFF. WELL, WHATEVER IT IS, THAT WAS INCREDIBLE. YOU'RE AMAZING.
NO, YOU'RE AMAZING. WHY DO YOU SMOKE THOSE THINGS?
THERE'S A TIME AND A PLACE TO CRITICIZE A GIRL'S BAD HABITS. AFTER HOT SEX IS NOT ONE OF THEM. JUST A LEAF FROM THE GUIDE TO UNDERSTANDING WOMEN FOR YOU TO TUCK AWAY, OKAY?
YEAH.
ROB, BABY, I'M HUNGRY. COULD YOU GET ME A SNACK TO NIBBLE ON? I DON'T WANNA GET DRESSED AND JACK IS HOME.
NO SWEAT. I'LL BE BACK IN A MINUTE.
HEY, BUD.
SEEDED RYE
SEEDED RYE

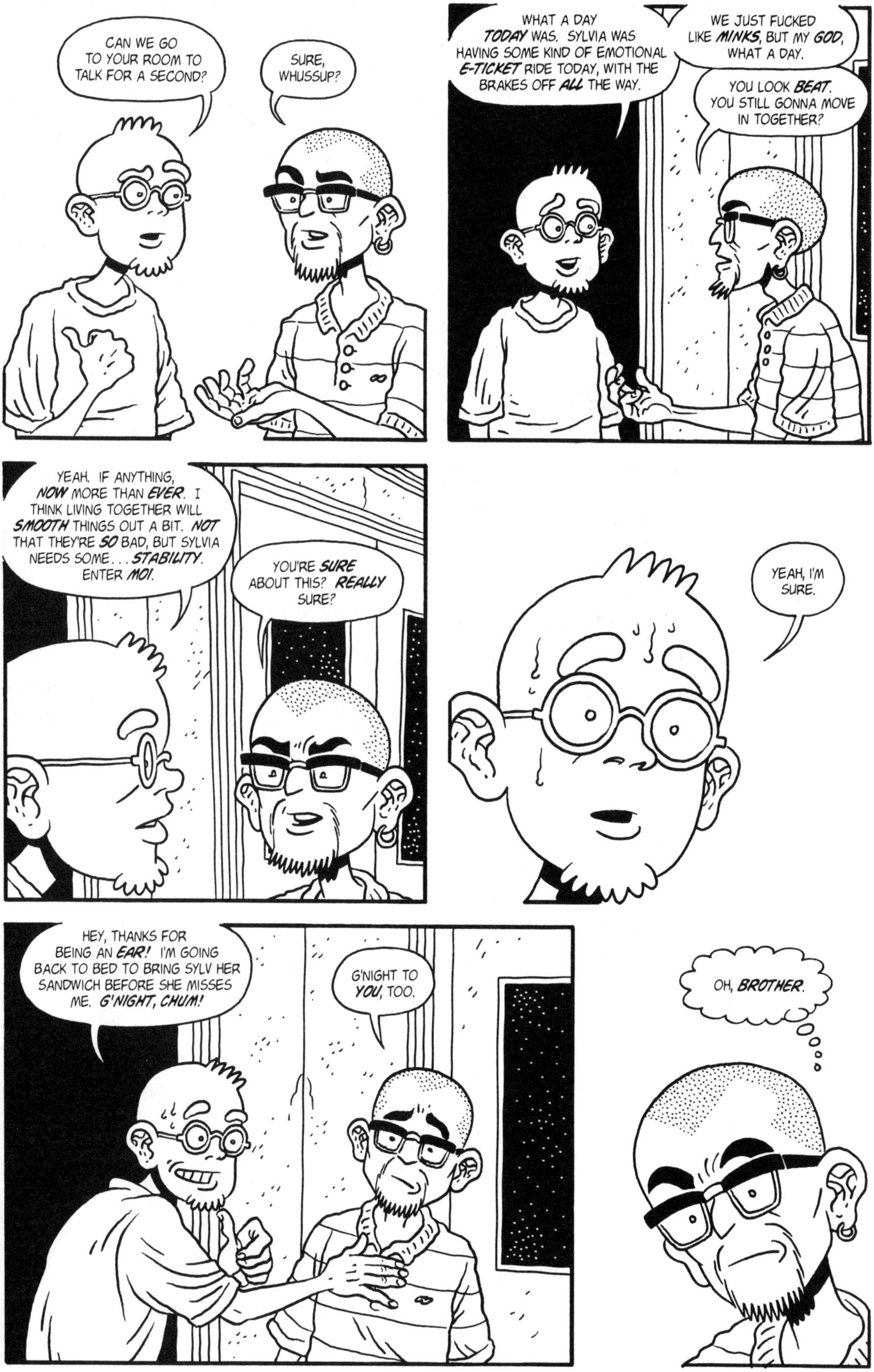
CAN WE GO TO YOUR ROOM TO TALK FOR A SECOND?
SURE, WHUSSUP?
WHAT A DAY TODAY WAS. SYLVIA WAS HAVING SOME KIND OF EMOTIONAL E-TICKET RIDE TODAY, WITH THE BRAKES OFF ALL THE WAY.
WE JUST FUCKED LIKE MINKS, BUT MY GOD, WHAT A DAY.
YOU LOOK BEAT. YOU STILL GONNA MOVE IN TOGETHER?
YEAH. IF ANYTHING, NOW MORE THAN EVER. I THINK LIVING TOGETHER WILL SMOOTH THINGS OUT A BIT. NOT THAT THEY'RE SO BAD, BUT SYLVIA NEEDS SOME. . . STABILITY. ENTER MOI.
YOU'RE SURE ABOUT THIS? REALLY SURE?
YEAH, I'M SURE.
HEY, THANKS FOR BEING AN EAR! I'M GOING BACK TO BED TO BRING SYLV HER SANDWICH BEFORE SHE MISSES ME. G'NIGHT, CHUM!
G'NIGHT TO YOU, TOO.
OH, BROTHER.

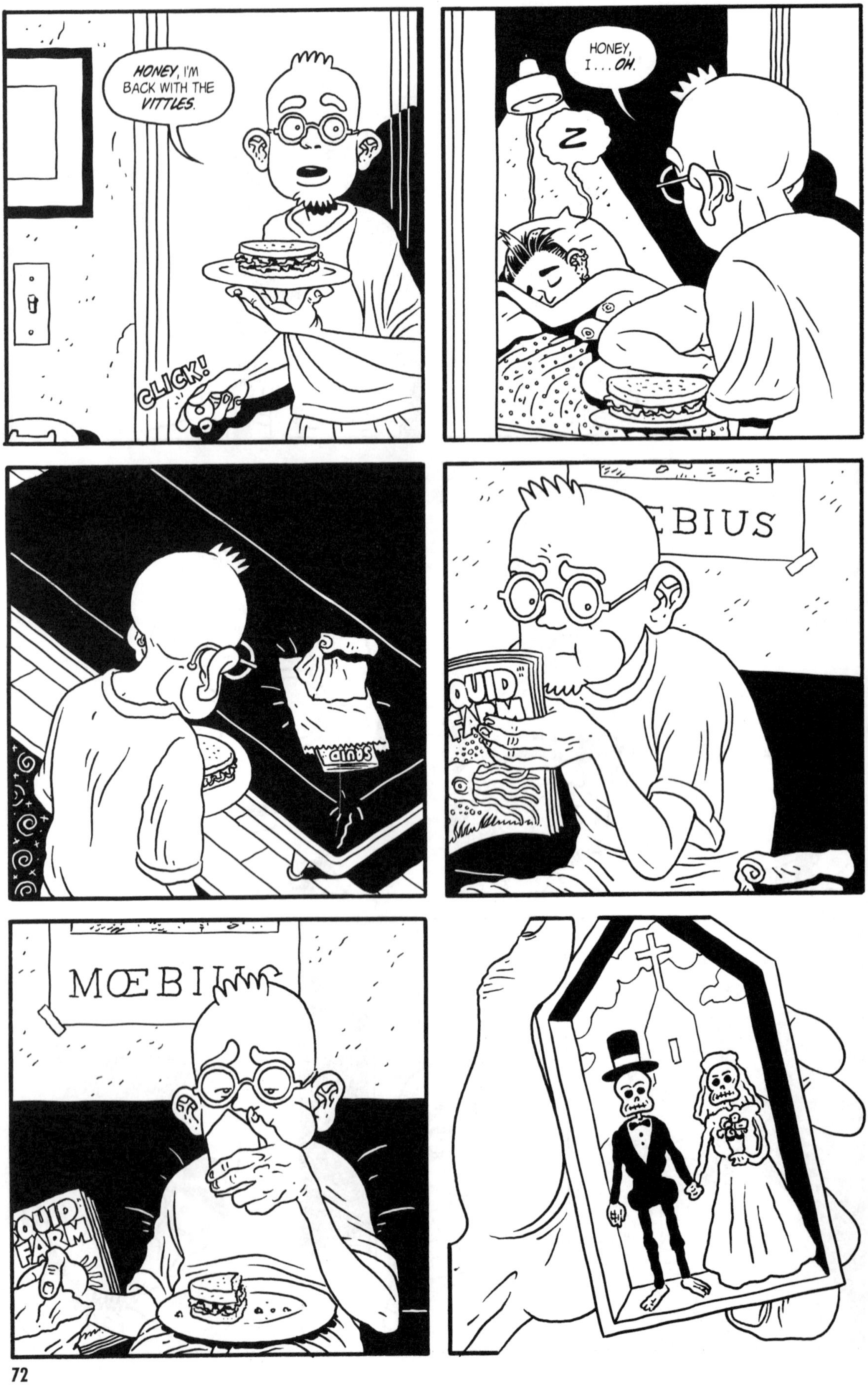
HONEY, I'M BACK WITH THE VITTLES.
CLICK!
HONEY, I... OH.
Z
SQUID
ŒBIUS
SQUID FARM
MŒBIU
SQUID FARM

PREPARATORY SKETCHES AND OTHER TIDBITS

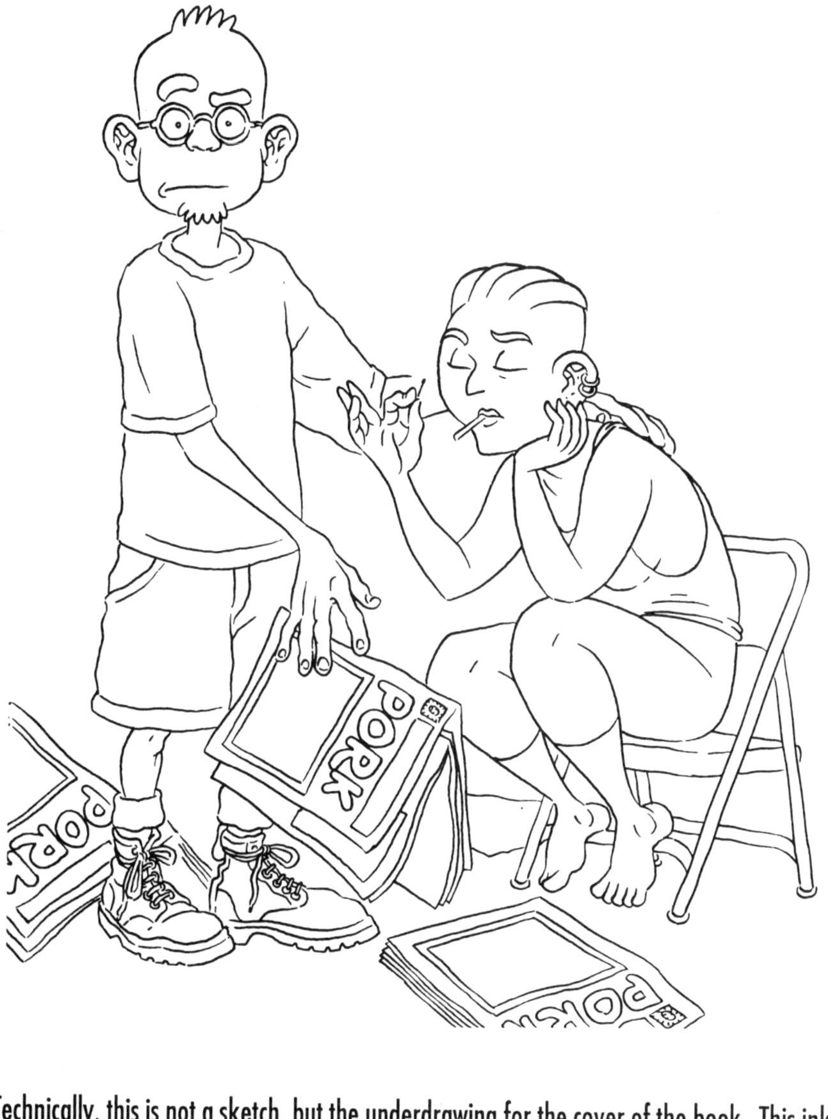
PORK
PORK
PORK

Technically, this is not a sketch, but the underdrawing for the cover of the book. This ink drawing was done on the board, then painted over. I liked the line quality, though, so I copied it before applying the paint. Fascinating, huh?

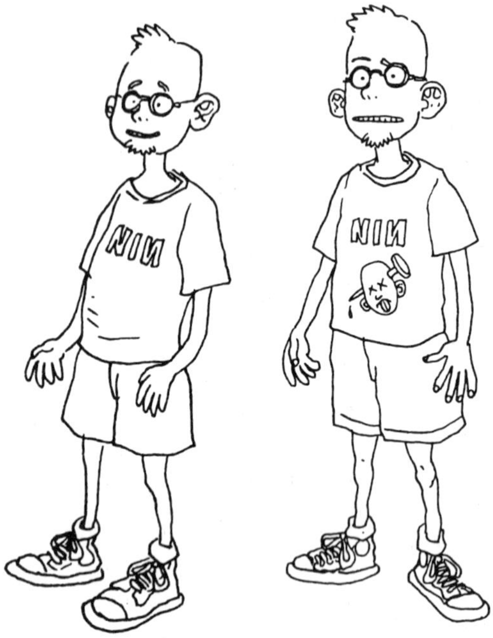

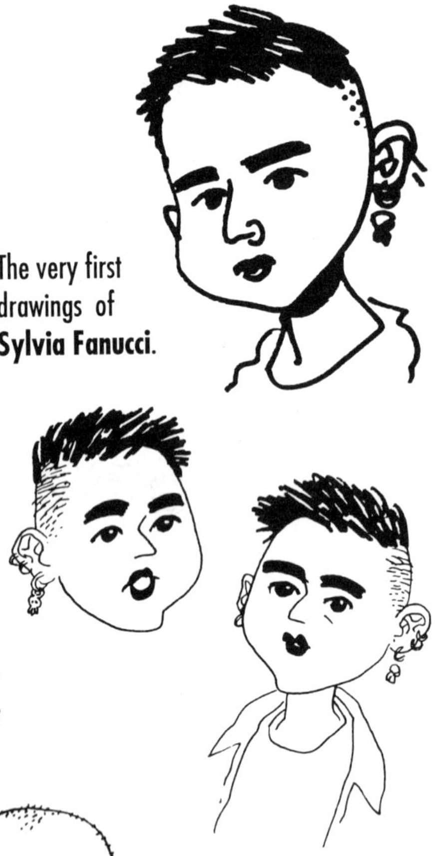

The very first drawings of **Sylvia Fanucci**.

Here are the first two drawings of **Rob Hoffman**. He's fairly pathetic-looking at this stage. Not that he became terribly imposing in the final version, but he didn't look quite *this* wimpy. Did he?

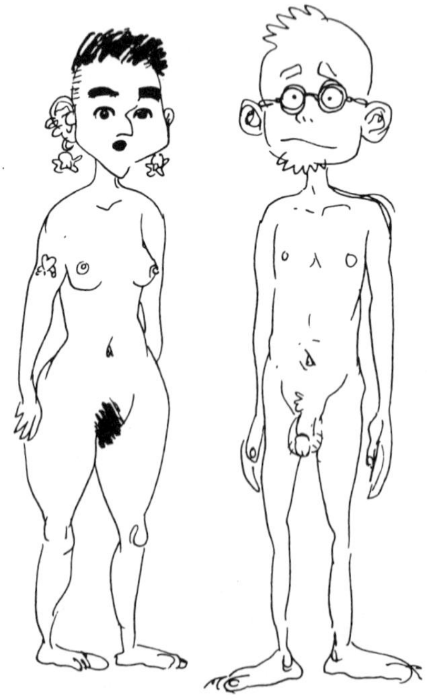

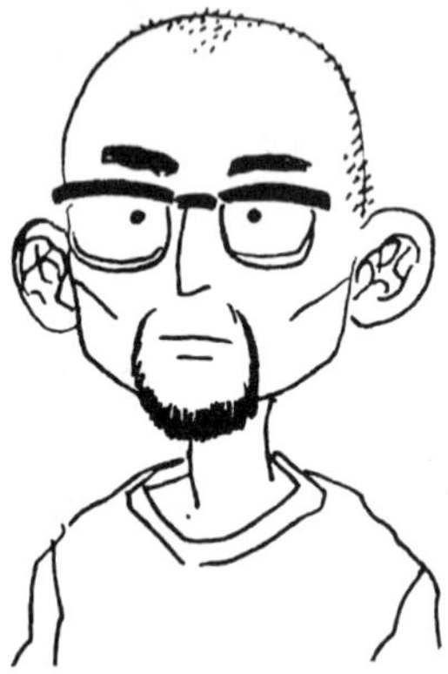

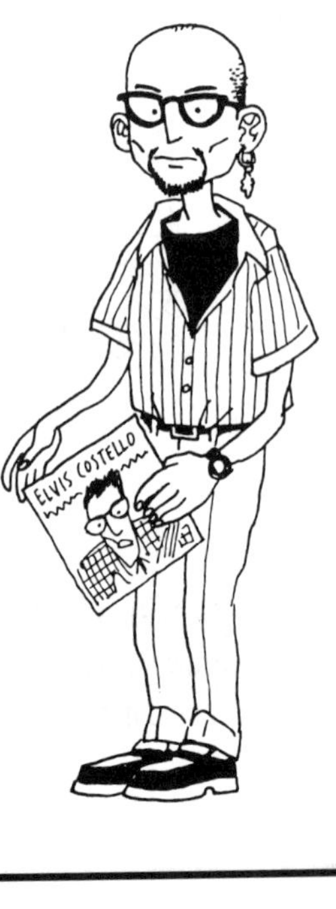
ELVIS COSTELLO

Here's **Jack Netzer**, Rob's book-loving roommate. I'm not so sure he should be this close to Sylvia and Rob when they're naked.

It wouldn't be a book by Bob Fingerman if it didn't have naked people in it, now would it? Naked people add vim and vigor to any project. Add some to your next project, whatever it might be.

Here are a couple of different views of our intrepid couple that were drawn as schematics for miniature figurines to be sculpted by ace action figure and collector's figurine artiste **Steve Kiwus**. These figures, once sculpted, will be available from yers truly for the duration of the series.

Yes, this is a plug for the upcoming onslaught of **Minimum Wage** merchandise. Soon the market will be flooded with tee-shirts, baseball caps, coffee mugs, Tarot card decks, thermoses, lunchboxes, ad nauseum, all bearing the distinctive likenesses of Rob, Sylvia, Jack and the whole gang! It will be such a huge money-making phenomenon that there will be counterfeiters pirating the stuff, leaking inferior quality knock-offs into the marketplace.

Like Rob says to Sylvia's brother Vinnie, "... The ancillary merchandise is where the bucks are."

I know, I'm quoting from my own characters. What can I say? Life imitates art, and vice versa.

Seriously, though, there will be at least these two figurines.

Here are some preliminary sketches of Rob's partners in crime in the wacky world of pornography. To the right is his editor, **Elvis Seward Foucault III**. He is what you might refer to in this day and age as a renaissance man. In addition to grinding out turgid copy for the estimable tabloid **Pork**, he also writes and performs pieces of his particular stripe of filth.

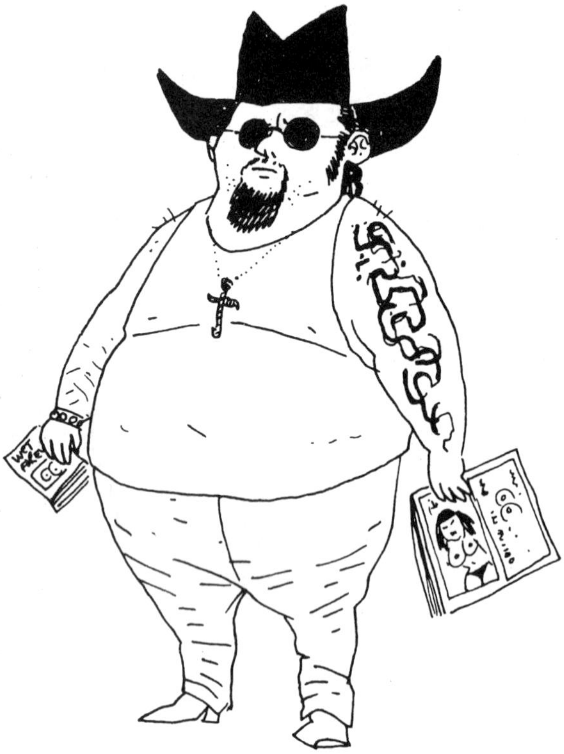

Below are, left to right, **Brian O'Brien** and **Ken Hinder**, two other long-suffering wage slaves of **Sheldon Glattsberg**, the cigar-chomping publishing despot of the **Pork** empire. We'll be seeing more of these fine lads in the continuation of this series.

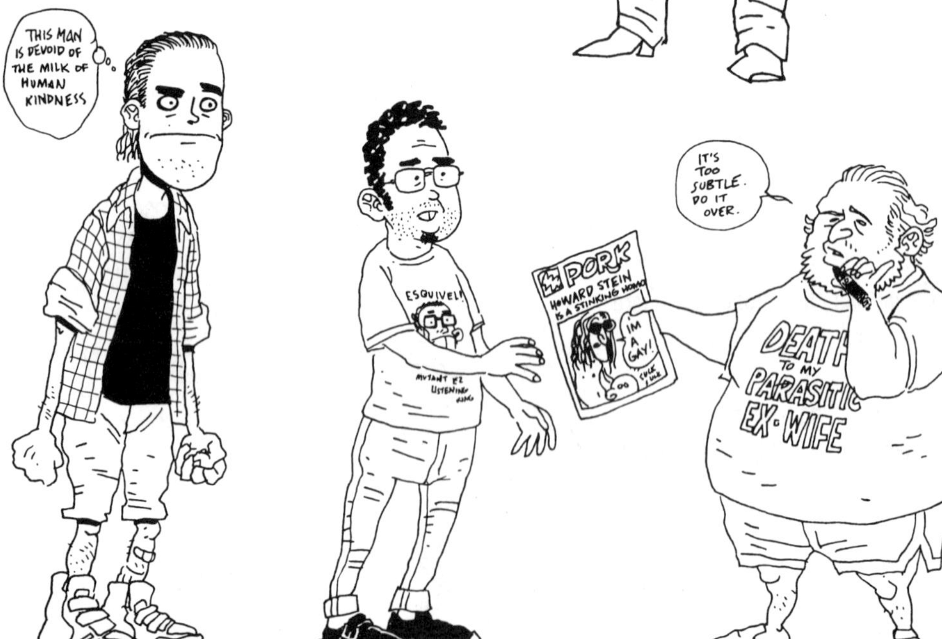
THIS MAN IS DEVOID OF THE MILK OF HUMAN KINDNESS
ESQUIVEL!
IT'S TOO SUBTLE. DO IT OVER.
PORK
HOWARD STEIN
I'M A GAY!
DEATH TO MY PARASITIC EX-WIFE

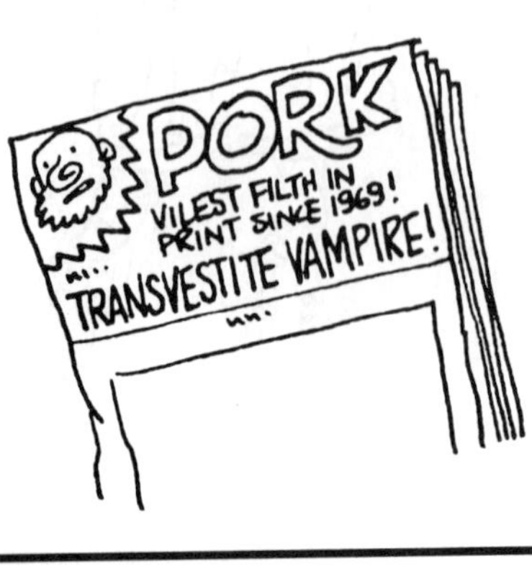
PORK
VILEST FILTH IN PRINT SINCE 1969!
TRANSVESTITE VAMPIRE!

Why is this rag called **Pork**? Stay tuned for Shel's unique explanation.